KNOCKING ON THE DOOR

KNOCKING ON THE DOOR

The Federal Government's Attempt
to Desegregate the Suburbs

Christopher Bonastia

PRINCETON UNIVERSITY PRESS

PRINCETON AND OXFORD

Library of Congress Cataloging-in-Publication data

Bonastia, Christopher, 1967–
Knocking on the door : the federal government's attempt to desegregate the suburbs /
Christopher Bonastia.
p. cm.
Includes bibliographical references and index.
ISBN-13: 978-0-691-11934-2 (cloth : alk. paper)
ISBN-10: 0-691-11934-1 (cloth : alk. paper)
1. Discrimination in housing—United States—History—20th century.
2. Discrimination in housing—Government policy—United States—History—20th
century.   3. Housing policy—United States—History—20th century.
4. Affirmative action programs—Government policy—United States—History—20th
century.   5. Suburbs—United States—History—20th century.   6. United States—
Politics and government—1969–1974.   I. Title.

HD7288.76.U5B66 2006
363.5'560973—dc22   2005054465

British Library Cataloging-in-Publication Data is available

This book has been composed in Sabon

Printed on acid-free paper. ∞

pup.princeton.edu

Printed in the United States of America

1 3 5 7 9 10 8 6 4 2

To Rebecca

CONTENTS

GROWING UP in suburban New Jersey, I was struck by the odd contours of racial segregation that I encountered. In the halls of my high school, you could count the black and Latino students on one hand. When I traveled thirty minutes to explore New York City with friends, fifteen minutes to a rival high school to lose another basketball game, or five minutes to the local mall, I was transported to a markedly more diverse (if not truly integrated) environment. The private schools that my basketball team played against seemed to have more diverse teams and student populations than my public school. I struggled to make sense of this racial landscape.

Years later, when it came time to choose a dissertation topic, I decided to study the small number of suburban towns that had taken it upon themselves to foster diverse, vibrant communities. In the preliminary stages of this study, my advisor asked how we had gotten to the point where the champions of residential integration had dwindled to these self-selected localities and neighborhoods. Intrigued, I expanded my dissertation into an exploration of why we as a nation have made so little progress in the area of residential desegregation. That dissertation mutated and expanded into this book.

In my attempt to explain the failure of residential desegregation policies, I have received help and gained wisdom from a wide array of generous individuals, within and beyond the boundaries of academia. Edwin Amenta supplied many insights on the trajectory of American social policies and on ways in which to study them. He also provided valuable personal and professional guidance, and the opportunity for me to release any displaced frustration by battling him on NYU's steamy basketball courts. Other faculty members at NYU—among them, Jeff Goodwin (another running partner on the basketball court), Dalton Conley, and Ruth Horowitz—also helped me to shape and refine this project. John Skrentny became an indispensable advisor, offering greatly needed guidance about racial politics in America. John's generosity with his time and energy is even more commendable given that he was a "nonresident" member of my dissertation committee, stationed all the way out in San Diego.

It is impossible to survive the marathon of graduate school without the support and good humor of your fellow graduate students. In particular, I would like to thank the Eastern Conference All-Stars dissertation group— Ellen Benoit, Nancy Cauthen, Tina Fetner, and Drew Halfmann—for reading endless iterations of dissertation chapters. Other friends from the NYU days—Karen Albright, Vanessa Barker, Lynn Krage, Carrie James, Miranda Martinez, and Karrie Snyder, to name just a few—allowed me to talk often about my work and then to forget completely about it.

One of the great things about attending graduate school in New York City is the easy access to scholars from nearby institutions. Taking courses with Phil Kasinitz (CUNY) and Norman Fainstein (then of New School University) gave me the chance to learn about subfields of sociology that were not strengths at NYU, and meet one of the coolest scholar/musicians out there, Raquel Rivera. Ingrid Gould Ellen, Robin D. G. Kelley, and Bruce Haynes also provided valuable encouragement along the way.

I had the good fortune to become a Robert Wood Johnson Scholar in Health Policy at the University of California, Berkeley, from 2001 to 2003. This postdoctoral fellowship spoiled me rotten with generous financial support, thought-provoking colleagues from Economics and Political Science as well as Sociology, and an office with a window (still my sole scholarly experience with natural light). It also spurred me to examine civil rights enforcement in health care, another area marked more by policy failure than success. Carroll Estes, Margaret Weir, Jill Quadagno, Richard Scheffler (the Berkeley site director), and Mark Schlesinger are especially deserving of my gratitude. My colleagues at Berkeley were a truly remarkable group of scholars. In particular, Michelle Berger, Tom Burke, Carol Caronna, Kevin Esterling, Dino Falaschetti, Jonah Gelbach, Kristen Harknett, Ann Keller, Karen Lutfey, and Adam Sheingate provided valuable commentary on my work, and helped this New York boy navigate and enjoy the charms of northern California. Nathan Jones and Louise Robertson also merit a shout out. My research assistant at Berkeley, Wendy Wong, showed remarkable creativity in tracking down data sources I had requested, and finding interesting ones that I hadn't.

Support from New York University, a National Science Foundation Doctoral Dissertation Improvement Grant and the Robert Wood Johnson Foundation afforded me the time and resources necessary to complete the research for this project. Archivists at the National Archives, the Richard Nixon and Jimmy Carter Presidential Libraries, the Library of Congress, the Bentley Historical Library, and the Schomburg Center for Research in Black Culture were always helpful in clearing up my confusion.

During my year at Queens College, Robin Rogers-Dillon, Victoria Pitts, Stephen Steinberg, and Mike Roberts kept my spirits up as I tried to finish my book, teach many classes, and get a job. I gratefully acknowledge my colleagues at Lehman College for finally giving me an academic home (in NYC, no less) and letting me eat. Bill Tramontano, Madeline Moran, Kofi Benefo, Tom Conroy, Herb Danzger, Fran Della

Cava, Elhum Haghighat, Barbara Jacobson, Miriam Medina, Elin Waring, and Esther Wilder made me feel welcome immediately.

I would like to recognize my undergraduate students, whose insights and curiosity continue to inspire. Suhadee Henriquez, my collaborator on a new (and completely different) project about flight attendants in the post–September 11th world, and Davira Jimenez deserve special recognition.

Friends and family outside of academia have been equally important to me, my work, and my sanity. Thanks to my brother Pete, my cousin Mark Costantin, Peter Kane (Luno Collision), Monica Grandy, Karl Thiel, Ebony Bostic, Mike O'Donnell, Karen Revis, and Monica Bhambhani for acting fascinated when I explained my "institutional homes" hypothesis to them. Thanks also to the nightcrawlers who shared my other passion, music, on the many nights I traded my computer for two turntables and a mixer. I am indebted to my parents, Peter and Bobbie, for their emotional support as I burrowed more deeply into the strange world of the scholar.

I am, of course, grateful to Chuck Myers, Jennifer Nippins, Jill Harris, and Linda Truilo at Princeton University Press for believing in this project, and helping it come to fruition. The comments of the anonymous reviewers resulted in a greatly improved manuscript. This book incorporates portions of articles that I wrote for *Social Problems* and *Social Science History*. I thank both those journals for granting the permission to do so.

I have been incredibly fortunate to have the support of so many people throughout the years. But fortune has never shone as brightly on me as the day in August 2003 when I met Rebecca Carroll on the "L" train platform in Brooklyn. She is an intellectual in the truest sense of the word: curious, engaged, thoughtful, brilliant. (Read her books . . . they rule.) And that does not even begin to describe what she means to me as a partner in crime for life. I dedicate this book to you, Rebecca. It thrills me to know that when you read this, our son, too, will no longer be "forthcoming," but out here in the world with us. Who says no one meets anyone on the subway platform?

Christopher Bonastia
Brooklyn
April 14, 2005

ABBREVIATIONS FOR FREQUENTLY CITED GOVERNMENT AGENCIES AND COMMISSIONS

EEOC Equal Employment Opportunity Commission
FHA   Federal Housing Administration
HEW   Department of Health, Education, and Welfare
HHFA Housing and Home Finance Agency
HOLC Home Owners' Loan Corporation
HUD   Department of Housing and Urban Development
OCR   Office for Civil Rights (Department of Health, Education, and
      Welfare)
OFCC Office of Federal Contract Compliance (Department of Labor)
USCCR U.S. Commission on Civil Rights

KNOCKING ON THE DOOR

Chapter One

Residential Segregation
The Forgotten Civil Rights Issue

EVERY FEW YEARS, Americans are left with another civil rights milestone to consider. Recently, journalists, scholars, movement participants, and politicians have pondered the impact of the Fair Housing Act of 1968 (the year 2003 marked its thirty-fifth anniversary), 1954's *Brown v. Board of Education* Supreme Court decision (fiftieth anniversary) and the Civil Rights Act of 1964 (fortieth anniversary). Some of these analyses bask in self-congratulation that we have "come so far," while others approach something close to despair over how much remains to be accomplished and how many opportunities have been wasted or lost.

Analysts often treat the array of contentious political actions, court decisions, legislation, and bureaucratic implementation that constitute the "civil rights revolution" as a coherent whole—again, either as inspirational triumph or tragic failure. The reality is more complex. We have, in fact, come a considerable way. The nation's largest corporations and most prestigious universities consider racial diversity (admittedly, a vaguely defined concept) to be in their self-interest, a nearly complete reversal over the past forty years. The most egregious forms of discrimination and segregation have diminished considerably. Yet there has also been unmistakable stagnation in the nation's commitment to racial equality, and even substantial backsliding. For example, after rapid reductions in primary and secondary educational segregation in the late 1960s and the first half of the 1970s, segregation levels peaked in 1988 and have been declining since.[1]

The most sobering legacy of dashed hopes in reducing racial segregation and discrimination is in housing. While Americans continue to believe that children are better off attending desegregated schools—at least if no sacrifices are required—residential segregation is largely a lost cause, or so it may appear. Some interpret the call for residential desegregation as implying that people of color need to be around whites to thrive. To others, residential desegregation simply lacks urgency. In this mistaken view, racial and ethnic clustering is a benign outcome of economic disparities and the preferences of people to "be with their own."

Lastly, the conventional wisdom about residential segregation is that the government can and should do little to tinker with the market forces that sort people into neighborhoods by class, race, and ethnicity. Residential segregation *is* a difficult problem to address, but not because it is beyond the government's purview. To the contrary, one important reason that residential segregation is so severe and resistant to effective solutions is that federal, state, and local governments had (and continue to have) such a large hand in creating and maintaining it. The consequences of residential segregation are numerous and far-reaching, though often obscured. Among other effects, segregation exacerbates black/white wealth disparities by affording African American homeowners lower returns on their investment, and it limits employment opportunities. Racially separate and unequal schools are a direct result of segregated housing patterns.

In the late 1960s and the early 1970s, the federal government had the opportunity to begin to correct the injustices that prevented African Americans and other racial and ethnic minorities from obtaining housing wherever they could afford. The federal government—in particular, the United States Department of Housing and Urban Development (HUD)—took this responsibility seriously, and worked to fashion desegregation policies that rivaled the intensity of those that were being implemented in employment and education. Without question, administrative agencies attempting to battle segregation faced different sets of obstacles and opportunities in the three primary areas of civil rights: employment, education, and housing. Congress enacted legal protections against housing discrimination four years after the historic Civil Rights Act of 1964, which prohibited discrimination in employment and education. From 1964 to 1968, federal bureaucrats began to discover what approaches to desegregation were more or less effective, civil rights opponents in Congress began to devise ways to restrain the more activist impulses of government agencies, and numerous riots and expressions of black militancy reduced white support for civil rights initiatives.

It was no accident that fair housing legislation lagged behind antidiscrimination protections in other areas. (In light of Congress' penchant for writing vague legislative language, it is also no accident that the legislature never defined what it meant by "fair housing.") A substantial proportion of Americans have the strong sense that the federal government has no business intervening in the private housing market. The fact that the federal government historically has acted quite forcefully in the housing market—on the side of segregation—is lost on many people. Given this heavy governmental influence on housing patterns, spurring significant reductions in residential segregation was a demanding responsibility for the federal government, but not an impossible one.

This book chronicles federal governmental involvement in residential segregation, placing particular focus on the years of the Nixon

Administration, when HUD attempted to reverse this legacy of enforced residential segregation. In the end the agency was unable to foster meaningful changes in segregation patterns. Scholars of social policy study success disproportionately because it is easier to study, and successful policies are more prominent than failed ones. To comprehend fully how a law may fulfill its stated objectives, however, we need to understand the many reasons why this often does not occur.

RESIDENTIAL SEGREGATION REACHES THE NATIONAL AGENDA

George Romney, secretary of HUD, had a reputation for speaking in blunt terms. "Our nation's metropolitan areas cannot endure . . . a run-down, festering black core, surrounded by a well-to-do, indifferent white ring," he said on one occasion in 1970.[2] On another, he insisted that "the most explosive threat to our nation is the confrontation between the poor and the minority groups who are concentrated in the central cities, and the middle income and affluent who live in the surrounding and separate communities. This confrontation is divisive. It is explosive. It must be resolved."[3]

Romney's sense of urgency had faded by the time he left HUD in early 1973, disillusioned by widespread scandals in the agency's housing production programs and his own inability to steer this massive, unwieldy bureaucracy. Nevertheless, he was correct in pointing to the destructive effects of racial and economic isolation, effects that continue to accrue today. At the dawn of the Nixon Administration, the time was ripe for federal action to foster residential desegregation. In fact, this opportunity to attack discrimination and segregation in housing was unprecedented. Though civil rights supporters typically had few positive things to say about President Richard Nixon, it was under Nixon that unmatched progress in Southern school desegregation took place and that affirmative action in employment took hold, beginning with the presidentially approved "Philadelphia Plan" to integrate the construction trades.[4]

At several junctures during this period, HUD appeared to be building the momentum to help forge elementary changes in segregated residential patterns by "opening up the suburbs" to groups historically excluded for racial or economic reasons. The door did not shut completely on this possibility until Nixon took the drastic step of freezing all federal housing funds in January 1973. *Knocking on the Door* assesses this "near-miss" in political history, exploring how HUD came surprisingly close to implementing unpopular antidiscrimination policies and why President Nixon derailed the agency's civil rights drive. It is perhaps obvious now that

HUD was, in the end, unsuccessful. It may not be so obvious why these initiatives failed or how they might have succeeded.[5] To be sure, one can identify some of the important elements in the failure of housing desegregation by highlighting commonly cited factors: substantial opposition from industry, considerable public resistance, inadequate mobilization of advocacy groups, and lukewarm support from Congress, to name a few. Yet, when we view housing desegregation in the context of other, relatively more successful civil rights policies such as affirmative action in employment and school desegregation (until it was abandoned), these factors alone fail to account for the varying trajectories of these policies. If one is to make sense of HUD's failure, it is crucial to understand how the structure of the agency made its component offices particularly apt to lose legitimacy, and how the array of missions within the agency resulted in various sectors of the agency working at cross-purposes from one another. These characteristics in particular made HUD acutely vulnerable to political attack, and President Nixon seized upon this vulnerability.

At first blush, the era of Richard Nixon's presidency (1969–74) may seem an unlikely period to identify as one in which effective federal attacks on residential segregation were most likely. Nixon is often remembered as an individual whose domestic political stances were calculated to gain the support of whites, especially Southern whites, who had grown resentful of the outbreaks of black rage in inner cities and of the expanding scope of federal civil rights enforcement. Internal disputes over philosophies and protest strategies severely weakened the civil rights movement, and public support for governmental attempts to fight discrimination appeared to be eroding. There is, however, a flip side to this picture. While Congress passed most of the prominent twentieth century civil rights legislation during the Johnson Administration, in the Civil Rights Acts of 1964 and 1968 and the Voting Rights Act of 1965, the specific policies that would carry out the aims of these laws took form during the Nixon Administration. During this time, federal agencies escalated their efforts to carry out federal civil rights laws, and courts largely deferred to the wisdom of the agencies.[6]

Led by the liberal George Romney, HUD was charged with enforcing the newly passed fair housing law "affirmatively." Moreover, a serious housing shortage had led Congress to make an enormous federal commitment to subsidizing housing production in the 1968 Housing and Urban Development Act. Historically, the federal government has had an easier time securing regulatory compliance from private sector and from other governmental actors when the incentive of federal funding, or the threat of withholding these funds, is present. Thus, the 1968 housing production legislation provided HUD with substantial leverage to carry out the antidiscrimination law.

HUD was on its way to spearheading a sustained attack on racial and economic exclusion. Ultimately, these efforts came unhinged. The Nixon Administration merits close examination as a pivotal period in explaining the divergence of federal civil rights policies in housing from those in other areas, such as employment and education, where the United States adopted stronger (though by no means flawless) race-conscious policies in trying to reduce inequality between African Americans and whites. This was the best opportunity that America had to devise political solutions to the problem of residential segregation. It also may have been the last one, at least for the foreseeable future. In accord with the dominant political focus of the time, I pay closest attention to issues of black/white inequality and segregation (and primarily use the terms "black" and "white" to reflect the common nomenclature of that era). While antidiscrimination initiatives later incorporated other racial and ethnic groups (Latinos, Asians, Native Americans) as well as other affected classes (women, the disabled), initial policies directed at African Americans served as a template for subsequent expansions; thus, said policies are important to decipher as the foundation upon which more broadly inclusive approaches were built.[7] This focus on the trajectory of residential desegregation policies during the Nixon Administration is supplemented by an assessment of the evolution of federal housing policies throughout the twentieth century, with particular attention to the ways in which these policies addressed or failed to address questions of racial discrimination. (Readers interested mainly in the historical narrative may wish to skip the theoretical discussion that follows, and proceed to page 16, "Hurdles to Housing Desegregation Initiatives.")

GOVERNMENT AGENCIES AS KEY POLITICAL PLAYERS

While studies that explore the processes and effects of segregation are numerous, relatively little scholarship seeks to understand the development of federal *policies* to address residential segregation. This study utilizes a comparative-historical framework to maximize analytical leverage in explaining the evolution of these policies. Employees of federal agencies are key players in the formation of social policies, despite the fact that the legislative and judicial branches are more visible political actors in the policy-making process. Legislative language is often vague, leaving a wide range of interpretation to the discretion of administrative agencies.[8] When courts have acted prior to legislative passage and agency action, little change has ensued. To wit, school desegregation after the landmark *Brown v. Board of Education* (1954) decision moved excruciatingly slowly until congressional passage of the 1964 Civil Rights Act. In the late 1960s and early 1970s, courts often responded to the actions of civil rights agencies, in most cases deferring to the expertise of the agencies in civil rights enforcement (see, for example, the Supreme Court's 1971 *Griggs v. Duke Power* decision). Moreover, ignoring the role of government agencies in policy formation "leaves the most important political outcomes—the impact of policies on citizens—unstudied."[9]

Skocpol argues that state bureaucracies are potentially capable of autonomous action, meaning that they may devise strategies of action independently of other branches of government, capitalists and organized business groups, political parties, interest groups, movement organizations, and public opinion. Some scholars have stressed the importance of organizational and intellectual capabilities in policy-making agencies seeking to establish autonomy.[10] Carpenter's study of executive agencies from 1862 to 1928 finds that the ability of government bureaucracies to achieve autonomy is predicated upon political insulation from actors who try to control them, the development of unique organizational capacities, and strong organizational reputations (political legitimacy).

To act autonomously, he argues, agencies must establish political legitimacy, "a reputation for expertise, efficiency, or moral protection and a uniquely diverse complex of ties to organized interests and the media."[11] Considering the cases of the Post Office, Agriculture Department, and Interior Department, Carpenter's account of American state-building is persuasive; however, his findings do not map neatly onto the civil rights agencies created in the 1960s. While agencies in the late nineteenth and early twentieth centuries typically employed strategies of incremental program expansion, Congress expected the civil rights agencies to act quickly to carry out their mandates. The mission of fighting racial discrimination had immediate legitimacy, though the agencies did need to develop legitimacy for the strategies that they employed to bring these mandates to life. Rather than being earned over the course of years, bureaucratic autonomy was in some sense built into the civil rights agencies, since Congress offered little specific guidance to the agencies in civil rights legislation. (This autonomy could be stripped away if civil rights agencies subsequently developed bad reputations.)

Whereas much previous work in this area focuses on the case of government agencies that attempt to secure passage of their legislative proposals, I investigate why certain agencies are able to initiate policy innovations based on existing law—even if these innovations are opposed by other political actors—while other, similarly situated agencies find themselves unable to do so.[12] One can better understand HUD's failure in civil rights by directing attention to its disadvantaged institutional home for these activities. The term "institutional home" refers to the government agency, agencies, or agency division(s) through which relevant policies are interpreted, articulated, and carried out. According to this approach, the structure and mission of an agency have important direct effects on policy outcomes. In addition, the institutional home of a policy has a marked influence on how prior policies and external factors that may influence policy development—such as interest and advocacy groups, other branches of government, and the media—play out in specific cases.

Activism in Government Agencies

Employees of government agencies, especially newly hatched ones, often have sizable aspirations for effecting change. Appointees with political ambitions typically want to develop reputations as instigators of action, not as overseers of slow-moving, unresponsive bureaucracies. What varies is the degree to which agencies successfully pursue and attain (or partially attain) their activist goals. One possibility is that Congress or the president exerts tight controls over administrative agencies, essentially dictating how boldly an agency may act. Congress may respond to public opposition directly by passing legislation to prohibit specific agency actions or policies, or indirectly by threatening budget cuts, refusing to confirm political appointees, or making administrators squirm while testifying on Capitol Hill.[13] It can be surprisingly difficult for Congress to limit unpopular agency actions, especially in cases where agency tasks are "hard to specify and difficult to evaluate" and "imbedded in conflict-ridden political environments."[14] While Congress can (and does) deny agency requests for new funding or authority, the legislative branch frequently has found it difficult to scale back agency efforts, especially when courts have supported these actions.

The White House has had similar problems. Wilson notes that "the White House repeatedly tries to tidy up these relationships and bring the regulatory agencies under close supervision, but the history of these attempts is one of dashed hopes and wasted energies."[15] Oftentimes, the president is unaware what individual agencies are doing, so long as the agencies do nothing newsworthy enough to demand his attention or intervention. Other factors contributing to this lack of presidential control include agency ties with interest groups and congressional committees, informational advantages of bureaucracies, and political appointees becoming ideological compatriots of agency employees rather than the White House.[16]

In more recent years, scholars have refined their conceptions of bureaucratic autonomy in light of increasing presidential success—especially by

Ronald Reagan—in controlling the bureaucracy. The centerpiece of this "administrative presidency" lies in appointments, where ideological compatibility with the president supercedes other factors, such as ties to interest groups, agency clients, or constituencies within the president's party.[17] Reagan took many of his cues from Richard Nixon, who began his second term determined to have federal agencies carry out his policy preferences more closely.

With respect to the judiciary, courts consistently backed forceful agency efforts in civil rights during the Johnson and Nixon administrations. While Rosenberg may be correct in arguing that court rulings *alone* may have only minor effects on social policies, he underestimates the extent to which judicial decisions may legitimate or undercut the actions of other governmental branches.[18] Nevertheless, an agency's ability to achieve its goals is not reducible to the preferences of other branches. Even skeptics of agency independence such as McCubbins and Weingast maintain that bureaucracies do sometimes exercise autonomy from the preferences of other branches, but only when there are missteps at the appointment stage.[19] Moreover, an agency's ability to convey legitimacy can strongly condition the responses of other branches.

Much early work on administrative agencies asserted that they may be "captured" by business or other powerful interest groups. According to some of these arguments, progressive social policies such as the Social Security Act are the result of the more liberal sector of the business class winning out over the more conservative one.[20] These works theorize policy adoption, though another strand of work makes a parallel argument about elites steering agency actions.[21] Business interests generally have not captured civil rights agencies, whose staffers are likely to sympathize with civil rights groups. Business elites may try to hamstring civil rights efforts by appealing to the larger agency (if civil rights responsibilities lie within a larger agency), Congress, or the White House, but they are unlikely to have success asking civil rights staffers to "ease up" and make the agency's efforts appear ineffectual.

In housing, the National Association of Real Estate Boards (NAREB) was the most influential business interest with a hostility toward civil rights enforcement. NAREB, however, had a tough case to make before HUD's housing production and civil rights staffers. Production staffers had no reason to support NAREB's contention that housing policies should de-emphasize new production, and civil rights staffers sharply disagreed with the association's laissez-faire stance toward antidiscrimination enforcement. On the other side of the equation, the National Association of Home Builders viewed HUD's attempt to increase subsidized housing production in suburbia as being in their self-interest, since this initiative would allow the association's members to build more housing.

Others claim that advocacy groups steer the actions of government agencies. Detlefsen and Belz argue this point in their explanation of the emergence of affirmative action in employment, though Skrentny and Graham offer strong proof to the contrary in showing that advocacy groups did not initiate the call for affirmative action and were initially wary of this approach.[22] After a social movement organization has succeeded in getting legislation passed, its means of influence may shift from pressure on elected officials to the installation in government bureaucracies of "institutional activists," social movement participants who hold positions within government and seek to attain social movement goals through normal bureaucratic channels.[23]

Even scholars who criticize sociologists for not taking public opinion seriously tend not to identify public attitudes as a direct cause of agency actions. One must nevertheless consider the simple explanation that public support for equal opportunity was greater in the areas of employment and education than in housing, and thus resulted in a stronger policy.[24] While public opinion is influential in much political decision-making, opinion and policy are, however, often coupled loosely.[25] Several policies may accord with public opinion, and citizens may often not know or care which specific policy options they prefer to carry out their broad preferences. Even when citizens do have clear preferences in a given policy area, in many cases this position is not strong enough to alter their support for a particular politician or party.

Comparing public opinion data among issue areas can be difficult, as methods and phrasing of questions often vary widely. Some surveys have shown that public support for intervention by the federal government in securing equal treatment for blacks in employment has been only slightly greater than that for open housing, though most observers assume that white opposition to affirmative action in housing has clearly outweighed opposition to employment-related affirmative action. White attitudes toward residential integration have shifted, at least in the abstract. The National Opinion Research Center has periodically asked respondents to agree or disagree, slightly or strongly, with the following statement: "White people have a right to keep (Negroes/blacks/African Americans) out of their neighborhoods if they want to, and (Negroes/blacks/African Americans) should respect that right." In the 1963 survey, 60 percent of white respondents agreed with the statement; that number declined to 56 percent in the 1968 survey and 41 percent in the 1972 survey, before rising back to 44 percent in 1977. Since then, white agreement with this statement has declined from 25 percent in 1988, to 20 percent in 1991 and 13 percent in 1996.[26]

In any case, using public opinion alone to explain the differing strengths of civil rights policies is problematic. Public opinion surveys reveal similar levels of support for school busing and housing desegregation, and vocal public opposition to school busing far outweighed opposition to housing desegregation. In employment, federal agencies implemented affirmative action without the support of Congress or the public—indeed largely without public knowledge. Thus, if public opinion does have an effect on agency actions, this effect is indirect, manifested in the responses of the media and other political actors to the initiatives in question, and reflected in the legitimacy that accrues to the agency.

A more direct cause of agency actions may be the views of the individuals who head them. Glazer contends that civil rights agencies tend to be staffed by advocates of the most ambitious measures to combat discrimination. In his view, staffers easily capture agency heads, who get more political mileage from heading an aggressive agency than being seen as "someone who presided over the reduction or dismantling of an unnecessarily bloated office."[27] The explanation for divergence in civil rights policies would hold that heads of the employment and education bureaucracies held more activist views than the HUD secretary. In light of HUD Secretary George Romney's repeated assertions that residential segregation was the greatest threat to the nation, this explanation is unconvincing. His career incentives to pursue civil rights issues single-mindedly, however, were not unambiguously clear. Though he spoke passionately in favor of desegregation, Romney's position as HUD chief compelled him to balance this objective with another goal he considered urgent: spurring housing production in light of the dire housing shortages faced at the time by the United States. This point notwithstanding, one cannot explain the differing outcomes of federal desegregation initiatives by examining the career considerations of the people who headed the agencies in question; a more systemic, institutional-level understanding of government bureaucracies is necessary.

STATE AUTONOMY AND INSTITUTIONAL CAPABILITY

The notion that state actors may pursue their own ideas or interests (in building their careers, for instance) through policy innovations is a key insight of historical institutionalism. State autonomy cannot be presumed, as it varies over time and across agencies.[28] Much historical institutional work that focuses on the constraints faced by political actors looks at state capacity. In short, these studies note, policy entrepreneurs will push policies that their agency is capable of carrying out given limits in staffing, information, resources, and so on.[29] While there is little agreement on how scholars should operationalize state capacity, agencies with more staffing, information, and resources might reasonably be expected to push more activist policies. HUD's civil rights office may have had a comparative advantage in terms of state capacity, as it could draw on the information, resources, and possibly the staffing of other sectors of the agency (and existing civil rights offices); the Equal Employment Opportunity Commission (EEOC), as a stand-alone agency, logically would not have had the same ease of access to information and resources. Ironically, in the case of the EEOC, limited state capacity led to innovation and aggressiveness, as staffers devised creative ways to fulfill the agency's mandate despite little enforcement authority and funding.[30]

Prior policies can influence state capacities.[31] These policy legacies (also known as policy feedbacks) may constrain some conceivable policy options and favor others. Policy-making is unavoidably historical, as all political actors react to previous governmental efforts that address the same sorts of problems. As Heclo argues, political actors engage in political learning, trying to apply the lessons of past policy successes and failures to current problems. The lessons of past policies are subject to varying interpretations and are often hotly contested.[32] This contention occurs in part because the prior policies that will impact current policy development are not always obvious: policymakers may draw upon a number of policy legacies, including a policy's immediate predecessor, policy in an analogous area, and the approach of another political jurisdiction. Moreover, the lessons of a particular policy may be interpreted in a number of different ways. For example, reformers portrayed Civil War veterans' benefits, once a broadly popular program, as emblematic of wasteful government spending and tools of political patronage; thus, they became "an obstacle rather than an entering wedge" for subsequent spending programs.[33]

Weir points helpfully to the creation of institutions as central to the restriction of policy possibilities. First, the existence of institutions channels action by directing research and political mobilization along some lines rather than others. Second, existing institutions affect the creation and operation of new institutions. The creation of new institutions, which appeals to those advocating rapid change, may be blocked by existing institutions with overlapping responsibilities. Even if the new institutions are created, existing institutions influence their character in important ways. Lastly, the failure to create policies and institutions may spur groups to make private arrangements that make subsequent public interventions harder to effect.[34]

The history of civil rights enforcement supports Weir's contentions about the importance of institutions in shaping policy possibilities.

Weir's insights can be developed further, however, by delving more deeply into how the institutional home of a policy conditions the responses of other political actors to agency attempts at articulating, developing, and carrying out their chosen policy prescriptions. HUD's civil rights office was clearly constrained by the institutional context under which it was created. Specifically, this office was part of a large, unwieldy bureaucracy with an unsavory policy legacy of tolerating and even encouraging racial segregation, and with other mandates (most notably, housing production) that could conflict with its antidiscrimination mission. Yet, one can best understand the failure of HUD's suburban integration efforts not as a story of institutions as such, but of how political actors opposed to fair housing efforts seized upon political vulnerabilities, which were fostered by the weak institutional basis for housing antidiscrimination policies. Institutions themselves are not actors; instead, institutions shape the political context—which political actors then respond to—in significant ways.

The interpretation of agency actions by other political actors can affect agency capabilities. Organizations face a "legitimacy imperative," which stresses the importance of symbolic actions that convey legitimacy to audiences capable of imposing sanctions if taken-for-granted "rules of the game" are violated.[35] Legitimation involves "explaining or justifying the social order in such a way as to make institutional arrangements subjectively plausible."[36] Because bureaucratic organizations such as government agencies are seen as following their own internal logic, often with significant arbitrariness, these sorts of organizations are keenly vulnerable to criticisms of their work arrangements and procedures, and thus have a particular need for legitimation. If agencies fail to achieve legitimacy, they will be incapable of autonomous action.[37] Meyer and Scott maintain that the legitimacy of a particular organization "is negatively affected by the number of different authorities sovereign over it and by the diversity or inconsistency of their accounts as how it is to function."[38] This point would suggest that agencies with multiple missions face an especially difficult task of legitimation.

The Importance of Institutional Homes

The approaches discussed thus far offer a number of perspectives that aid understanding of the empirical puzzle presented here. Weir's emphasis on the importance of institutions in shaping policy is a good starting point. Other factors such as interest groups, social movements, and policy legacies are also indispensable parts of the story. However, one must consider these factors in the context of a policy's institutional home, which mediates the impact of other factors that may be important in determining policy outcomes. In addition, the key elements of an institutional home—structure and mission—have direct effects on policy outcomes. An advantaged institutional home will increase the odds of policy success—as measured by the degree to which agency goals as understood by employees are fulfilled—while a disadvantaged home will decrease these odds. An advantaged institutional home is one where agency employees consider the mission in question to be primary, other agency missions do not conflict with the mission in question, the agency's legitimacy will be judged by the achievement of that mission, and achievement of the agency's primary mission is relatively easy to convey to a broader audience. In a strong institutional home, the agency does not house numerous other programs, particularly ones with a tendency toward mismanagement or an unfavorable policy legacy.[39]

In contrast, a disadvantaged home is one where the mission in question is secondary and may conflict with other missions, legitimacy may be gauged by the achievement of other agency goals, and fulfillment of the mission is difficult to communicate. A weak institutional home may encompass other programs with a tendency toward mismanagement or a policy legacy that contradicts the mission in question. Multiple missions are likely to spawn competing agency cultures, which may result in inefficiency and ineffectiveness. "Organizations in which two or more cultures struggle for supremacy will," Wilson says, "experience serious conflict as defenders of one seek to dominate representatives of the others."[40]

Consider the case of an agency whose primary mission is to stimulate private enterprise but has other missions as well. One of these secondary missions is to enforce antidiscrimination laws. To take the example of housing production, a government agency might provide subsidies to a developer who plans to build 5,000 new units of needed housing in a metropolitan area. Bureaucrats responsible for housing production are thrilled. Bureaucrats in the civil rights office want to ensure that the housing units are located so as to promote racial integration and marketed to a wide cross-section of potential buyers so that the units are racially and economically integrated. The housing production staff has little interest in losing the good will of the builders or endangering the project itself by placing additional constraints on the developers.

The interest group for the builders will likely lobby the housing production staff, while civil rights advocacy groups will lobby the civil rights staff. This scenario goes against the implicit assumption in most explanations that opposing groups are vying for the attention of the same agency staffers. Bureaucrats in a disadvantaged institutional home not only have to justify their policy approaches to outside audiences, such as other branches of government and the media, but to agency employees not directly involved in that mission. Other agency employees may view the aggressive approach as directly threatening their own career objectives and may seek to undermine bold action. So, while an advocacy group may capture a civil rights staff, this capture may be only marginally effective if the staff has little power within the agency. By the same token, the presence of many institutional activists may have little effect if they are part of a civil rights office within a larger agency.

Agency mission and structure mediate other factors as well. A disadvantaged institutional home will tend to encourage policy feedback that constrains rather than enables aggressive action. In the enforcement of antidiscrimination laws, political actors may plausibly model their approach on previous policies in the particular policy area (e.g., housing, employment, education), or existing civil rights policies in other policy areas (or by other political jurisdictions). After passage of the Civil Rights Act of 1968, which extended antidiscrimination protections to the area of housing, HUD had two plausible paths to follow. On the one hand, the agency could carry out fair housing laws in a muted way (using a colorblind, case-by-case approach), reflecting the federal government's legacy of tolerating and even encouraging residential racial segregation. One might expect this direction if long-time employees of the agency remained there after passage of fair housing laws. On the other hand, the agency could implement fair housing laws in an aggressive, race-conscious manner, as government agencies in employment and education were doing, with judicial support. If civil rights policies were housed in a disadvantaged institutional home, we would expect to see the former scenario play out, as civil rights staffers might lack the power within the agency to enact the aggressive measures that they favored. In the case of an advantaged institutional home, the latter would be more likely.

An advantaged institutional home also decreases the chances of presidential sanctions. This has to do with presidential concerns about legitimacy. When attempting retrenchment in civil rights policies, a president runs a greater risk to his own legitimacy if he takes on an agency with the sole mission of enforcing civil rights laws.[41] Of course, a president may want a highly publicized dispute with agency heads to dramatize his position. In most cases—and certainly with Nixon—the president interested in civil rights retrenchment will attempt to portray himself as committed to civil rights goals, while opposing bureaucratic overreaching.

A similar risk applies for delegitimation more generally, as larger agencies with multiple missions have greater chances of scandals or mismanagement in one section of the agency tainting the agency's repu-tation as a whole.[42] Policy feedback approaches do not capture this dif-fusion of delegitimation, which may pose a danger equal to or greater than the constraining effects of prior policies. As noted earlier, policy legacies may be an important determinant of whether an institutional home is relatively strong or weak. The institutional home, however, me-diates *which* policy legacies are drawn upon and *how* these prior policies affect new policies. The presence of multiple missions—even absent pol-icy legacies that are, for instance, hostile to civil rights goals—may pres-ent serious obstacles to the fulfillment of one or more agency objectives and offer additional opportunities for agency opponents to attack these initiatives.

The institutional context is not an explanation in itself, but provides a framework for unraveling how and why agencies act in particular ways, and how various governmental and private interests in the political pro-cess respond to these actions. Stated another way, institutional homes are not merely the starting point that affects which path a policy takes. They are enduring parts of the political landscape; paying attention to them allows us a more complete understanding of the reactions, strate-gies, and decisions of political actors as policy is continually shaped and reshaped.

Political Strategies of Blame Avoidance

Scholars of social policy often assume that policymakers, whenever pos-sible, will act and vote in an attempt to claim credit with constituents and clientele groups that benefit from these actions.[43] Thus, in the case examined here, one would expect the Nixon White House to battle civil rights agencies aggressively and explicitly, making clear that the relax-ation of enforcement efforts is a gift to its political supporters. A com-peting expectation follows from Weaver's assertion that "when push comes to shove, most officeholders seek above all not to maximize the credit they receive but to minimize blame."[44] This objective entails a more subtle strategy, in which the White House balances its attempts to receive credit from its conservative supporters with occasional efforts to placate civil rights supporters and, more importantly, convey to ob-servers that it is constrained by factors beyond its control: courts, the Congress, and so on. Consequently, the White House can pin less-than-optimal policy outcomes on other political actors. This blame avoidance strategy seems particularly useful for complex, contentious issues where ideal outcomes are hard to specify and even harder to realize. Such an approach would also accord with studies revealing that constituencies respond more strongly to losses than they do to gains.[45] In the two-party system of the United States, taking ambiguous positions, especially on divisive issues, may often represent the best strategy for electoral candidates.

For officeholders, however, the strategy of blame avoidance does not always entail "ambiguity and inaction."[46] This point rings especially loudly when one considers presidential decision-making regarding government agencies. In many cases, the president cannot escape blame for the actions of executive agencies merely by claiming unawareness of agency actions or inability to stop them. When advisers or agencies attract criticism, they may serve as "lightning rods" that deflect blame from the president himself. Alternatively, they may become a political liability to the president, as occurred with Ronald Reagan's interior secretary, James Watt.[47]

Administrative agencies may have goals that conflict with White House objectives. The president may attempt to rid an agency of troublesome employees by firing them or forcing their resignations. As discussed in the previous section, the White House has struggled to get agencies to act as the executive wishes. Given the difficulty with which agency actions can be brought into line with White House desires, the president will choose which battles to fight based on his perceived odds of winning, as it is a clear political disaster to try publicly and unsuccessfully to redirect an agency's activities.[48] To understand the political calculus involved in deciding which agency (or agencies) to take on, it is necessary to examine the characteristics of the agencies themselves.

Examining comparable agencies affords substantial analytical leverage. By doing so, one can identify the qualities that make agencies more likely to achieve the goals they set. This perspective also permits a grounded evaluation of success. If one were to examine any civil rights agency in isolation, measuring success by whether it has eliminated inequality, then each agency would rank as a failure. This criterion, however, is not realistic, nor is it particularly helpful. By investigating comparable agencies, one can evaluate *relative* success in relation to what other agencies have accomplished.

HURDLES TO HOUSING DESEGREGATION INITIATIVES

Despite facing their own, formidable obstacles, the employment and education bureaucracies both managed to interpret their limited congressional mandates creatively to justify taking bold, race-conscious action in their respective areas. Title VI of the 1964 Civil Rights Act prohibits entities receiving federal funds from engaging in racial discrimination. The 1964 legislation exempted federal mortgage insurance, including the Federal Housing Administration (FHA) and Veterans Administration (VA) loan programs, from coverage. Title VII of the 1964 legislation, which addresses employment discrimination, specifically prohibits the use of "preferential treatment" to correct racial imbalance. The Civil Rights Act of 1968 states that "it is the policy of the United States to provide, within constitutional limitations, for fair housing throughout the United States," and directs the secretary of Housing and Urban Development to act "affirmatively" to enforce the provisions of the law. In antidiscrimination laws, terms such as "discrimination," "fair housing," and "affirmative action" are not defined, and thus are subject to varying interpretations.

One way in which housing antidiscrimination laws differ from those in employment and education is in their later passage, lagging four years behind protections in the other two areas. Antidiscrimination initiatives in employment and education did not develop much in the four years that transpired between passage of the two civil rights laws. Yet the head start of the employment and education bureaucracies probably did mean that, by 1968, they had some experience in identifying which desegregation strategies might work best; HUD did not. Federal agencies intensified desegregation policies in employment and education during the Nixon Administration, after the fair housing law was passed. Within the broad political context, civil rights efforts in all three areas were up against public resistance and an administration that was ambivalent, at best, about extensions of existing policies.

In more specific terms, however, each area featured distinct political dynamics. Housing is typically viewed as an area ruled by local prerogatives. This is not an entirely accurate view. First, as subsequent chapters will detail, the federal government was intimately involved in the perpetuation and maintenance of residential segregation. Most pivotally in the massive suburban migration following World War II, the FHA and the VA reinforced all-white neighborhoods by refusing to insure mortgages in multiracial neighborhoods, and in many all-black neighborhoods as well. In doing so, the federal government affirmed the beliefs of prospective white homeowners and private interests that investment in racially exclusive neighborhoods was the only sensible financial decision one could make. During the years after World War II, and again during the Nixon Administration, the great public demand for housing afforded the federal government substantial leverage in ensuring the equitable treatment of all its citizens. This leverage remained largely untapped. Left to their own devices, localities believed that their self-interest rested in excluding nonwhites, and—whenever possible—families of low and moderate income, regardless of race. The belief in local sovereignty existed in education as it did in land use, reflected in the pervasive unwillingness of Southern communities to desegregate their schools in the absence of severe federal arm-twisting.

Much of the struggle to foster suburban desegregation has butted up against the practice of exclusionary zoning by municipalities. In legal theory, states are invested with complete power over local governments; however, states have typically granted local governments "home rule" authority for decisions affecting the locality. Many localities have passed ordinances requiring minimum sizes for homes or lots, and banning multi-family housing, mobile homes, and subsidized housing.[49] Towns designed these ordinances consciously to maintain economic segregation to the greatest extent possible.

Debates over interpretation of the Fair Housing Act have focused largely on the question of whether showing that a policy or practice has a disproportionate racial impact (regardless of intent) is enough to prove a violation of the right to fair housing. In employment, the Supreme Court established the disparate impact standard in the pivotal *Griggs v. Duke Power Co.* (1971) (401 U.S. 424) decision, then progressively narrowed it, culminating in *Wards Cove Packing Co. v. Atonio* (1989) (490 U.S. 642). Congress passed the Civil Rights Act of 1991 to codify the disparate impact standard under Title VII of the Civil Rights Act of 1964, which protects against discrimination in employment. The legal situation is considerably cloudier in housing. The Supreme Court has never ruled on whether a case can be brought under the Fair Housing Act based exclusively on disparate impact theory. Appeals courts have been divided, making for "an increasingly incoherent body of case law."[50] The 1988 amendments to the Fair Housing Act did little to clarify this confusion, as political actors differed widely on whether a disproportionate impact standard held sway in housing.

Housing is also an industry with many moving parts, including builders, lending institutions, and real-estate brokers, as well as governmental entities concerned with housing. The most results-oriented approach to combating racial inequality has proven to be addressing broad patterns, rather than strictly investigating individual cases of discrimination. This approach, typically labeled "affirmative action," has been used extensively in both employment and education. Lending institutions and big building firms are clearly large enough to monitor broad racial patterns. Given average income, racial makeup of the metropolitan area, and other demographic data, one can identify towns whose populations deviate from reasonable expectations of racial diversity. It is then relatively simple to identify those towns that *may be* practicing or condoning racially discriminatory behavior. Mustering the political will to investigate possible offenders, and compelling these towns to take some form of affirmative action, has been considerably more difficult.

DEFINING AFFIRMATIVE ACTION POLICIES

Affirmative action itself is a notoriously muddy concept. The term is used most often to mean "race-conscious," as opposed to "color-blind," efforts by employers or educational institutions to increase the proportion of underrepresented groups within their ranks. The idea of affirmative action is rooted in an English legal concept of equity dating back several centuries, in which the administration of justice is guided by what is considered fair in a particular situation rather than by a rigid set of legal rules. The phrase "affirmative action" first appeared in the 1935 National Labor Relations Act. Under this law, affirmative action meant that employers found to be discriminating against union members would not only be required to stop the discrimination but also "to take such affirmative action including reinstatement of employees with or without back pay."[51]

When first used in the civil rights context, the concept of affirmative action was tied to a color-blind approach. Executive orders by Presidents Kennedy and Johnson required firms contracting with the federal government to "take affirmative action to ensure that applicants are employed, and that employees are treated during employment, without regard to their race, creed, color or national origin." The Civil Rights Acts of 1964 and 1968 both require the relevant agencies to act affirmatively to promote the antidiscrimination objectives of the legislation.

Skrentny identifies five primary tenets of race-conscious affirmative action in employment that distinguish it from the traditional color-blind model: (1) a requirement that employers in hiring and promotion decisions view race as real rather than unreal or irrelevant; (2) "an emphasis on counting anonymous minorities in the workforce," as opposed to treating each employee as an individual; (3) a de-emphasis on discriminatory or racist intent and on identifying individual victims of discrimination; (4) a de-emphasis or reevaluation of traditional standards of merit; and (5) an overarching concern with representation or utilization of minorities rather than stopping individual acts of discrimination.[52] This set of ideas appears to hold sway in university admissions policies as well—particularly the emphasis on counting anonymous minorities and the de-emphasis on individual victims of discrimination and on traditional standards of merit (e.g., SAT scores). One might also view busing for the purposes of school desegregation as a form of affirmative action, in that it focuses on racial representation in schools rather than individual acts of discrimination.

Few along the political spectrum would suggest that affirmative action is the ideal means to attack discrimination. Conservatives typically argue that such policies constitute reverse discrimination and violate the ideal of a meritocracy. Even defenders of affirmative action are likely to acknowledge that attempting to treat the root causes of discrimination and inequality would, in the long run, be more effective than affirmative action approaches, which attempt to alter the consequences of disadvantage. Nevertheless, this approach has yielded more demonstrable results than case-by-case, color-blind strategies.

While affirmative action in employment has been the subject of considerable scholarly attention in recent years, very little work has examined housing as a civil rights policy on the national level.[53] Affirmative action approaches in housing can take a number of forms. To one extent or another, HUD tried several approaches to encourage residential desegregation. These included the following: (1) site selection of public or subsidized housing in predominantly white or racially mixed neighborhoods; (2) requiring housing builders receiving government funds to foster integration in their advertising strategies and tenant selection; (3) requiring real-estate brokers to inform clients of all residential options, rather than showing families homes in different neighborhoods according to their race (as was customary); and (4) withholding government funds from localities or other entities whose actions (or inaction) promoted segregation. These strategies, if pursued more aggressively and effectively, likely would have engendered greater change in residential patterns. Subsidies for "pro-integrative" housing moves, a requirement that localities or metropolitan agencies develop and implement plans to foster neighborhood integration, and race-conscious tenant assignments in public housing represent other policy possibilities.

This book focuses on federally subsidized housing and private housing, rather than project-based, "bricks and mortar" public housing. For many years, local housing authorities—without objection by the federal government—segregated residents of public housing by race.[54] By the time these practices came under close scrutiny, many cities found few non-elderly whites willing to live in public housing with significant numbers of racial minorities; as a result, integration within buildings became virtually impossible.[55] During the Nixon Administration, policy deliberations about "opening the suburbs" seldom considered the possibility of integration via the placement of public housing, often with a primarily nonwhite tenant population, in white neighborhoods. Many political actors believed that suburban towns were considerably more resistant to traditional public housing than to subsidized housing. In a number of cases, however, suburban residents seemed to consider all housing associated with the federal government to be "public housing." Of the options that were on the table, formation of regional boards to plan for and manage economic and racial desegregation represented the best possibility for notable progress (see chapter 5).

CIVIL RIGHTS POLICIES DURING THE NIXON ERA

An understanding of HUD's failure to implement effective desegregation policies must account for the political context that the agency faced under the Nixon Administration. Scholars in recent years have offered a number of different takes on Nixon's civil rights policies generally, and specifically on Nixon's support for affirmative action in employment. O'Reilly's analysis of the racial politics of American presidents labels Nixon a "demographer," concerned only with placing himself in the most advantageous political position possible in a given situation. Graham paints a similar portrait, arguing that Nixon designed his civil rights policies to maximize political dividends.[56] The fact that he occupied the White House at a pivotal time for civil rights policy, coupled with his often-unpredictable positions on specific issues, makes Nixon's tenure as president a particularly revealing period to examine.

Critics often emphasize that President Nixon was guided by a "Southern strategy" that sought to secure the support of whites, especially from the South, who might be receptive to the more blatant racial appeals of George Wallace.[57] True enough, Wallace was a concern to Nixon. But Nixon had other political concerns as well. "Turning back the clock" completely on civil rights was not a viable strategy. First, many politicians across the political spectrum feared that pulling back too far on civil rights enforcement would reignite the black anger and violence that had swept through numerous urban areas in the preceding years. In O'Reilly's take, "[T]he President wanted manageable division and bitterness between the races, not the chaos that would have followed unqualified success" in turning back civil rights movement goals in areas such as school desegregation and voting rights.[58]

Even if violence did not occur, Nixon knew that any sign of civil rights retreat would be met harshly by advocacy groups and covered widely by the media. While the civil rights movement during the Nixon era was in many respects sharply divided, several established organizations—such as the NAACP, the Urban League, and the Leadership Conference on Civil Rights—were still able to gain the attention of Washington and the news media, if not always the younger generation of African Americans.[59] Civil rights agencies were staffed by institutional activists who were ready to fight any attempts to dismantle government efforts. While Nixon was to become more and more impatient with the career bureaucrats who would not bend to his wishes, he also created problems for himself by appointing independent progressives to head domestic policy departments.[60]

Lastly, at least in the case of busing, it is not entirely clear that Nixon alone could have halted court-ordered desegregation.[61] While many members of Congress shared Nixon's distaste for busing as a means of desegregation, the president was never able to sign legislation that slowed the use of this approach in any significant way. He did, nevertheless, try repeatedly to avoid blame for the continuance of busing by attributing responsibility to the courts. In housing, Nixon ended desegregation policies indirectly by cutting off all housing funding. He did this at no electoral risk, since he waited until after his reelection to do so. The remainder of this book explores the causes and consequences of this abandonment of housing desegregation policies, at a time when the potential for changes in racially separate living patterns was virtually unparalleled.

How This Book Unfolds

Chapter 2 develops the comparative aspect of the study, situating housing antidiscrimination policies via concise analyses of civil rights policies in employment and education, as carried out by federal civil rights agencies. In employment and education, federal bureaucrats overcame factors such as presidential disapproval, public resistance, and limited authority to institute relatively strong, race-conscious policies, at least for a period of time. This chapter also considers the field of health care, where civil rights enforcement was virtually nonexistent after a brief flurry of activity when the Medicare program was launched. Faced with limited funding and resources, the Department of Health, Education, and Welfare's Office for Civil Rights (OCR) paid nearly exclusive attention to school desegregation, at the expense of discrimination in the health care system. The last part of chapter 2 establishes residential segregation as a crucial policy problem, reviewing research on the extent and effects of racial isolation in housing.

Chapter 3 begins the historical narrative about housing, recounting federal involvement in residential segregation prior to the Nixon Administration. This chapter shows that federal action or inaction can have dramatic consequences for residential patterns and racial inequality, and it illustrates that the legacy of pro-segregative policies and deferential treatment of the housing industry constrained HUD's efforts during the

Nixon Administration. I utilize several archival sources often left un-tapped in such inquiries, including the papers of several civil rights or-ganizations and those of Robert C. Weaver, a pivotal figure in fighting housing discrimination throughout the twentieth century and the first secretary of HUD, a distinction that also made him the first black cabi-net member in American history. In presenting this account of govern-mental policy-making, *Knocking on the Door* also makes use of HUD agency files, the presidential papers of Presidents Johnson, Nixon, and Carter, and the papers of HUD Secretary George Romney, as well as congressional testimony, court decisions, and secondary accounts.

In addition to documenting the evolution of federal housing policies, chapter 3 examines the long legislative battle to establish a cabinet de-partment for housing and urban development, and the unlikely passage of the Civil Rights Act of 1968 (the Fair Housing Act). Legislative de-bates reflect a Congress concerned with the growing power of federal civil rights bureaucracies, and debating whether a housing antidiscrimi-nation law would foster or forestall riots, which occurred with alarming frequency in the latter half of the 1960s. The chapter concludes with a discussion of HUD's early fair housing activities in the waning days of the Johnson Administration.

Chapter 4 describes HUD's bright civil rights prospects early in the Nixon Administration, marked by new legislative protections against housing discrimination, a greatly increased federal commitment to hous-ing production, and support for suburban desegregation within the agency and the White House. HUD had some early successes in "open-ing up the suburbs" by withholding needed agency funding from locali-ties that failed to provide low- and moderate-income housing, or that discriminated against racial minorities. Its ill-fated attempts to bring about open housing in Warren, Mich., proved highly consequential, gen-erating negative publicity and the scrutiny of the White House. This chapter documents some of the early struggles between HUD and the White House. It also assesses some of the opportunities and constraints that HUD faced, considering the ways in which external political forces such as business elites, advocacy groups, and the public at large influ-enced and responded to the agency's civil rights initiatives.

Chapter 5 focuses on tensions and vulnerabilities within the agency that are traceable to its weak institutional home. HUD's housing produc-tion staffers worked furiously to process applications for HUD assis-tance, showing little concern for civil rights issues. This myopic attention to housing production led to scandals in the FHA that resulted in a loss of legitimacy by the agency. Before these scandals fully came to light, hopes for aggressive desegregation were bolstered by a series of court decisions that broadly interpreted HUD's mandate to ensure "affirmatively" the

right to fair housing. Corruption in the FHA's inner-city housing programs, which were unrelated to suburban desegregation, wiped away the
prospects for such an attack on segregation. Despite evidence that the
problems in these programs were capable of repair, President Nixon
seized this political opportunity by declaring a housing "freeze" shortly
after his 1972 reelection. In doing so, Nixon was able to halt federal expenditures on increasingly costly subsidy programs and to stop the housing desegregation drive indirectly. Such a move helped Nixon to sidestep
much of the blame normally pinned on politicians pursuing civil rights retrenchment. It was HUD's weak institutional home for civil rights, in the
context of public resistance, that gave Nixon this political opening.

   Chapter 6 brings the story up to date, providing a survey of American
policy approaches to residential integration since the 1973 housing
freeze. The most noteworthy federal effort has been Moving to Opportunity, a voucher-based mobility program modeled on the Chicago-area
Gautreaux program that ran from 1976 to 1998. Under this approach, a
limited number of families eligible for public housing receive assistance
in locating private housing, typically in predominantly white, suburban
neighborhoods. This chapter also looks briefly at several state-level interventions to encourage racial and economic integration in housing and
at the small number of suburban towns that have taken it upon themselves to promote and maintain residential integration, rather than
falling prey to "white flight" and resegregation. As the towns themselves
will attest, these pro-integrative policies are extraordinarily difficult to
sustain in the absence of coordination among localities at the metropolitan level. Indeed, the specific policy lessons of this book are that solutions
to the vexing problems of economic and racial segregation are unlikely to
be realized in the absence of metropolitan-level planning.

   The final chapter continues the comparative aspect of the study by examining civil rights policies in employment and education since the
Nixon era, explaining retrenchment in school desegregation and the re-
silience of affirmative action in employment in the face of President Reagan's attempts to dismantle it. The final section summarizes the book's
key theoretical and empirical findings, and examines the implications of
these findings for scholarship on social policy and the development of
more effective regulatory policies.

Chapter Two

The Divergence of Civil Rights Policies in Housing, Education, and Employment

THE CIVIL RIGHTS ACT of 1964 profoundly changed federal governmental treatment of racial discrimination. Ending the Senate debate on cloture, Minority Leader Everett Dirksen (R-IL) stressed the inevitability of such a change, quoting Victor Hugo's aphorism: "Stronger than all the armies is an idea whose time has come." Dirksen added, "The time has come for equality of opportunity in sharing in government, in education and in employment. It will not be stayed or denied. It is here."[1] Those opposing the legislation also foresaw profound changes resulting from its passage. Howard W. Smith (D-VA), chair of the House Rules Committee, warned apocalyptically of fallout from the legislation: "Already the second invasion of the Southland has begun. Hordes of beatniks, misfits and agitators from the North, with the admitted aid of the Communists, are streaming into the Southland mischief-bent, backed and defended by other hordes of federal marshals, federal agents, and federal power."[2]

Important as this legislative accomplishment was, it was far from inevitable. "When President Kennedy sent his civil rights bill to Congress June 19, 1963," *Congressional Quarterly* observed, "the wildest optimist would not have predicted enactment of the bill which President Johnson soon will sign into law."[3] In fact, two sections of the law that would prove most influential in the evolution of antidiscrimination policies were nearly not included in the version passed by Congress. The provision allowing the government to cut off federal funding from entities found to be discriminating was added to the original Kennedy bill "at the last minute for bargaining purposes"; this authority has been the single greatest weapon used by the federal government to fight discriminatory behavior. The original Kennedy bill did not include equal employment opportunity provisions. His message to Congress merely expressed "renewed" support for equal employment bills already before congressional committees. Fair employment practices legislation was added to the House bill "in the expectation that the Senate would drop it in order to get the bill through . . . The Administration stood ready, if necessary, to drop both [fair employment practices and funding cut-off] provisions in order to get a bill."[4] Had Southern Democrats opposed to the bill bargained with the Senate leadership on amendments, rather than adhering

to their ultimately failing filibuster strategy, a substantially weaker law—
or possibly no law at all—likely would have resulted.[5]

After passage of the Civil Rights Acts of 1964 and 1968, antidiscrimination protections in U.S. civil rights laws covering housing, employment, and education diverged in practice in significant and sometimes
surprising ways. One influence in the disparate development of these
policies was the distinct policy legacies that existed in these areas prior
to the groundbreaking civil rights laws passed in the 1960s.

Early Experience with Affirmative Action in Employment

Two main factors stand out in the history of civil rights enforcement in
employment. First, statistical monitoring of the workforce was not a foreign concept to business prior to government mandates to do so in the
mid-1960s. Businesses have always kept records of their workers, even if
many did not record the race of each employee. (Those companies with
all-white work forces would have little rationale for doing so.) Prior to
federal monitoring requirements, around 200 large corporations voluntarily did so through an initiative called "Plans for Progress," which fa-
miliarized participating firms with the racial monitoring approach.

More significant than this relatively mild legacy was the strong institutional home for civil rights that developed within the EEOC after its birth
in 1965. On its face, this assertion may seem odd. After all, the EEOC was
created with little enforcement authority and meager funding. What the
agency did possess was a unity of purpose that propelled its employees to
search for ways that it could fulfill its basic mandate of fighting discrimination in employment. Early in the EEOC's life, employees realized that
the relative ineffectiveness of investigating individual complaints of discrimination was frustrating—and it made them look bad. They had ample
incentives to try to find a better way, a way that produced tangible results.
When they did, they found that courts were willing to yield to their expertise. The Office of Federal Contract Compliance (OFCC) was also an
advantaged home for civil rights. Though not a stand-alone agency, the
OFCC had the power to cut off funding to federal contractors that did not
comply with antidiscrimination requirements, and the support of the Department of Labor (in which it was situated) to use this authority.

The federal government made its first real attempt to address employment discrimination during World War II. In the wake of a threatened
March on Washington led by A. Phillip Randolph of the Brotherhood
of Sleeping Car Porters, President Franklin D. Roosevelt signed Executive Order 8802, which established a policy of nondiscrimination in government employment and defense contracts.[6] EO 8802 also created a

five-person Fair Employment Practices Committee (FEPC), which was charged with receiving and investigating complaints of discrimination, taking "appropriate steps" to address verified grievances, and recommending to the president and federal agencies ways by which the order could be carried out. Roosevelt's Executive Order 9346 of May 1943 formally dissolved the first FEPC, and established a new one under the president's wartime authority as commander-in-chief. This second version of the FEPC asserted the duty of all employers and labor organizations "to provide for the full and equitable participation of all workers in defense industries without discrimination."[7] The new commission was authorized to hold hearings and issue findings of fact. The two FEPCs combined were able to resolve successfully roughly one-third of the 14,000 complaints that they received; their success ratio in the South was one-fifth. Employers and unions found that they could, if so inclined, stall the FEPC for considerable lengths of time. While the push to establish a permanent FEPC gained some congressional support, the commission was dissolved in 1946. Beginning in 1948, a series of executive orders prohibited discrimination in government contracts and in the federal civil service. Government contract committees could publicize and attempt to conciliate disputes but lacked the power to impose sanctions. Contracting officers in executive departments and agencies had the power to cancel contracts due to findings of discrimination, but they were typically more concerned with procuring goods and services.

Between 1945 and 1964, twenty-six states passed fair employment practices laws. A typical statute declared it illegal to discriminate against or refuse to hire an individual based on his/her race, color, religion, or national origin. State commissions sought voluntary compliance, under which the committee would try to convince the company to offer the prospective employee the first appropriate job opening and to stop discriminating. When conciliation was unsuccessful, the commission could hold a public hearing and order the employer to cease and desist from practices found to be unlawful. In addition, the employer could be ordered to hire, reinstate, or upgrade an employee, and a union ordered to grant an individual membership.[8] Relying on an individual complaint model, these state panels had little recourse against all-white companies that hired via personal references and other job search methods from which blacks were informally but not explicitly excluded.[9]

COLLECTING RACIAL STATISTICS

Under President Dwight Eisenhower, the President's Committee on Government Contracts (PCGC), directed by Vice President Richard Nixon, was an important precursor to later federal affirmative action efforts. The panel examined the racial composition of the federal work force in several cities, "gathering statistical data that raised questions about possible discrimination and indirectly pressuring contractors to hire blacks."[10] The committee's executive director, Jacob Seidenberg, remarked in 1957 that "the occupational breakdown of the work force by race probably is the most important information to be gathered during the survey. This is the yardstick by which the contractor's compliance . . . is measured." The PCGC began to view integration as the "affirmative duty to make specific commitments. These are specific only when they spell out the fact that a definite number of qualified Negroes will be employed within a given period of time."[11] Despite the bold new rhetoric, the panel still had minimal leverage in its negotiations with employers. In addition, the PCGC's efforts were complicated by the fact that states with fair employment practices laws made racial data collection illegal.

John F. Kennedy assumed the presidency as civil rights protests were beginning to spread throughout the South. During the campaign, Kennedy had supported civil rights sit-ins and memorably phoned Coretta Scott King when her husband, Martin Luther King, Jr., was jailed in Reidsville, Georgia.[12] Perhaps unsurprisingly, Kennedy's support for civil rights became more muted after his inauguration. Rather than urging Congress to pass civil rights legislation and risking Southern support for other initiatives, he took the safer step of issuing another executive order and forming another committee. EO 10925 prohibited discrimination in the government contract program and in government employment, created the President's Committee on Equal Employment Opportunity (PCEEO), and required contractors to take "affirmative action" to ensure that individuals were treated without regard to race, creed, color, or national origin. Contractor obligations included an agreement to provide information and reports about their employment practices, including work force statistics. The PCEEO had the authority to cancel contracts or debar contractors and was charged with reviewing and publicizing statistical surveys of the federal work force that were to be conducted by departments and agencies. EO 10925 was the first to provide such enforcement authority.

Much of the PCEEO's effort revolved around negotiating with large firms to adopt voluntary "Plans for Progress" (PFP). After signing a ten-year, billion dollar defense contract with the Pentagon, the Lockheed Corporation was the subject of thirty-two complaints by black workers of employment discrimination at its new Marietta, Georgia, plant. The filing of these complaints, led by the NAACP, spurred negotiations between Marietta and the PCEEO for the contractor to abandon its Jim Crow cafeteria, washrooms, and water fountains, and—more importantly—to agree to accelerated hiring, upgrading, and access to apprenticeships for African Americans. In May 1961, Lockheed president Courtlandt S. Gross joined President Kennedy and Vice President Johnson at the White House to announce a Plan for Progress in the desegregation of its work force. By May 1964, 192 companies had signed such agreements, in which firms were exempted from standard contract compliance enforcement by agreeing to undertake racial surveys of their work force and change their practices to enhance equal opportunity.[13]

The PFP's Board of Directors was an advisory council of around twenty representatives from member corporations whose chairman (who changed annually) was typically the president or CEO of a major defense contractor. In addition to recruiting new companies, the staff published "educational materials" such as newsletters, statistical reports of members' minority work forces, and "how to" manuals, and it sponsored job fairs and seminars on equal opportunity policies.[14] A survey of the first 101 signers of these plans reported that the percentage of minority employees increased from 5.1 percent in 1963 to 9.3 percent in 1966; the gross number of minority employees jumped from 200,000 to 471,000 over this time period. Minorities represented 1.5 percent of these firms' white-collar workers in 1963, and 4 percent in 1966; the aggregate number of minority, white-collar employees rose from 29,000 in 1963 to 93,000 three years later.[15] The EEOC had a more skeptical take on the effectiveness of these voluntary efforts, finding in 1968 that the largest hundred PFP members headquartered in New York City had fewer minority white-collar employees than did non-PFP members.[16] While these voluntary efforts were insufficient stand-ins for binding government protections, Plans for Progress did provide early experience for government and business in utilizing an affirmative action approach concerned more with increasing hiring and promotion of blacks than policing individual acts of discrimination.[17] As the civil rights movement in the South drew increasing attention and sympathy from the media and the public, the clamor for federal protection against employment discrimination grew.

The movement achieved its first major legislative victory with the passage of the Civil Rights Act of 1964. Title VII of the 1964 Civil Rights Act makes it unlawful for an employer "to fail or refuse to hire or to discharge any individual . . . because of such individual's race, color, religion, sex, or national origin," while Title VI provides the power to withhold government funds from federally assisted programs that are found to be noncompliant with antidiscrimination laws. Opponents of the historic civil rights legislation were concerned that Title VII of the bill would be used to justify racial quotas in employment. An interpretive memorandum by Sen. Clark (D-PA) and Sen. Case (R-NJ), the bipartisan floor managers of the Senate debate, insisted that "there is no requirement in Title VII that an employer maintain a racial balance in his work force. On the contrary, any deliberate attempt to maintain a racial balance . . . would involve a violation of Title VII because maintaining such a balance would require an employer to hire or to refuse to hire on the basis of race."[18] To allay some of these concerns, Section 703(j) was added to Title VII as part of the Senate leadership compromise brokered to gain sufficient legislative support. This provision states plainly that the title does not "require any employer . . . to grant preferential treatment to any individual or group on account of an imbalance which may exist with respect to the total number or percentage of persons of any race . . . employed by an employer . . . in comparison with the total number or percentage of persons of such race . . . in any community . . . or in the available workforce in any community." The Senate compromise also included Section 706(g), which specified that the legislation aimed only at discriminatory acts that were intentional; inadvertent discrimination did not violate the law.

The Civil Rights Act of 1964 created the Equal Employment Opportunity Commission (EEOC) to enforce Title VII. When provided with a sworn charge of alleged discrimination by a private employer, labor organization, or employment agency, the EEOC could engage in conciliation with the accused party. If conciliation was unsuccessful, the commission would merely notify the complainant, who then had the option to file a lawsuit. The U.S. Attorney General and the Justice Department could take part in the suit if they felt that a "pattern or practice" of intentional discrimination existed and that the case was a matter of public importance.[19]

The commission's first chair, Franklin D. Roosevelt, Jr., predicted that the need for the commission would last fifteen to twenty years. He remarked in 1965 that he hoped "we could end job discrimination within 10 years, but I think it is going to take a little longer."[20] Civil rights advocates typically did not share this optimism in the EEOC's early days, finding the commission wanting in its statutory authority, congressional funding, and day-to-day operations. Eleanor Holmes Norton, a long-time civil rights activist who became EEOC chair under President Jimmy Carter, recalled that when the commission was created, civil rights supporters "were inclined not to expect too much."[21] Inadequate funding, combined with questionable leadership at the top and the difficulty of proving discrimination on a case-by-case basis, led to a mounting backlog of unresolved complaints. Out of a desire for self-preservation and a real commitment to root out discrimination, EEOC employees searched for more efficient ways to fulfill their mandate. Ultimately, the EEOC shifted its focus from determining whether individual discriminatory acts had taken place (an "intent" standard) to whether businesses hired minorities (and women) in what were considered to be fair proportions (an "effects" standard).[22]

How could an administrative agency with such limited powers spearhead such profound changes in social policy? Because Congress often passes legislation that leaves wide room for interpretation, administrative agencies may have substantial opportunities to shape how laws are carried out in practice. Alfred Blumrosen, a former EEOC staffer himself, observes that the decisions of administrators "are often taken in an atmosphere where the choice is free, where judgement is unencumbered by immediate political pressure or judicial precedent, where administrators can either be creative or cautious, and where the larger forces of the bureaucracy and the courts will support their decisions." For its part, the EEOC minimized the formal requirements for invoking Title VII, simplified federal-state relations, instituted a national reporting system despite apparently restrictive statutory language, developed an in-depth compliance procedure, established a framework for multilateral negotiation among labor, management, and civil rights groups, and utilized guidelines in the absence of official rule-making authority.[23] In addition, the EEOC was thought in some quarters to play fast and loose with the law. A commission staffer reportedly told the *Harvard Law Review* that "the anti-preferential provisions [of Title VII] are a big zero, a nothing, a nullity. They don't mean anything at all to us."[24]

That the EEOC was able to take these bold steps is even more noteworthy in light of its rather chaotic and ineffective early years. Staffing was an ongoing problem, as the new agency ran through four commissioners in its first five years, with no commissioner serving for even two years. Many employees felt that the first head of the EEOC, Franklin D. Roosevelt, Jr., lacked dedication, more concerned with planning a run for Governor of New York than with running the agency.[25] In April 1969, EEOC Chair Clifford Alexander resigned in frustration over the absence of support from the Nixon Administration.[26] Staff turnover at the upper levels was also frequent.

On top of this internal bickering, Congress consistently was stingy in its allocations to the commission. As its coverage increased each year to its widest in fiscal 1968, the EEOC requested greater budgets, which Congress denied. Given its lack of organization, funding and statutory authority, the EEOC quickly accumulated a staggering backlog of discrimination complaints from individuals around the country. From the first 15,000 complaints it received, the agency tabbed 6,040 for investigation, and completed 3,319 of these investigations. Due to the EEOC's weak means of recourse against companies and a nationwide staff of only five conciliators, a mere 111 cases were conciliated successfully in the commission's first year.[27]

But Title VII of the law also provided authority to the EEOC to collect data from employers and labor organizations that the commission deemed necessary, so long as this data was not already required by state or local FEPCs, or by previous executive orders. Alfred Blumrosen, the commission's chief liaison for federal, state, and local agencies, reports having discovered "underutilization" lists at the PCEEO offices that recorded employers with few or no black employees. This was just the sort of data that the new agency needed. This information was, however, not easy to tap. Most importantly, the establishment of a national reporting system required an interpretation of the relevant statute in the Civil Rights Act that was "contrary to the plain meaning" of it.[28] In addition, the PCEEO was less than willing to share their lists with an agency viewed as something of an upstart competitor. (Blumrosen initially obtained a copy of the PCEEO's underutilization lists unofficially through one of its staffers who was interested in a post at the EEOC.)

This move toward required racial record-keeping created some controversy. In fact, civil rights groups and other liberals were initially quite skeptical about the government sanctioning racial identification, which had historically been a tool to exclude African Americans. At an August 1965 White House conference on equal employment opportunity, Clarence Mitchell, the NAACP's chief lobbyist in Washington, chastened supporters of the EEOC's nascent approach for their naiveté: "It seems to me incredible that the Government of the United States, recognizing that there is a nasty, underhanded little system for keeping track of people through a cute little code system . . . would make it easy for discrimination by saying 'Oh, no, you don't use obscure little marks. You put a nice big thing which shows this is a Negro so you don't have to put on your glasses to find out.'"[29] It was not until 1968 that the NAACP switched its position from opposition to support of governmental collection of racial data.[30] The EEOC's account of the conference—which was attended by 600 individuals identified as leaders from communities, industries, labor unions, and government agencies—reported that participants largely agreed that affirmative action programs and racial record-keeping requirements were essential elements in the agency's fight against employment discrimination.[31] The commission's new approach survived a December 1965 public hearing, resistance from the Budget Bureau, and reservations from some of its own commissioners, and in March 1966 the agency began to require the submission of a master EEO-1 reporting form from companies with one hundred or more employees.[32]

Using the data gathered from the EEO-1 reporting forms, the EEOC began to sponsor public hearings that convened representatives of specific industries, discussing data on minority underrepresentation and urging firms to change their business practices voluntarily to address this problem. Between 1967 and 1971, hearing topics included discrimination in the textile industry in the South and white-collar employment in New York City, as well as the nationwide practices of the pharmaceutical and utility industries. The EEOC's 1966 Guidelines on Employment Testing Procedures were the first public delineation of the principle that Title VII of the Civil Rights Act prohibited facially neutral practices that had a discriminatory impact and could not be justified by business necessity.[33] While the EEOC was laying important groundwork in investigating broad patterns (rather than individual instances) of discrimination and documenting the extent to which these patterns existed, it was the other major civil rights enforcement agency for employment, the Office of Federal Contract Compliance (OFCC), with greater fiscal leverage against businesses under its purview, that really began to flex its muscles in the area of minority underutilization.

THE OFFICE OF FEDERAL CONTRACT COMPLIANCE JOINS THE FIGHT

The OFCC was created by a September 1965 executive order, EO 11246, that required firms under contract with the federal government to "take affirmative action to ensure" that job applicants and employees "are treated . . . without regard to their race, creed, color, or national origin." (The order was amended in 1967 to forbid discrimination on the basis of gender as well.) Most of the initial OFCC employees were culled from the PCEEO. While EO 11246 resembled previous presidential orders on job discrimination, the Johnson initiative was something of a departure because it made the OFCC part of the Department of Labor, rather than a stand-alone presidential commission. Thus, the contract compliance function moved from a highly politicized organization to a more technical one that needed to produce tangible results if it wished to establish and maintain legitimacy.[34]

The labor secretary, through the OFCC, was to submit regulations, investigate complaints, review compliance, hold hearings, and penalize violators. The compliance office could cancel contracts with firms that did not devise satisfactory affirmative action plans, though the agency had not invoked this sanction as of 1969. What exactly constituted affirmative action was left fuzzy. OFCC Director Edward C. Sylvester, Jr., explained that "there is no fixed and firm definition of affirmative action. I would say in a general way, affirmative action is anything that you have to do to get results."[35] Like the EEOC, the OFCC scrambled for ways to carry out its mandate efficiently and effectively given budgetary and staffing shortcomings.

The OFCC also struggled early on to build credibility among more established and considerably more powerful government agencies whose cooperation it required. When the new agency's proposed rules and regulations included OFCC clearance prior to the award of a contract, the Department of Defense, which was handling over 15 million contracts annually, ignored the OFCC's directive as unworkable. Defense awarded $9.4 million in contracts to three textile companies that had been found noncompliant with equal employment standards.[36] In its first couple of years, the OFCC settled for pursuing companies, mainly but not exclusively in the South, with blatantly segregationist policies. Its most public triumph was a March 1966 conciliation agreement that the OFCC, the EEOC, and the Department of Defense reached with the Newport News Shipbuilding and Drydock Company. The accord provided class relief for 5,000 of the firm's black employees and secured the company's promise to appoint 100 blacks to become supervisors.[37]

Despite the Defense Department's dismissal of early agency efforts, the OFCC maintained its view that pre-award clearance afforded the most leverage in fighting discrimination. Indeed, Executive Order 11246 specified that bidders could be asked to submit "Compliance Reports prior to or as an initial part of their bid or negotiations of a contract." In May 1966, the OFCC established this way of doing business in the construction industry only. Construction differed in a number of important respects from other industries that contracted with the government. For one thing, jobs were generally channeled through union hiring halls rather than employers, and employees typically worked intermittently.[38] Moreover, because construction firms typically sought contracts with multiple government agencies at the federal, state, and local levels, the OFCC could not feasibly assign compliance monitoring to one lead agency, as it did in other fields. Instead, the Department of Labor began to monitor the construction industry on a metropolitan or labor market basis. Unlike its monitoring of other industries, in which compliance officers were situated in other agencies, officers on the OFCC's payroll monitored construction.[39]

THE PHILADELPHIA PLAN

In 1966–67, during the Johnson Administration, the OFCC sought to ensure compliance in construction contracts in St. Louis, San Francisco, Cleveland, and Philadelphia. The construction industry was a sensible target for government action because the typically all-white makeup of construction crews was highly visible, the work that they performed seemed relatively simple, and civil rights organizations had demonstrated against and picketed all-white construction sites beginning in the early 1960s.[40] After the St. Louis and San Francisco plans produced few tangible results, the OFCC put additional pressure on Cleveland to come up with an approach that would show demonstrable progress. During the bidding process, one contractor included "manning tables" that specified the number of minorities to be hired in each trade. Seizing on this idea, the OFCC subsequently required such tables for all Cleveland-area contractors. The Cleveland Plan became the model for the Philadelphia Plan, which fully included suggested ranges of minority hires. The Comptroller General in the General Accounting Office subsequently ruled that both the Cleveland and Philadelphia Plans were illegal (in May 1968 and November 1968, respectively) because they did not include specific minimum standards for affirmative action set forth prior to bidding. Since the rules did not offer equal and unambiguous terms and conditions to all bidders, a contract might be unfairly denied to the low bidder as a result of a contract compliance officer's arbitrary decision.[41]

The following year, the Nixon Administration revived the Philadelphia Plan for the integration of the construction trades.[42] Arthur Fletcher, who was then an assistant secretary at Labor, recalled that he defended the plan to the White House by explaining it as "workfare, not welfare. And President Nixon and the folks in the White House say, 'Oh, nobody's ever explained it that way.' "[43] The revised edition of the plan required contractors to select a specific minority hiring goal within ranges provided in the invitation for bids. These percentages were described as targets rather than quotas; employers that did not reach their targets would have to show that they had made a "good faith" effort to reach the target. Attorney General John Mitchell, responding to the Comptroller General's claim that the Philadelphia Plan violated the color-blind principle of Title VII in the 1964 Civil Rights Act, asserted that "the obligation of nondiscrimination . . . does not require and, in some circumstances, may not permit obliviousness or indifference to the racial consequences of alternative courses of action which involve the application of outwardly neutral criteria." He argued that "there is no inherent inconsistency between a requirement that each qualified employee and applicant be individually treated without regard to race, and a requirement that an employer make every good faith effort to achieve a certain range of minority employment."[44]

Scholars have identified several motivations for this Republican president, who appealed—sometimes blatantly—to white racial resentment, to throw his support behind an apparently liberal antidiscrimination strategy wrought with controversy. This decision had the political benefit of dividing two core Democratic constituencies: African Americans, who would support it, and labor, which would oppose it; top domestic policy aide John Ehrlichman highlights this political calculation as a major reason for Nixon's support of the Philadelphia Plan.[45] Skrentny develops a related argument, which draws on Skowronek, maintaining that Nixon was practicing the "politics of preemption" by exploiting existing political divisions and thus creating a wider political base for creative presidential leadership. Kotlowski argues that presidential support for affirmative action in employment was based on pragmatic politics: Nixon believed his stance in this area would gain the support of civil rights organizations, while not arousing the intensity of opposition that housing or educational desegregation would. Other scholars claim that the primary motivation for White House backing was economic, as increasing minority employment in the construction industry would lower construction costs and housing prices, thus increasing housing production.[46] Nixon surely knew that his support for the Philadelphia Plan would not transform him suddenly into a hero of the civil rights movement. By taking the side of civil rights supporters in this instance, Nixon could, however, avoid being tagged as a president who wished unequivocally to turn back the gains that had accrued for blacks during the previous administration, and show that he was capable of initiating his own equal opportunity efforts.

Nixon's resuscitation of the Philadelphia Plan was all the more surprising due to the deep suspicions of Congress. In December 1969, the Senate Appropriations Committee attached a rider to a supplemental appropriations bill that prevented any government funds from being spent on contracts disapproved by the Comptroller General. The Senate passed the bill, 73-13, and sent it to a conference committee. The Nixon White House publicly opposed the rider, with the president threatening a veto of the entire bill. The strategy was successful, as the House rejected the rider (208-156), and the Senate reversed its previous vote (39-29). Legal challenges to the plan similarly failed, enabling the Philadelphia Plan to take hold.[47]

George Shultz, the Secretary of Labor (which housed the OFCC), subsequently warned nineteen major cities that their failure to adopt Philadelphia-type plans to integrate the construction trades would provoke the imposition of a more rigorous plan from the OFCC's Washington office. In early 1970, with Nixon apparently unaware, the Labor Department issued Order No. 4, which expanded the newly validated affirmative action model from the construction trade to all federal contractors.[48] In addition to requiring contractors to take affirmative action in hiring through positive recruitment, the agency began to require a self-analysis of employer practices, data collection on hiring and promotional

practices in the context of the relevant labor market, and the establishment of goals and timetables in hiring and promotion.[49] The order also
specified that affirmative action is a "set of specific and result-oriented
procedures to which a contractor commits himself to apply every good
faith effort."[50]

The OFCC, like HUD's civil rights staff, was part of a larger agency.
The Labor Department, however, strongly backed affirmative action initiatives as a high-priority mission and was perfectly willing to use its financial leverage to compel compliance. Why the different stances by
HUD and Labor? Whereas the fair housing mission at HUD was a vague
responsibility piled on an already overwhelmed, difficult-to-administer
agency, the assignment of primary contract compliance functions to Labor significantly enhanced the agency's strength and reputation by giving
it a clear-cut responsibility and the authority to carry it out. As a result,
Labor defended the OFCC from political attacks.[51]

By the end of 1970, Nixon was again keyed into the affirmative action
issue, and was again changing course. Feeling that civil rights groups
never gave him credit for his progressive actions and encouraged by the
thousands of construction workers who had marched in support of his
Vietnam War policy, Nixon began distancing himself from these race-
conscious employment policies, though "he never publicly repudiated"
the Philadelphia Plan.[52] Union leadership remained angry with Nixon,
whose wage freeze was viewed by the AFL-CIO as hurting workers in
the building trades.[53] Local unions and civil rights organizations were
given the option of negotiating their own "hometown" plans in lieu of
the Philadelphia Plan. In what seemed to be more a public relations ploy
than a needed clarification, Nixon sent out a directive in August 1972
barring hiring quotas for federal government workers. That fall, on the
cusp of the presidential election, the Nixon Administration was reported
to be on the verge of weakening the Philadelphia Plan substantially or
eliminating it altogether. Nixon and the Democratic presidential candidate, George McGovern, both took pains to assert that they supported
hiring goals but were firmly opposed to quotas.[54]

While the Philadelphia Plan set an important precedent for federal use
of affirmative action approaches, the plan itself was not terribly effective
at opening jobs for African Americans. Under the plan, federal contractors were required to set hiring goals for minority workers in six prestigious crafts, which employed a mere 4 percent of the area's construction
workers. African Americans comprised 35 percent of the Philadelphia
region's construction workers, but only 2 percent of workers in the me-
chanical trades that the plans targeted. As a result, even aggressive efforts were unlikely to affect large numbers of black workers. Moreover,
in August 1969, the administration slashed federal construction by 75

percent, a move that the Office of Management and Budget later acknowledged had depressed minority entrance into the construction trades.[55] Nationwide, 17.4 percent of the 2.5 million local union members were identified as "Negro, Spanish American, Oriental, or American Indian"; members of these groups comprised 13.2 percent of the 1.5 million members of the building trades, and 23.3 percent of the 1.05 million members of nonbuilding trade unions.[56] In any event, the federal government had established the precedent of monitoring the racial composition of workplaces.

Judicial and Congressional Support for Affirmative Action

The affirmative action model received judicial and congressional support in 1971 and 1972. The Supreme Court offered its stamp of approval in 1971's *Griggs v. Duke Power Co.* (401 U.S. 424), which held that employers could be in violation of the Civil Rights Act of 1964 even in the absence of discriminatory intent. In this case, employees of Duke Power Company charged that hiring, transfer, and promotion policies requiring a high school diploma and a passing grade on two aptitude tests were discriminatory. When the suit was filed, fourteen of Duke's ninety-five employees were black; the company relegated black workers to its essentially custodial labor department. On the day (July 2, 1965) that Title VII of the Civil Rights Act took effect, the company instituted its testing requirement for new employees working outside of its labor department. The Supreme Court, in reversing a decision by the Fourth Circuit Court, maintained that under the Civil Rights Act of 1964, "practices, procedures, or tests neutral on their face, and even neutral in terms of intent, cannot be maintained if they operate to 'freeze' the status quo of prior discriminatory employment practices." The decision noted that the company's black employees had received an inferior education in North Carolina's then-segregated schools. Citing EEOC guidelines that permitted only job-related tests, the court stated that the "administrative interpretation of [the 1964 Civil Rights] Act by the enforcing agency is *entitled to great deference*" (emphasis added). The *Griggs* decision was particularly important for civil rights law in establishing the use of statistical evidence and requiring the demonstration of "business necessity" for employer practices with a disparate impact.[57]

In March 1972, Congress granted the EEOC authority to sue employers that were believed to be acting in a discriminatory fashion, thus giving employers a strong legal incentive to get their numbers "right." The Equal Employment Opportunity Act of 1972 did not grant the commission cease and desist authority, as some members of Congress had sought.

The legislation extended equal opportunity requirements to include employers and unions with fifteen or more full-time workers (down from twenty-five), employees of state and local government, and workers in religious institutions. It also created the Equal Employment Opportunity Coordinating Council, which consisted of the attorney general, the secretary of labor, and the chairs of the EEOC, the Civil Service Commission, and the U.S. Commission on Civil Rights (USCCR). The purpose of the council was, as its name suggests, to get the various government agencies involved in this field "singing off of the same page," and to stop employers from pitting one agency against another. During debate over the bill, the Senate rejected two amendments offered by Sen. Sam Ervin (D-NC). The first, which the Nixon Administration publicly opposed, would have banned "discrimination in reverse by employing persons of a particular race . . . in either fixed or variable numbers, proportions, percentages, quotas, goals or ranges." The second would have applied Title VII's prohibition of preferential treatment to executive orders as well.[58]

With its enhanced authority, the EEOC also received increased funding and an expanded roster of employees. The commission had a budget of $32 million for fiscal 1973, compared to $6.5 million in fiscal 1968. Its staff of attorneys swelled from 40 in November 1972 to 222 in June 1973. Business began to take serious note of the EEOC's activities after the commission reached a $38 million back-pay and promotion settlement with the American Telephone & Telegraph Company (AT&T) in January 1973. The commission discovered in 1970 that 7 percent of its workload was related to AT&T cases. Under the agreement, AT&T agreed to make $15 million in one-time payments to 13,000 women and 2,000 minority male workers who allegedly suffered discrimination due to the firm's employment policies, and $23 million in pay-policy and wage adjustments to 36,000 workers whose advancement may have been blocked.[59]

The agreement took shape before the EEOC got its court enforcement powers. The agency had intervened when AT&T—a public monopoly—had petitioned the Federal Trade Commission for a rate increase in its long-distance charges. The EEOC contended that a company with discriminatory employment policies should not receive a rate increase, and the FTC delayed its decision, affording the EEOC leverage in negotiations with AT&T. In the wake of the settlement, a U.S. Chamber of Commerce attorney commented that "fear is not too strong a word to use about the way companies feel about the EEOC now."[60] The EEOC seemed to encourage this response, with one staff attorney commenting that the AT&T settlement showed other employers that "we can take on some of the nation's biggest employers and beat the socks off them."[61]

The EEOC went on to file over 300 lawuits in less than two years, concentrating on large corporations such as General Motors, General Electric, and Sears, Roebuck. In a move that sent waves of fear through the corporate world, nine major steel companies reached a settlement with the EEOC in which they agreed to furnish $31 million in back pay to 40,000 African American, Latino, and female employees who allegedly experienced discrimination, and to set aside substantial percentages of future openings to racial minorities and women.[62] During the 1970s, the EEOC also wrung six-figure consent decrees from United Airlines (1976), Duquesne Light Company (1977) and Bechtel Corp. (1979), the nation's largest construction company. Employers took note: a study by the Bureau of National Affairs found that over 80 percent of large employers had equal employment opportunity policies, and follow-up on hiring and promotion decisions, by 1976.[63]

From its inception as a small agency charged with processing individual complaints of discrimination and gently persuading businesses to change their hiring practices, the EEOC evolved into an organization with the weapons to convince—or compel—businesses to make demonstrable changes in their recruitment, hiring, and promotion practices. With a shared sense of mission, EEOC employees developed innovative, far-reaching approaches to fight discrimination. Some observers felt strongly that these approaches extended well beyond the intent of the law. Fortunately for the agency, the courts offered their support. As Eleanor Holmes Norton, EEOC head under President Carter, recalled about the agency's early years: "The courts . . . were not much interested in whether EEOC was a true regulatory agency or had enforcement power. Lacking precedents in the American experience for civil rights enforcement, the courts accepted the expertise of the Commission and its view of the law. Never in the history of administrative law has an agency done so much with so little."[64]

PLODDING PROGRESS IN THE EARLY YEARS
OF SCHOOL DESEGREGATION

The Department of Health, Education, and Welfare's (HEW) Office for Civil Rights (OCR) also achieved some impressive results in its desegregation efforts. Though invested with more power initially than the EEOC, OCR operated in the face of considerable hostility from white citizens, as well as from the executive and legislative branches. The case of school desegregation provides an instructive middle case between the failure of race-conscious policies in housing and the relative effectiveness of them in employment. School desegregation initiatives started slowly, underwent a period of substantial progress, then largely fizzled after 1974. Two factors make the case of school busing distinctive. First, the development of school desegregation polices has been more strongly guided by judicial decision-making than affirmative action in housing or employment. This is not to suggest that the evolution of school desegregation is a story that can be told strictly from the perspective of the courtroom. As in other areas of civil rights, the actions of the department responsible for civil rights—in this case, HEW's Office for Civil Rights— played a key role in shaping the approach and reach of school desegregation policies. Second, school desegregation was the most prominent civil rights issue in the public eye: the volume of popular protest and maneuvering by politicians wishing to publicize their opposition to school busing dwarfed comparable activities in employment and housing.

The brief account of school desegregation that follows directs attention to dynamics within HEW, and between HEW and the White House, that shaped school desegregation efforts. The assignment of civil rights responsibilities within HEW—first within the individual program agencies, and later within a department-wide OCR—posed specific constraints and opportunities for the enforcement of antidiscrimination protections. Judicial decisions and public resistance also influenced the evolution of policy, as did the presidential strategy of blame avoidance.

In one of the most significant judicial decisions of the twentieth century, the Supreme Court's 1954 *Brown v. Board of Education of Topeka, Kansas* (347 U.S. 483) decision struck down the legality of public school systems explicitly divided by race, ruling that "separate educational facilities are inherently unequal." At the time, seventeen Southern and border states required that schools be segregated by race; Arizona, Indiana, Kansas, New Mexico, New York, and Wyoming explicitly permitted segregation.[65] The Supreme Court ruled in the *Brown II* decision (1955) (349 U.S. 294) that public school segregation must be ended with "all deliberate speed," but did not set a deadline for the accomplishment of this goal. Many states and school districts reacted to the ruling with defiance. *Southern School News* reported in 1962 that over 92 percent of Southern black students were still attending segregated schools.[66] Simply stated, Southern school desegregation moved at a glacial place in the decade following the *Brown* decision.

Nevertheless, the America of the late 1950s and early 1960s was in the midst of a historic transformation. Public awareness of discrimination against African Americans grew considerably from 1961 to 1965, as America witnessed jail-ins, Freedom Rides, dramatic campaigns against local discrimination (in Birmingham, Selma, and Albany), and the March on Washington. During the years 1961 to 1965, "the heyday of black insurgency," local civil rights protestors "sought to broaden the conflict by inducing their opponents to disrupt public order to the point where supportive federal intervention was required. As a by-product of the drama associated with these flagrant displays of public violence [by local white authorities], the movement was also able to sustain member commitment, generate broad public sympathy, and mobilize financial support from external groups."[67] From 1963 to 1965, civil rights was at or near the top of issues that Americans identified as "the most important problem facing this country today." In June 1963, 55 percent of whites in the North and 12 percent in the South supported passage of a law assuring equal rights in public accommodations. By the following January, in the wake of the March on Washington and the assassination of President Kennedy, support rose to 71 and 20 percent respectively.[68]

Passage of the Civil Rights Act of 1964 began the real move toward dismantlement of legally segregated primary and secondary education in the South. The key provision in terms of school segregation was Title VI, which bars discrimination in any federally funded activity and empowers the federal government to withhold aid from activities in which discrimination is found to exist. Also important was Title IV, which directed the Office of Education to furnish financial and technical assistance to de-segregating schools, and to undertake an examination of the equality of educational opportunity in schools nationwide. This section of the law also authorized the Attorney General to bring school desegregation suits.[69] In December 1964, HEW began its first formal actions to implement Title VI, informing state agencies administering Office of Education grants of their new responsibilities under the Civil Rights Act.

Individual program agencies had primary responsibility for implementing Title VI. Within HEW, five departmental units—the Office of Education, the Public Health Service, the Surplus Property Division, the Vocational Rehabilitation Administration, and the Welfare Administration—had Title VI obligations. This arrangement meant that each of these agencies was asked to convey grants and to refuse to do so if justified. An internal history of the department noted that HEW's "grant administrators had in past years demonstrated a general coolness to the idea of grant conditioning; now, in 1965, the function of conditioning grants was assigned to the agencies whose operations were conducted by these same administrators."[70]

The HEW assistant secretary was directed to evaluate and supervise Title VI activities within the agencies and to represent the department in government-wide Title VI activities. The assistant secretary, with a staff of two, was responsible also for other civil rights obligations (including those stemming from two executive orders covering equal employment opportunities), air and water pollution control, international affairs, and patent policy. James M. Quigley, the assistant secretary at the time, quickly became troubled by uneven handling of Title VI compliance across HEW's component agencies. "Let's quit acting like the Balkans and start performing like a Department," he scolded them.[71] He proceeded to offer department-wide, procedural guidance on Title VI compliance.

According to HEW estimates circa 1969, the department was responsible for monitoring the possible presence of racial discrimination in approximately 200 state agencies administering continuing programs under as many as 400 or 500 state plans; roughly 10,000 hospitals; about 23,000 public school districts; and about 2,000 colleges. Of the public school districts, around 2,000 had a regulatory exemption from immediate and actual desegregation in 1965. These districts could establish formal compliance by showing significant changes enabling them to be certified as desegregated, submitting acceptable voluntary plans for desegregation, or filing assurances of compliance with court orders for desegregation. (HEW was typically not involved in the filing of court orders, and had no authority to review court orders, though it could ask Justice to intervene if HEW felt that steps taken to obey court orders were inadequate.) The remaining 21,000 districts were assumed to be in compliance with Title VI if they filed formal assurances with HEW.[72]

In comparison to other agencies within HEW, the Office of Education (OE) had an advantage in building its Title VI team, owing to the existence of staff to administer Title IV, which offered funds to aid in school desegregation. In addition to widespread resistance to desegregation in the South, the technical aspects of securing acceptable school desegregation were daunting. This difficulty was heightened because it was impossible for OE to "borrow" staffers experienced with civil rights compliance— this was a new enterprise. Moreover, the stakes were high, particularly after the passage of the Elementary and Secondary Education Act (ESEA) of 1965. For example, Mississippi, which had been receiving around $9 million under Education programs, stood to receive an additional $31 million under ESEA.

HEW attempted to clarify its expectations for desegregating schools with the release of guidelines in April 1965. It announced that public schools failing to desegregate completely by September 1967 would not receive federal funding. HEW directed school systems to show good faith by desegregating at least four grades by the fall of 1965. The guidelines angered Southern school officials, who deemed them unconstitutional, shocking extensions of federal authority, and groups sympathetic to desegregation, which found them unsatisfactorily timid. The determination of Southern school officials to fight desegregation plans was stoked by HEW's capitulation to political pressure from Mayor Richard J. Daley after the agency attempted to withhold ESEA funds from Chicago for rampant segregation in the city's schools. President Johnson, usually one to stand by civil rights enforcement efforts, let HEW know that the matter should be settled quickly. ESEA funds were released to the city, with the school board promising to look into problems of segregation in the schools.[73]

In summer 1967—due to the insistence of Congress, which wanted greater control over how agency funds were spent—a reluctant HEW shifted Title VI responsibilities from its constituent programs to a new Office for Civil Rights that was accountable directly to the HEW secretary.[74] While some civil rights organizations initially believed the reorganization signified a retreat from the government's commitment, HEW's internal history maintains that "the relationship between the new centralized Office for Civil Rights and the program agencies showed substantial improvement. There was no longer presence in the program agencies of a unit which program administrators saw as an irritant and a block to their desire to distribute the funds so generously endowed on them by the Congress." It continues, "Through the centralization in the Office of the Secretary, [OCR Director F. Peter] Libassi was able to exert more influence directly through the Secretary and from a more responsible hierarchical position high in the bureaucracy, rather than from a position of what can almost be termed subservience to the program directors."[75]

By late fall, Libassi began to make clear in public forums that school districts would be required to take immediate steps toward the elimination of the dual school system by the beginning of the school term in September 1969, and show good faith via intermediate steps during the 1968–69 school year. As of October 1967, fifty-seven school districts had allowed federal financial assistance to be stopped, and another 130 were involved in termination proceedings. By this time, around 1,000 of the 2,300 Southern school districts were desegregating under voluntary plans; the remainder had already desegregated, were under court order, or had been terminated.[76]

The Supreme Court's 1968 *Green v. New Kent County* (391 U.S. 430) decision specified that the only acceptable desegregation plan is one "that promises realistically to work, and promises realistically to work now." HEW's revised guidelines of March 1968 were, for the first time, directed at Northern as well as Southern schools. Though not requiring correction of racial imbalance due to segregated housing patterns, they prohibited school systems from denying a student (because of race, religion, or national origin) the education "generally obtained" by others in the system.[77] The 1968 guidelines continued to include sample forms and sample letters to parents regarding "freedom of choice," suggesting that this was still an acceptable means of desegregating schools.[78] Under a freedom of choice plan, black families brave enough to risk reprisals from local whites could request that their children be transferred to white schools.

SCHOOL DESEGREGATION UNDER PRESIDENT NIXON

The election of Richard M. Nixon elicited uncertainty on all sides as to how stringently school desegregation requirements would be enforced under the new administration. On the one hand, as widely reported, Nixon had brokered a deal with Southerners at the 1968 Republican convention, gaining their support in exchange for assurances that federal pressure on desegregation would be eased.[79] On the other hand, Nixon's appointees for HEW secretary (Robert H. Finch) and assistant secretary for education/commissioner of education (James E. Allen, Jr.) were known to support school desegregation efforts. Also on the side of desegregation were the committed staff of 350 in OCR.[80]

The views of the public lacked sharp definition. For example, a 1968 Institute for Social Research survey asked respondents whether "the government in Washington should see to it that white and black children go to the same schools, or stay out of this area, as it is not its business?" A little over half (53 percent) of white respondents said that the government should stay out, 36 percent said that the government should see to it, and the remainder expressed no interest in the issue. Nine in ten black respondents said that the government should "see to it."[81]

The first clear sign that Nixon's desegregation policies would reside in the murky middle came in leftover business from the Johnson Administration. Outgoing HEW Secretary Wilbur Cohen had signed an order on December 30, 1968, specifying that five school districts in North Carolina, South Carolina, and Mississippi would forfeit federal funds due to noncompliance with Title VI. The cutoff date (January 29, 1969) would arrive nine days after Nixon's inauguration, and Southern politicians pressured the White House and HEW to delay deadlines and weaken enforcement. The decision to grant a sixty-day extension during which time the districts could come into compliance and have their funds restored satisfied no one.[82]

As of January 30, 1969, the federal government had cut off funds from 129 school districts, over half of which were in Mississippi (39) and Georgia (38).[83] In July of that year, HEW Secretary Finch and Attorney General John Mitchell issued "new, realistic administrative procedures," which largely affirmed the requirements of the old guidelines but offered exceptions for schools "with bona fide educational and administrative problems," such as "a serious shortage of necessary physical facilities, financial resources or faculty."[84] Nixon's liaison to the South, Harry Dent, observed that "it was difficult for many to understand the actual content of the statement because of conflicting reports." The White House welcomed the confusion. In Dent's view, "Senator [Strom] Thurmond's reaction was just right: 'This is an improvement, but not the real freedom of choice I wanted.' "[85] Less than a week later, Dent reported that "tough" actions by the administration—particularly the Justice Department filing suit in Georgia—left some Southern political leaders feeling "they have been fooled" by the Nixon Administration.[86]

Under the exception specified in the new guidelines, the Administration sent Justice Department attorneys into the Court of Appeals to request delays of the desegregation deadlines for thirty-one Mississippi school districts. This move was widely seen as an attempt by the administration to secure Mississippi Sen. John Stennis's vote for the antiballistic missile program. It was the first and only time that Nixon sought directly to delay desegregation.[87] In an embarrassment to the White House, the Supreme Court—headed by Nixon's pick for chief justice, Warren Burger—subsequently ruled in 1969's *Alexander v. Holmes County* (396 U.S. 218) that *all* dual school systems be dismantled "at once" and replaced with unitary systems immediately. The White House came to see a political benefit from the verdict, since it put the onus on the courts for integration.[88]

In contrast, the White House was aware that they could not dodge political responsibility for any desegregation actions taken by HEW. Nixon and his staff were clearly displeased with the forcefulness that HEW used to carry out its desegregation mandate. Attorney General John Mitchell and HEW Secretary Robert Finch announced in July 1969 that the administration would shift its enforcement emphasis from HEW funding cutoffs to lawsuits brought by the Justice Department against noncomplying school districts.[89] As one school board lawyer told OCR chief Leon Panetta, "I'd be nuts to advise my district to buy an HEW plan. The court affords us a longer time frame; it might offer us more than HEW; and politically, it is a hell of a lot better for the court to force it than for us to stick our neck out with you."[90] In February 1970, the White House forced Panetta to resign. In response, 125 HEW employees wrote to Nixon to express their "profound dismay" and "bitter disappointment" with Panetta's departure.[91]

The next month, President Nixon released his first statement on school desegregation, a release clouded in vagueness and offering little insight as to how far the Administration was willing to go in this area. While affirming that the government would continue its attempt to undo de jure segregation, Nixon maintained that he could not and would not require dismantling of de facto segregation, and that "transportation of pupils beyond normal geographic school zones for the purpose of achieving racial balance will not be required."[92] Two weeks after the statement, HEW Secretary Finch said that the president's statement would result in little or no change to the department's enforcement of school desegregation guidelines, and that busing would continue to be one means of enforcing court- and HEW-ordered desegregation in the South. The White House fired Education Commissioner James Allen, a strong supporter of desegregation, in June 1970, and moved HEW Secretary Robert Finch to an advisory position in the White House.[93]

In July 1970, Nixon told top staffers, "Our people have got to quit bragging about school desegregation. We do what the law requires— nothing more . . . [B]elieve me, all this bragging doesn't help. It doesn't cool the blacks. We'll just quietly do our job." Later that summer, at a school strategy meeting that included top HEW and White House staffers, Nixon warned, "I don't want a young attorney going down there [to the South] being a big hero kicking a school superintendent around; that is not to be done. I'll not have such a pipsqueak, snot-nosed attitude from the bowels of HEW."[94] While Nixon became increasingly intent on restraining the more ambitious desires of OCR, the judiciary was supporting desegregation efforts. The Supreme Court's 1971 *Swann v. Charlotte-Mecklenburg Board of Education* (402 U.S. 1) decision approved a federal district judge's order for an extensive busing program throughout a 550-square mile school district in North Carolina. More broadly, it upheld the permissibility of using busing, alteration of school attendance zones, and pairing of noncontiguous zones as remedies to end segregation.

Conflicts between the White House and HEW came to a head in Austin, Texas, where the agency recommended "extensive" cross-town busing to bring about integration between the white majority, African Americans (about 15 percent of the city's school population), and Mexican Americans (about 20 percent). In August 1971 (three months after HEW's proposal), President Nixon disavowed HEW's recommendations, inviting Austin school officials to devise an alternate plan.[95] That same month, White House Press Secretary Ronald Ziegler remarked pointedly that government bureaucrats "who are not responsive [to the wishes of the White House] will find themselves in other assignments or quite possibly in assignments other than the federal government."[96] The number of school districts that were desegregated administratively and judicially peaked historically in 1970–71, when HEW desegregated sixty-one school districts, and the courts another 107 districts. In the subsequent two-year period, 1972–73, the numbers declined to twelve and five, respectively.[97]

Nixon made his next major gambit in school desegregation with his March 1972 call for Congress to enact a moratorium on new or additional court-ordered busing.[98] This freeze would last until Congress passed substantive legislation addressing "the questions raised by school desegregation cases," or until July 1, 1973, whichever came first. The president coupled this proposal with another asking Congress to allocate additional funding for districts that were desegregating or that had heavy concentrations of poor children. "These measures," Nixon asserted, "would protect the right of a community to maintain neighborhood schools—while also establishing a shared local and federal responsibility to raise the level of education in the neediest neighborhoods."[99] Part of Nixon's rationale, which he would later echo when he declared a housing moratorium in January 1973, was equity. He reasoned, "Rather than require the spending of scarce resources on ever-longer bus rides for those who happen to live where busing is possible, we should encourage the putting of those resources directly into education—serving all the disadvantaged children, not merely those on the bus routes."[100] Civil rights groups, joined by ninety-five of the 148 lawyers who worked in the Civil Rights Division of the Justice Department, vehemently objected to the proposal. Antibusing Southerners were less than enthusiastic, since the moratorium would have no effect on existing busing orders.[101] Congress did not enact the freeze, but that was not the White House's main concern: letting the public know that Nixon opposed busing was. Nevertheless, in summer 1972, "Despite four years of badgering from the White House, HEW and Justice lawyers continued to bring desegregation cases to the courts."[102]

ENFORCEMENT IN HEALTH CARE WITHERS

OCR's activism in school desegregation was accompanied by a virtual absence of activity in enforcing civil rights in health care. This had not always been the case. In the six months prior to the implementation of the Medicare program in July 1966, the federal government undertook a massive effort to ensure that hospitals slated to receive funds did not discriminate on the basis of race. By the day of Medicare's launch, all but 10 percent of the nation's hospitals were found to be in compliance with Title VI of the 1964 Civil Rights Act, which prohibits the provision of federal funds to entities that discriminate. Two years later, only 2 percent of hospital and health facilities that had applied for Medicare payments were found to be noncompliant. Compared to other areas of civil rights, hospital desegregation was both smooth and successful.[103]

"HEW, by virtue of the nature and scope of its programs, is the most important federal department or agency to be affected by Title VI," the USCCR wrote in 1970. "To a large extent, the success or failure of that law is measured by the success or failure of HEW's effort."[104] By 1969, HEW had more than 100,000 employees and comprised "some 250 separate programs under hundreds of authorizations supported by approximately 100 appropriations categories." HEW's 1969 expenditures of $45 billion represented nearly one-fourth of total federal expenditures. Moreover, the agency's civil rights compliance program, beginning in the summer and fall of 1964, "was to occupy more space in the public print, more presidential attention, and more political controversy for the ensuing decade than any other HEW program."[105]

In the area of health, the General Accounting Office found in a 1973 report that "HEW has significantly reduced its title VI compliance staff to the point where the staff's principal duties are to prevent hospitals, ECFs [extended care facilities], and nursing homes from reverting to previous overt discriminatory policies and practices."[106] At a congressional hearing that same year, recently appointed OCR director Peter Holmes acknowledged that civil rights enforcement in the Medicare and Medicaid programs had "not received the same level of emphasis or attention by the Office for Civil Rights as has the elementary and secondary education program. That is an admission on the record by me of that fact. And we are trying to do something about it." At the time of Holmes's testimony, OCR had no full-time health expert on its staff.[107] The situation did not improve in subsequent years. In 1976, the acting director of OCR's Health and Social Services Branch testified in a deposition that the number of professional staff positions—which had declined from eighty-seven in 1973–74 to less than nineteen in the 1977 operating plan—meant that the branch could do a "less than minimum [job] . . . It is just not adequate in any sense of the word to meet our responsibilities."[108]

One reason for the absence of enforcement in this area is that health-related claims historically have constituted a small percentage of Title VI complaints. This situation creates disincentives within government agencies and Congress to allocate resources to civil rights enforcement in health. Numbers of complaints "served to justify certain policies, such as the priority which was given to particular field investigations and particular programs at the expense of others. They also served to justify, by their absence, inactivity in other areas."[109] The incentive for an individual to file a discrimination complaint may be weaker in housing or health than in employment or education. If a court finds that one has convincingly made a case that she has been a victim of racial discrimination, it is still unlikely that she will be able to acquire *that* house, or receive health treatment that truly compensates for the inadequate care received.[110] For example, in a recent survey of residents in the Washington metropolitan area, 95 percent of black respondents who reported having experienced racial discrimination in housing did not file a complaint with a civil rights or fair housing organization. Half of these respondents said that one reason they did not file a complaint was that nothing would come of it.[111]

OCR's emphasis on education was not merely the result of greater prioritization within the agency and higher numbers of complaints, but also of judicial mandates. Most important in this regard is the *Adams* litigation, filed in 1970. The litigation charged HEW with failure to enforce Title VI of the 1964 Civil Rights Act by granting federal funds to numerous school districts and state higher education systems in the seventeen Southern and border states that were discriminating against African Americans on the basis of race. The U.S. District Court and the Court of Appeals issued orders in 1973, 1975, 1976, and 1977 obligating HEW to adopt strict time frames for complaint processing and other procedures to assure compliance with Title VI.[112] Other requirements included finishing all compliance reviews begun prior to the beginning of the current fiscal year; undertaking a number of compliance reviews in elementary, secondary, and postsecondary education; completing reviews of formerly dual postsecondary systems of education; negotiating acceptable state-wide desegregation plans; and initiating enforcement proceedings in all cases where voluntary compliance could not be achieved. Because the *Adams* orders were limited to educational institutions, OCR "was required to give priority attention to education activities," resulting in "almost total neglect of health and human service policy development activities and greatly reduced compliance efforts."[113]

The courts continued to be active in school desegregation. In *Keyes v. Denver School District No. 1* (1973) (413 U.S. 189), the Supreme Court ruled for the first time on school segregation in the North and West, where no explicit segregation statutes existed. The court found that school districts were responsible for policies that resulted in racially segregated schools, such as locating schools in racially homogenous neighborhoods and creating attendance zones that segregated schools. The whole district was presumed to be segregated illegally if intentional segregation was identified by a school board in a part of the district. In addition, the case recognized that Latinos, like African Americans, had a right to desegregation.

Milliken v. Bradley (1974) (418 U.S. 717), which is largely viewed as marking the end of aggressive school desegregation, reversed a District Court desegregation plan that included suburban school districts along with the city of Detroit. *Milliken* marked the first time the Supreme Court had overruled a desegregation order in the three years since the

Swann decision supported broad remedial powers for district courts.[114] The Supreme Court edict sharply circumscribed the remedies available for school desegregation. By a 5-4 margin—all four of Nixon's appointees voted with the majority—the court ruled that Detroit's suburbs could not be compelled to participate in a school desegregation remedy unless the localities themselves could be found guilty of intentional segregation, or the state could be shown to have created the situation of a predominantly black Detroit ringed by virtually all-white suburbs. The court did not consider the extent to which discriminatory housing practices had resulted in intensive residential segregation and, consequently, school segregation.[115]

In the wake of *Milliken*, Congress passed the Elementary and Secondary Education Act Amendments of 1974, which banned busing "beyond the school next closest" to a student's home, but permitted courts to require additional busing if needed to guarantee the student's civil rights. The Senate had earlier rejected, by a 46–47 vote, a rider passed by the House that would have prohibited agencies or courts from ordering busing to any school but the closest or second-closest, and that would have allowed any school district under a federal court order or desegregation plan to have its case reopened. The Education Act Amendments reached Nixon's desk on August 7, two days before he resigned in the midst of the Watergate scandal. President Gerald Ford signed the bill on August 21.[116]

Nixon presided over the most intense period of Southern school desegregation in American history. He did so grudgingly, for the most part. Perhaps Leonard Garment, one of Nixon's primary advisors on civil rights, captured it best: "He backed and filled, catered and compromised, spoke in contradictory ways to different constituencies, yielded here, stiffened there, drew on every play in his voluminous book, but did, in the end, get the job done."[117]

The development of desegregation policies in education and employment suggests several lessons about bureaucratic politics. As noted earlier, the executive and legislative branches may find it quite difficult to stop bureaucratic initiatives. Congress can, of course, starve agencies of funding and refuse to pass laws that an agency deems critical to its mission. It is substantially harder, however, to pass legislation that prevents administrative agencies from doing business as they see fit. Likewise, as demonstrated most vividly in the case of education, the president may also be frustrated in his attempts to get government agencies to act according to his wishes. Large agencies such as HEW juggle numerous missions, even within the area of civil rights. Those that top the list of priorities, such as school desegregation, stand a decent chance of some progress. Those further down the list, such as civil rights enforcement in health care, are unlikely to be pursued with much enthusiasm. Agencies where civil rights missions do not compete with other missions may not suffer the same internal conflicts over prioritization as multi-mission agencies do.

Clearly, courts may force government agencies to change their policies and practices. In the late 1960s and early 1970s, however, courts typically deferred to agency expertise in deciding what policies accorded with the intentions of Congress. These agencies tended to fare best when the judiciary evaluated practices already in effect. That is, courts were much more likely to sanction existing agency practices than to prescribe new ones. As a result, agency action (or inaction) was a central factor in determining how civil rights laws were carried out.

The Need to Intervene in Residential Segregation

As subsequent chapters reveal, housing desegregation initiatives faced similar presidential resistance to agency activism. Reducing racial residential segregation was (and is) perhaps even more crucial than desegregation in employment and education, since ongoing progress in either of these areas (particularly the latter) is extraordinarily difficult in the face of continued racial isolation at home. Compared to the unlikely success of affirmative action in employment, and the early victories in school desegregation, civil rights initiatives in housing were largely unimpressive. The federal record of tolerating and even promoting segregation in housing made the problem at hand more severe, and arguably made governmental responsibility in this area greater than in other areas. Moreover, when the federal government did finally commit itself to fighting discrimination in housing, the relevant agencies—particularly the Federal Housing Administration—faced the prospect of completely reshaping the culture within them.

Residential segregation is not a trivial occurrence, but a social and public policy problem with profound consequences. Black socioeconomic characteristics, housing preferences, and degree of knowledge of white housing markets do not sufficiently explain the persistence of black residential segregation.[118] Nor can high segregation levels be written off as a state of affairs that has always existed. Residential segregation at the turn of the nineteenth century appears to have been less pervasive than in later decades. In the urban North of the working class, some blacks lived in neighborhoods with poor European immigrants. Groups of blacks living among poor whites occurred in the urban South as well. In both regions, the numerically small black elite lived among whites in well-to-do neighborhoods.[119] The typical northern, urban black resident in 1890 lived in a neighborhood that was only 13 percent black.[120] While the South subsequently developed Jim Crow laws to enforce segregation, racial separation prevailed in the North in more patchwork—though still quite effective—fashion, via white refusal to sell or rent to blacks (often enforced by restrictive covenant), governmental support of exclusionary practices, intimidation, and violence. During the first forty years of the twentieth century, widespread industrialization and the migration of rural blacks to urban areas led to large increases in residential segregation.

The years following World War II were pivotal in the entrenchment of residential segregation. During this time, the "Great Migration" of blacks from the rural South to the industrial North continued, causing many black ghettoes to become severely overcrowded and many white neighborhoods to resist black incursion forcefully. The Federal Housing Administration and the Veterans Administration financed the mass movement of families, the overwhelming majority of them white, to the expanding suburbs.[121]

In the 1950s, intense residential segregation existed in virtually all American cities. The suburbs consisted of predominantly white enclaves, dotted by a limited number of formerly rural black enclaves that had been established prior to the postwar suburban expansion. Some older satellite suburbs had black residents, as did some spillover ghettoes adjacent to central-city areas of black concentration. Residential segregation in the 1960s lessened to a certain degree, as the overall SMSA (Standard Metropolitan Statistical Areas) scores for the index of dissimilarity (for 137 fully tracted areas) decreased from 75.4 in 1960 to 69.5 in 1970.[122] The index, which ranges from 0 (individuals randomly assigned to residence regardless of race) to 100 (absolute segregation), can be interpreted as the percentages of either blacks or whites who would have to change their block group of residence to eliminate racial concentration. Larger numbers of blacks moved to the suburbs during the 1960s, though mainly to areas already housing black residents. As a result, these moves typically had little impact on housing integration.

Black suburbanization continued to increase in the 1970s, albeit with the same trend of movement mainly to existing areas of black settlement. Of the sixty SMSAs examined by Massey and Denton, the average index of dissimilarity declined 10 percentage points, from 79 to 69 percent. Lieberson and Carter estimated that 85 percent of black segregation in the 1970s was attributable to involuntary causes. In the 1980s, Farley and Frey found "a pervasive pattern of modest declines," with the average index of similarity in metropolitan areas with substantial black populations declining from 69 in 1980 to 65 in 1990. The average score for both Asians and Latinos in 1990 was roughly 43, over twenty points lower than for blacks.[123]

Glaeser and Vigdor's analysis of the 2000 census found some encouraging news: overall black/nonblack segregation levels are at their lowest levels since 1920, and all but nineteen of the 291 Metropolitan Statistical Areas studied experienced declines in segregation.[124] The authors attribute these decreases primarily to the integration of formerly all-white census tracts. Areas with relatively small black populations tend to experience substantially steeper segregation declines than those with larger black populations. Also worth noting is that the fastest-growing metropolitan areas, such as Las Vegas, Phoenix, Austin, and Raleigh-Durham, are characterized by especially low and declining segregation levels. Despite these somewhat optimistic findings, overall segregation levels remain high in the United States.

THE HARMS OF RESIDENTIAL SEGREGATION

The maintenance of high levels of racial isolation is cause for concern. The detrimental effects of residential segregation can be summarized by three broad claims: (1) segregation has negative financial consequences for African Americans in the form of reduced home appreciation, and in fewer public benefits (such as services, quality schools, recreation areas, and so on) for their home investment; (2) segregation isolates blacks by constraining employment opportunities, maintaining racially separate schools, and limiting the potential for political alliances; and (3) segregation naturalizes and reinforces racial differences.

Much of the scholarship on residential segregation focuses on its effects on lower-income blacks. As a consequence of residential segregation, lower-income African Americans find themselves in neighborhoods of concentrated poverty, which tend to have high rates of crime, drugs, teenage childbearing, and so on. In addition, isolated African Americans may find themselves excluded from the informal social networks that are often the best source for finding jobs. For middle-class individuals, "the spatial payoffs of upward mobility are lower for blacks than for whites because of racial segregation." For example, one study found that a middle-income black family is three times as likely as a similar white family to have neighbors on welfare. While there may be no irrefutable social scientific proof that the proximity of low-income neighbors has serious consequences for middle-class families, "nearly every black and white family in America assumes that inferior neighbors will drag them down and tries to distance itself from those beneath it."[125] Succinctly stated, as a result of residential segregation, "poor blacks live under unrivaled conditions of poverty and affluent blacks live in neighborhoods that are far less advantageous than those experienced by the middle class of other groups."[126]

Continuing research by Massey, Charles, and colleagues suggests that African American and Latino students growing up in segregated environments later perform less well academically than their more integrated counterparts. According to Charles, "[T]he negative effect holds after controlling for socioeconomic status and is not attributable to differences in school quality or variations in intellectual, social, or psychological preparation among students from segregated and integrated neighborhoods." Instead, segregation is important "because it results in exposure to unusually high levels of violence while growing up."[127]

Oliver and Shapiro argue that differences in housing prospects are the key to understanding racial wealth disparities and, in turn, disparities in the transmission of class status. In 1992, net housing wealth comprised 31 percent of total net household wealth in the United States. Oliver and Shapiro estimate that "discrimination in housing markets costs the current generation of blacks about $82 billion."[128] Of this sum, $13.5 billion is lost through denied mortgages. If black mortgage approval rates equaled those of comparable whites, an estimated 8 percent of African Americans who are denied mortgages annually (roughly 14,200 out of 177,501 applicants in 1992) would be homeowners today. One primary reason cited for these differences in mortgage rejection rates was a greater "presumption of creditworthiness"—based on race alone—for white applicants than for black or Latino ones. They attribute an additional loss of $10.5 billion to higher interest rates on mortgages paid by blacks in comparison to similarly situated whites.[129]

The biggest price of being black—and the most important in the context of racial segregation—in the housing market is a slower rate of home appreciation, a factor Oliver and Shapiro tag at $58 billion. From 1967 through 1988, the mean value of the average white home escalated $53,000, compared to $31,000 for the average black home. With nonrace factors taken into account, race still remains important in differential home appreciation. Yinger contends that one-fifth to one-quarter of nonwhite-white gaps in homeownership rates and overall housing wealth are attributable to current discrimination, estimating that African Americans implicitly pay out an average of $2.6 billion per year in the form of higher search costs and lost housing opportunities due to discrimination.[130] In 1990, the mean value of owner-occupied homes in the nation's 100 largest metropolitan areas was $143,000 for whites, $83,000 for blacks, $129,000 for Hispanics, $225,000 for Asians, and $113,000 for Native Americans. Controlling for income, the homes of black owners have an average value that is 18 percent less than their white counterparts. According to Rusk, "[T]his gap in home values, or 'segregation tax' imposed on black homeowners, primarily results from a high degree of racial segregation in neighborhoods."[131]

One cannot measure the costs of segregation solely in financial terms. Sugrue argues in his study of Detroit that "the most visible and intractable manifestation of racial inequality of the [post–World War II] city was residential segregation," under which ghettoization came to be seen by whites as "an inevitable, natural consequence of profound racial differences" reflecting moral shortcomings rather than structural barriers.[132] In reality, residential segregation is not a natural state of being. Indeed, racially biased governmental policies, and the examples they set for the private sector, were key factors in the sedimentation of residential segregation. As Jackson describes it, "The lasting damage done by the national government was that it put its seal of approval on ethnic and racial discrimination and developed policies which had the result of the practical abandonment of older, industrial cities. More seriously, Washington actions were later picked up by private interests. . . . The financial community saw blighted neighborhoods as physical evidence of the melting-pot mistake."[133] Residential segregation has exacerbated inequality between blacks and whites, adversely impacting the lives of African Americans in largely unseen ways. Policies condoning or encouraging residential segregation have limited policy alternatives on issues ranging from school desegregation to energy.[134] The next three chapters examine the evolution of policies related to residential segregation.

Chapter Three

The Federal Government and Residential Segregation, 1866–1968

"WHO ARE WE KIDDING when we say—on the one hand—that minority groups 'prefer to live together'—and then proceed to utilize every device available in the market place to dictate that they do so?" a Federal Housing Administration official wondered in a 1955 speech.[1] Questions of housing and race confronted public and private actors well before the congressional debates of the 1960s. Indeed, one can scarcely understand the passage of the Civil Rights Act of 1968 and HUD's subsequent development of fair housing policies without grasping the historical sweep of governmental involvement in residential segregation. Deference to private-sector practices and attitudes marked federal housing policy throughout much of the twentieth century. The close links forged between employees of FHA and private-sector actors (builders, realtors, bankers, and so on) had two important consequences for housing policy. The first is that the coziness between FHA and the private sector made corruption within the agency more likely. These close ties also led the federal government to accept without objection the segregationist practices of the private sector; in turn, the federal acceptance of, and even preference for, segregation legitimated private-sector practices with respect to race. By choosing to do business overwhelmingly with white families in white neighborhoods, FHA became a darling of Congress, arousing little controversy (except when scandals emerged) and costing the federal government little money—in fact, FHA turned a small profit in some years.

The first part of this chapter examines residential segregation prior to 1968. While incorporating the necessary context of private-sector and local actions relevant to this topic, this chapter places particular emphasis on the role of the federal government in shaping patterns of residential distribution by race. Because public housing has always constituted such a small portion (less than 2 percent) of U.S. housing stock, government involvement in the private sector, including mortgage insurance and housing subsidies, has proven especially consequential. Even when the federal government took small steps away from racial exclusion in official policy, it was reluctant to use its authority to change private-sector or local governmental practices that increased segregation. The second section takes a close look at congressional debates over fair housing legislation, providing a window into the political and historical context from which the last significant legislation of the civil rights era was signed into law. The debates reveal a Congress grappling with the questions of whether passage would dissuade or encourage rioters, whether the fair housing law would be a laudable achievement or a source of disappointment to all involved parties, and whether it would create another bureaucracy that would, in the eyes of civil rights opponents, ignore congressional intent and develop an overzealous approach to enforcement. This last concern reflected the realization that once an enforcement agency (such as HEW's Office for Civil Rights) established aggressive methods to promote desegregation, Congress could do remarkably little to stop it.

EARLY PROMISE, DASHED HOPES

As with many civil rights issues, housing policy began optimistically enough during post–Civil War Reconstruction. The Civil Rights Act of 1866 banned all racial discrimination, public or private, in the rental or sale of residential property. This law, however, was essentially ignored for the next century. Another law enacted that year, the Southern Homestead Act, also had the potential to improve the lot of African Americans. This law opened federal lands in the South to homesteaders, specifying that applicants could not be discriminated against on the basis of color. Previous Homestead Acts had excluded blacks from eligibility, explicitly or by implication. The volume of applications from African Americans betrayed a strong desire for land ownership. For the first six months that the act was in effect, only freedmen and whites loyal to the Union were permitted to settle these lands. After that period, anyone meeting age and citizenship requirements could apply. The act was deemed a failure and repealed in 1876, due to factors that included the poor quality of available lands, bureaucratic ineptitude (with some corruption) on the federal and local levels, and the opposition of Southern white landowners to black land ownership.[2]

White resistance also dampened African American prospects on the private market. Early in the twentieth century, a number of localities began to experiment with measures to enforce residential segregation.[3] Baltimore, the first city to do so (in 1910), designated all-white and all-black blocks in areas where individuals of both races lived. Atlanta and Greenville adopted similar provisions. Virginia empowered city councils to create segregated districts and prohibit individuals of another race from living there; Roanoke and Portsmouth adopted such plans. Another Virginia city, Richmond, designated blocks by race according to the majority of residents living there, forbidding residence in cases "where the majority of residents on such streets are occupied by those with whom said person is forbidden to intermarry." A New Orleans law required that a person (of either race) obtain the consent of the majority of persons living in an area before establishing a residence there. St. Louis (1916), Dallas (1917), and Indianapolis (1926) also passed segregation ordinances.[4]

A 1917 Supreme Court decision, *Buchanan v. Warley* (245 U.S. 60), found Louisville, Kentucky's residential segregation ordinance to be unconstitutional. That ordinance was purportedly designed "to prevent conflict and ill-feeling between the white and colored races . . . [by requiring] the use of separate blocks for residence, places of abode and places of assembly by white and colored people respectively." The decision had a limited impact, as it did nothing to prevent private acts of discrimination or indirect efforts by the government to foster segregation.[5] Moreover, Southern cities such as Richmond, Charlotte, Atlanta, and New Orleans enacted replacement ordinances that scarcely differed from the one that was struck down by the Supreme Court. The New Orleans ordinance, also subsequently declared unconstitutional, would have required at least 8,000 whites and 18,000 blacks to move.[6]

The federal government made its first foray into housing production in 1918, authorizing the U.S. Shipping Board Emergency Fleet Corporation to provide housing for shipyard employees. Congress expanded these activities by authorizing and appropriating funds for housing war workers. An executive order created the U.S. Housing Corporation in the same year. Operating through the USHC, the Bureau of Industrial Housing and Transportation acted quickly, building, organizing, and managing twenty-five community projects containing more than 5,000 single-dwelling units. Work had begun on additional 140 projects when, after only 109 days in operation, the USHC was discontinued as World War I came to an end. This abrupt stoppage was an early sign that the federal government would work to aid the private housing industry, rather than compete with it or attempt to control it. The government withdrew abruptly from the housing field, to return only when the national economy collapsed in the 1930s.[7]

The end of World War I did not stem the flow of African Americans escaping the oppression of the rural South for the supposed "Promised Land" of the North. From 1916 to 1919, half a million black Americans moved North, and another million followed in the 1920s. The existence of formal and informal mechanisms to restrict black residence resulted in the creation of overcrowded black ghettoes. As African Americans moved to cities in substantial numbers, residential segregation grew dramatically. By 1930, a full 63 percent of black Chicagoans lived in areas that were at least 90 percent black. In the period from 1910 to 1930, the black populations of numerous Northern cities increased exponentially. New York, Philadelphia, Chicago, and Detroit all saw their numbers of black residents exceed 100,000. Detroit's black population multiplied by more than twenty times, from less than 6,000 in 1910 to over 120,000 in 1930; the black share of the city population rose in that time from 1.2 to 7.7 percent.[8]

Chicago's black population increased more than five-fold in those two decades, from 44,000 to nearly 234,000; African Americans accounted for 2 percent of the city's population in 1910, and nearly 7 percent two decades later. In 1910, no communities existed where blacks constituted over 61 percent of the population; more than two-thirds lived in areas less than one-half black, and one-third lived in areas that were under 10 percent black. By 1920, 87 percent of African Americans lived in areas that were at least half-black. One year later, the Chicago Real Estate Board voted to expel any member who sold a property to an African American on a previously all-white block.[9]

When ordinances, discrimination by real-estate interests, or insufficient economic means did not prevent some black families from moving into all-white neighborhoods, violence often kept them from remaining there. During a forty-five-month period between 1917 and 1921 in Chicago, fifty-eight racially motivated bombings occurred. The racial violence reached its apex in 1919, when a dispute between whites and blacks at a beach escalated into a riot whose seriousness is reflected in raw numbers: thirteen days, thirty-eight dead, 537 injured, and more than 1,000 left homeless. The Chicago race riot was one of twenty-six in American cities in the year 1919 alone.[10]

Instances of violence stemming from neighborhood "turf wars" decreased somewhat after the Supreme Court's 1926 *Corrigan v. Buckley* (271 U.S. 323) decision, which held that restrictive covenants, as private action, were beyond the scope of the due process clause of the Fourteenth Amendment. The decision read, in part: "The constitutional right of a Negro to acquire, own, and occupy property does not carry with it the constitutional power to compel sale and conveyance to him of any particular property. The individual citizen, whether he be black or white, may refuse to sell or lease his property to any particular individual or class of individuals." Consequently, neighborhoods could retain their all-white character through legal means. Racially restrictive covenants spread widely and rapidly, with fifteen state courts upholding their validity. In some cities, restrictive covenants were estimated to cover as much as 80 percent of residential property. In addition to restricting the movement of African Americans, some covenants were used to bar Mexicans, Chinese, Japanese, Jews, Filipinos, Native Americans, and others considered to be nonwhite.[11] Real estate "experts" typically accepted and even endorsed racial segregation. For example, one textbook entitled *Real Estate Fundamentals* maintained that "the solution of the negro problem seems to depend upon rigid segregation."[12] The Great Depression also led to decreased levels of neighborhood racial conflict, as black migration from the South slowed and middle-class blacks were less able to move to upscale neighborhoods. Small pockets of integration also began to emerge. In 1937, under sponsorship by the American Friends Service Committee (the Quakers), the Penn-Craft cooperative in rural, southwestern Pennsylvania became the first known, intentionally integrated housing development in the United States.[13]

Beginning in the 1930s, the federal government began to pay greater attention to the racial aspects of housing problems. A 1931 conference on home building and ownership called by President Herbert Hoover produced little along the lines of legislation; significantly, however, one full volume of the eleven-volume committee report focused on the housing problems of African Americans. The one notable legislative outcome was the creation of the Federal Home Loan Bank system, a move signaling that the future role of the federal government would be to facilitate credit rather than build houses.[14]

FEDERAL SUPPORT FOR SEGREGATION

The Hoover committee also found that, as a result of the Great Depression, half of all home mortgages in the United States were in default, and foreclosures neared one thousand per working day in late 1931 and 1932. Over the next few years, Congress created a number of agencies designed to stimulate the private-sector housing market. The Home Owners' Loan Corporation (HOLC), formed in 1933, was the first federal agency to reinforce and encourage private-sector trends of racial residential segregation. The HOLC was created to take over and refinance mortgages on one- to four-family dwellings that were either delinquent or held in lending institutions whose assets were frozen. In its first three years of operation, the HOLC financed over one million homes, or one in five of all mortgages on owner-occupied homes in non-farm areas. The HOLC introduced and perfected the feasibility of the long-term, self-amortizing mortgage with uniform payments throughout the life of the debt. Because its business mission was to take over problem mortgages, the agency had to make assumptions and predictions concerning the useful life of the housing it financed. As part of this effort, HOLC appraisers developed profiles of neighborhoods based on such characteristics as occupation, income, race and ethnicity, and housing stock.[15]

HOLC assigned neighborhoods one of four grades, with the lowest of these assigned the color red; it was from this classification system that the term "redlining" came into use. Top-rated neighborhoods were new and homogenous on racial and ethnic grounds. Jewish neighborhoods or ones with an "infiltration of Jews" could not be top-rated. Black neighborhoods invariably received the lowest grade, and even neighborhoods with small proportions of blacks typically received red grades. Individuals in lower-ranked neighborhoods could still receive HOLC assistance. In fact, the HOLC issued the majority of its mortgage insurance assistance in areas ranked third ("definitely declining") or fourth ("hazardous"). This was not mere beneficence: the residents of lower-income sections actually maintained better pay-back records than HOLC customers in higher-income areas. Blacks received a little less than 5 percent of HOLC mortgages in 1940. When the HOLC acquired homes in white neighborhoods, the agency prevented blacks from buying them. Private-sector companies had considered race and ethnicity in their appraisals prior to the establishment of the HOLC, but the public-sector corporation did it on a far larger scale. As Jackson writes, "The damage caused by the HOLC came not through its own actions, but through the influence of its appraisal system on the financial decisions of other institutions."[16]

The Federal Housing Administration, created as part of the 1934 National Housing Act, adopted the HOLC's methods, and probably its maps as well. FHA insures long-term mortgage loans made by private lenders for home construction and sale. The agency collects premiums, establishes reserves for losses, and indemnifies the lender in the event of default. FHA does not build houses or lend money. Prior to the establishment of FHA, home buyers needed down payments of at least 30 percent; FHA insurance made down payments of more than 10 percent unnecessary. Like the HOLC, FHA extended the repayment period for guaranteed mortgages to twenty-five or thirty years and insisted that all loans be fully amortized. FHA employees emphasized that the agency was a "conservative business operation," becoming self-sustaining by 1940 and at times even earning a small profit from fees, premiums, and interest income.[17]

As with most agencies, "FHA adopted the professional beliefs and prejudices of the interests it served. The real-estate trade, the building industry, and financial institutions supplied FHA with most of its personnel and guidelines, and each of these groups accepted, as an iron law of economics, the concept that racial homogeneity was essential if residential districts were to retain their stability and desirability."[18] Moreover, the housing industry earned a reputation for its myopic outlook. In Wolfe's estimation, "Words fail in describing the housing industry. Many businessmen approach the political arena with a short-sighted and selfish point of view, but at the top of the list for sheer venality would have to be the real-estate and building lobby."[19] These views are revealed in a 1943 brochure of the National Association of Real Estate Boards, which lumps "a colored man of means" with a bootlegger, a gangster, and a madame as examples of prospective buyers that "would instigate a form of blight" and thus should be denied purchase of a listed home. NAREB considered the refusal to introduce nonwhites into white areas not just a matter of good business but also an ethical principle.[20]

FHA reflected a similar perspective. The agency's 1938 *Underwriting Manual* stated that "if a neighborhood is to retain stability, it is necessary that properties shall continue to be occupied by the same social and racial groups." The manual contained a model covenant, which recommended "prohibition of the occupancy of properties except by the race for which they are intended."[21] Indeed, "inclusion of the restrictive covenant in real estate sales contracts became almost a prerequisite of FHA mortgage insurance."[22] Under FHA policy, when land was sold to Mexican or African Americans, adjoining land typically would be classified as a poor risk to retain its value and thus was undesirable. Unlike the HOLC, FHA allowed personal and professional bias in favor of all-white, suburban subdivisions to affect its loan decisions. FHA policies "supported the income and racial segregation of suburbia. FHA exhorted segregation and enshrined it as public policy." Real-estate operators, builders, and developers typically cited the agency's underwriting manuals as justification for excluding blacks from most new housing built between 1934 and 1940.[23]

One particularly absurd illustration of FHA policies occurred in Detroit in the late 1930s, when white families began to move near a black enclave adjacent to Eight Mile Road. By 1940, neither the black nor the white families could get FHA insurance due to the presence of an "inharmonious" racial group nearby. Finally, when a developer built a concrete wall to separate the black and white areas, the white families, but not the black ones, were able to secure FHA approval of their mortgages.[24] FHA, as a risk-averse business operation closely tied to the private sector, preferred the predictability of segregation. In turn, this governmental embrace of segregation reassured the private sector that this way of doing business was logical, even natural. Thus, the practice of deference to the industry was becoming deeply entrenched in federal housing agencies.

On the public housing front, Congress created the U.S. Housing Authority (USHA) with the passage of the Housing Act of 1937. In contrast to earlier public housing laws, this legislation was long range in purpose, establishing the agency as a permanent corporate body. The construction, ownership, and operation of public housing was placed under the

jurisdiction of local housing authorities. This deference to local prerogatives would later prove to be a formidable obstacle to federal enforcement of the fair housing mandate specified in the Civil Rights Act of
1968. Congress authorized the new federal agency to make loans covering
90 percent of the cost and pay annual subsidies on the housing. Municipalities contributed annual amounts equivalent to 20 percent of federal
payments.[25]

Housing followed other social policies in its design as a two-tiered system, whereby public housing was created as a stingy, stigmatized, means-
tested program for the poor, and FHA mortgage guarantees were a popular, middle-class entitlement. Drawing on the work of Lieberman, one
might think of public housing as similar in scope to Aid to Families with
Dependent Children (later Temporary Assistance to Needy Families), a
policy with a weak and parochial institutional structure, which included
African Americans from the outset. FHA programs, in contrast, have
more in common with Old-Age Insurance, with their strong, national institutional structure and their initial exclusion of African Americans.[26]

FHA created the Office of Race Relations, which was headed by
Robert Weaver, who would go on to become the first HUD Secretary and
the first African American cabinet officer in national history. Continuing
policies established by Harold Ickes's leadership of the Public Works Administration, the USHA required localities to give blacks an equitable
share of the new dwellings that the agency helped to construct.[27] By May
1940, about 48,000 of the 140,000 USHA-aided housing units under
contract were for black occupancy. In 1941, the Federal Works
Agency—which had taken over the USHA after a 1939 reorganization—
issued an order forbidding discrimination against black defense workers
in emergency war housing. Myrdal concluded that "the U.S.H.A. has
given [the Negro] a better deal than has any other major federal public
welfare agency." Nevertheless, the USHA did little to attack residential
segregation, as the majority of projects were exclusively occupied by
one race. As with other programs directed at aiding the poor, local prerogatives limited the racial progressivity of public housing policies.
With construction and site selection decisions left to the discretion of
local governments, most cities chose to carry out "separate but equal"
policies.[28]

In the few years prior to World War II, the federal government was beginning to show signs that it wished to withdraw from the public housing market. The defense effort, however, required further expansion of
the housing supply, and Congress passed the Lanham Act in October
1940 to provide funds for temporary and permanent housing for war
workers. The housing industry insisted that these 700,000 housing units
be sold or destroyed at war's end.[29] Following the attack on Pearl Harbor,

when white males left factories to join the segregated armed forces, approximately 700,000 African Americans migrated within the United States during a three and a half-year period. Blacks were just one part of a massive civilian migration that cut across racial lines; from December 1941 to March 1945, 15 million Americans changed their county of residence.[30]

A 1942 executive order combined the federal housing agencies—the Federal Home Loan Bank Board, FHA, the USHA (renamed the Federal Public Housing Authority), and the new wartime agencies—into a new super agency, the National Housing Agency (NHA). This action represented the first attempt to place housing agencies under one administrative umbrella, while doing little to bridge the widely varying cultures and practices of these units. The NHA announced a basic policy of no discrimination on the basis of race, creed, color, or national origin. These directives were not antisegregation orders, but were intended to assure an equitable distribution of war housing for minorities in racially separate projects. Blacks ultimately received about 15 percent of NHA war housing, nearly six times as many units (totalling 84,000) as were provided for black occupancy under the larger FHA program of private war housing (15,000 units). Only 4.3 percent of the total private, priority war housing and 2.4 percent of the nonpriority war housing was allocated to African Americans. The failure of NHA and FHA to encourage nonsegregated, privately financed housing during World War II was a lost opportunity, as FHA-insured financing during this time removed nearly all the risk from private enterprise in housing, while preserving the profit.[31]

In 1944, Congress passed the Servicemen's Readjustment Act (aka the GI Bill), which provided Veterans Administration guarantees for financing homes and business ventures at low interest rates. In contrast to the FHA method of reimbursing the insured lender with long-term debentures, the GI loan plan provided cash payments in cases of default. In most other aspects of operation, including its preference for racial residential segregation, the Veterans Administration followed FHA policies and procedures. The two agencies had a huge impact on the workings of the dual housing market: by 1956, over 40 percent of all mortgages on owner-occupied, single-unit, nonfarm properties were either insured by FHA or guaranteed by the VA.[32]

FHA's Grudging Move Away from Segregation

In Washington, the Federal Housing Administration was remarkably slow to change its pro-segregation policies. In 1943, for example, FHA commissioner Abner H. Ferguson tried to convince senators not to include an antidiscrimination provision into federal housing legislation. FHA became a part of the Housing and Home Financing Agency established by Congress in 1947. Running under a single administrator, HHFA made permanent the centralized direction of housing policies established through the wartime NHA. That same year, FHA began to take some halting steps in the direction of nondiscrimination, establishing its own Racial Relations Service to serve minority housing needs.[33] The 1947 edition of the FHA's *Underwriting Manual* made no direct reference to race, substituting terms such as "user groups" and "incompatible groups." The guide asked appraisers to study the significance of "a mixture of user groups" or change from one group to another, but added that "additional risk is not necessarily involved in such a change."[34]

The Supreme Court's 1948 *Shelley v. Kraemer* (334 U.S. 1) decision, which declared restrictive covenants to be "unenforceable as law and contrary to public policy," nudged FHA further from its pro-segregative policies. FHA's first official reaction was to claim that the verdict was not applicable to its own operations, and the agency continued to insure mortgages on properties with restrictive covenants.[35] Given the underwhelming history of federal housing agencies, civil rights groups were not deluded into believing that the racial landscape would transform itself overnight. The short-term effect of the decision, according to the Urban League's housing coordinator, would be to allow "hundreds of minority families to occupy property they have owned but could not live in because of the covenant prohibition."[36]

FHA insured a public housing project with a nonsegregated tenant population for the first time in 1949. It took the agency until February 1950—nearly two years after the *Shelley* decision—to announce that it would not provide mortgage insurance on properties on which restrictive covenants were recorded. Even this step was half-hearted, as the agency assured housing interests that it was not attempting to prohibit segregation or deny benefits to individuals who chose to discriminate racially in their selection of purchasers or tenants.[37] Also in 1950, the agency announced that all repossessed FHA-insured housing would be administered and sold on a nonsegregated basis.

The following year, in connection with housing for nonwhite defense workers during the Korean War, FHA directed its field offices to give "some preference" to proposals for open-occupancy developments versus all-minority ones. FHA announced its intention of "taking active steps to encourage the development of demonstration open-occupancy projects in suitable key areas." By 1957, HHFA counted forty-one open-occupancy projects involving $53 million.[38] Fair housing groups contended that the agency's actions lagged behind its rhetoric. In 1954 the

National Committee Against Discrimination in Housing complained that FHA "had done almost nothing to implement" these stated changes in policies and that district offices often ignored or were unaware of agency policy shifts.[39]

Moreover, despite these announced changes, FHA maintained the principle that builders and lenders should be unrestrained in their decisions about who could buy or rent houses built using federal mortgage insurance. Developers built large FHA-insured projects with an acknowledged policy of excluding blacks.[40] Federal agencies largely viewed themselves as allies of the private housing industry, rather than as regulators. This policy legacy of deference to the housing industry later made it difficult for federal agencies to change course and impose more stringent requirements—such as those prohibiting racial discrimination—on the private sector. Indeed, this is why civil rights organizations were concerned when the Fair Housing Act of 1968 placed responsibility for civil rights enforcement within the Department of Housing and Urban Development (created in 1965), rather than a separate fair housing board that did not include employees who had condoned residential segregation for years.

The private-sector preference for segregation left civil rights organizations with the unsavory alternatives of accepting the construction of minority-only projects or relinquishing the possibility of greatly needed housing to insist on integration. The National Association of Home Builders—who would later support the spread of subsidized, integrated housing—proposed the construction of a small number of all-black housing projects to meet demand, even after the historic *Brown v. Board of Education* decision on school segregation. Ultimately, the NAACP and the National Urban League rejected the NAHB's proposal, arguing that additional segregated housing would "confuse the campaign for integration," and concluded that "we do not want Jim Crow dwellings whether they are new or not."[41] On the local level, however, black leaders often found it difficult to reject much-needed low-income housing, even if its construction would increase segregation. "We think that public housing is wrong in the way it's being handled," one black newspaper editor in Chicago said in the late 1950s. "But on the other hand, we can't oppose it too much because we don't want to penalize people who need housing somewhere of some kind. . . . So what do we do? We just mumble about it."[42] This call for desegregation entailed more costly trade-offs in housing than in other policy areas. Though all forms of desegregation are likely to subject African Americans to some form of hardship and hostility, the direct sacrifice of more housing in the interest of desegregation does not exist in parallel form in the areas of employment and education.

Federal Support for Segregation

FHA played a significant role in the urban renewal efforts instituted by the National Housing Act of 1949. Debate over the bill sparked intense emotions, even causing a fistfight on the floor of the House between sixty-nine-year-old E. E. Cox, a Democrat opponent of the bill from Georgia, and the chair of the Rules Committee, Chicago's Adolph Sabath (also a Democrat), who was in his eighties at the time of the impromptu bout.[43] During the course of the debate, Cox labeled the legislation a "Socialist scheme" to create "a vast omnivorous bureaucracy," and predicted that "no home in America will be free from its invasion or sacred from its trespass." The housing industry used rhetoric similar to Cox's. A number of bill supporters echoed Sen. Allen Ellender (D-LA), who argued that passage of the housing legislation was "the most realistic way to defeat Communism, Fascism or in fact any other 'ism.' "[44] During the 1949 debate, the conservative bloc in the Senate introduced an amendment requiring the elimination of segregation in public housing. This move obviously did not represent an enlightened breakthrough, but an attempt to embarrass the coalition of Senators favoring passage. The amendment was defeated, as "growth priorities dictated to the reformers that they abandon liberal goals."[45]

The landmark law included a congressional statement that called for "the realization as soon as feasible of the goal of a decent home and a suitable living environment for every American family." It also authorized loans of up to $1 billion and grants up to $500 million to localities undertaking urban redevelopment and slum clearance.[46] The result was the replacement of deteriorating commercial buildings and decaying residential areas with new office buildings, convention centers, and apartment houses typically catering to higher-income individuals. While Congress required localities to develop a feasible plan for the temporary relocation of displaced families, most cities completed the paperwork and, in the words of one federal official, "gave the families a few dollars and told them to get lost." HHFA was aware that many localities were failing to fulfill their obligations, but "like most institutions, the agency was most concerned with self-preservation and expansion."[47] Most applications for urban renewal funds did not receive a thorough review or a follow-up. As a result, urban renewal led to slum overcrowding, a quicker transition of many neighborhoods from "gray areas" to slums, and higher rents.[48]

From the beginning, FHA's responsibility for most of the construction under the act aroused considerable concern among groups concerned with nonwhite housing. Speaking on behalf of civil rights groups, Robert Weaver (who would later become HUD's first secretary) maintained that FHA "has little in its past operations to commend it as an instrument for facilitating the equitable participation of minorities."[49] These fears were well-founded. HHFA maintained that "a main objective of the urban renewal program is to make sure urban renewal not only does not adversely affect the housing situation of minority groups, but increasingly improves their housing conditions and opportunities."[50] The reality was quite different. Southern and border cities demolished integrated slums for reuse by whites only, while Northern communities built new housing well beyond the financial means of most blacks. The USCCR concluded in 1959 that urban renewal was "accentuating or creating clear-cut racial separation."[51] Black leaders had feared from its inception that urban renewal would amount to "negro removal," displacing African Americans from good neighborhoods, reducing the supply of living space open to them, and forcing the breakup of integrated neighborhoods. During congressional debate over the 1949 Housing Act, civil rights leaders urged that a nondiscrimination clause be included and that site occupants be given first preference for housing in renewal areas. They were ignored. It is during these times of federal investment in housing that the government is particularly poised to fight discrimination. In this case, as in many others, the government did not make use of this opportunity.

The news was not entirely bleak in the fight against residential segregation. The Supreme Court made a small but important move in 1953's *Banks v. Housing Authority of San Francisco* by denying a writ of certiorari to the San Francisco Housing Authority, which had appealed a lower court decision that invalidated its "separate but equal" public housing policy. The *Banks* case essentially banned segregation in public housing across the nation, at least in theory. In 1955, the federal Public Housing Authority took a couple of steps backward, including the discontinuation of its requirement that segregated facilities be equal. Still, the PHA took credit for increasing integration in public housing projects from 11 percent nationally in 1953, to 55 percent in 1960. The agency could claim this seemingly impressive change largely because it began to consider any project with more than one family of another race as "completely integrated," and because Southern states were excluded from the 1960 tallies. With Southern states included, 19 percent of projects nationwide were deemed integrated.

Congress took several small steps in the 1950s to correct some of the more flagrant inequities in the urban renewal plan. In 1956, it authorized payment of moving expenses for displaced families. Three years later, Congress made it possible to construct public housing on renewal sites, and required municipalities to compile long-range inventories of needs and assets. On the whole, the harm to African Americans caused by urban renewal overwhelmed any benefits. As of 1956, 60 percent of individuals displaced by urban renewal were nonwhites. Nine out of ten dislocated families moving into public housing were black.[52]

As the agency charged with oversight of urban renewal, HHFA was "hardly the paragon of harmony," with each of its three main constituent units—FHA, the Public Housing Administration (PHA), and the Urban Renewal Administration (URA)—"run as an independent fiefdom." As each unit remained concerned more with its particular clientele than HHFA's supervisory power, "FHA sabotaged urban renewal while URA went ahead with its projects oblivious of what PHA was doing."[53] It did not help that HHFA was a second-tier agency battling with other similarly positioned ones for congressional and White House attention. As an institutional home for fulfilling the goals of urban renewal and other policies, the HHFA was a decidedly weak one.

President Eisenhower signaled his low expectations for HHFA by appointing as administrator one Albert Cole, a defeated four-term congressman from rural Kansas who had voted against the creation of the National Housing Agency and HHFA, and had opposed many housing programs.[54] He began his term by announcing his intention to turn thirty race relations service jobs from civil service to patronage appointments, which would presumably weaken their power. Despite his assertion that housing discrimination was the "number one domestic problem," Cole argued that federal open-occupancy requirements "would make just about everything much tougher and increase the abrasive factors that slow down the real—the permanent—progress of integration."[55] He maintained that such a step would adversely affect housing production; the competing goals of housing production and integration would reappear as a central conflict within HUD during the Nixon Administration. After noting in congressional testimony that racial minorities represented at least two-thirds of slum families, Cole maintained that "federal intervention is incompatible with our idea of political and economic freedom." At this time, the Public Housing Authority and Urban Renewal Administration similarly affirmed that it was not their policy to condition aid on requirements of nondiscrimination.[56] This stance was not unusual, as agencies responsible for grant administration typically have been unenthusiastic about grant conditioning.[57]

On the ground, racial violence stemming from disputes over residential territory became increasingly commonplace, in locales that included Redwood City, Calif.; Dallas; Nashville; Miami; and Rome, Ga. Over an eighteen-month period in 1951 and 1952, more than forty racially or religiously motivated bombings occurred in the South, with not a single perpetrator convicted. In 1953, Chicago, East St. Louis, Cleveland, Indianapolis, Long Island, and Los Angeles County reported violence or bomb-throwing. Substantial migrations of blacks to American cities inflamed white fears. Between 1940 and 1950, the black population increased more than 100 percent in Buffalo, Denver, Detroit, Flint, Los Angeles, and Milwaukee, among other locales. As black populations grew rapidly, the shortage of housing for black families became increasingly severe. In Philadelphia, for example, the black population increased 32 percent between 1940 and 1949, but only 200 of the 38,000 new housing units built during that time were available to black families. In Detroit, where blacks made up 14 percent of the population and roughly 25 percent of the housing need, around 1 percent of newly built units were available to African Americans during this period.[58] In Chicago, long a focal point of racial tensions, the city's Housing Authority attempted to move a few black families into a housing project on the Southwest Side in 1946. After the first two black families moved in, over one-thousand whites rioted; the families moved out after two weeks. Four years later, the Housing Authority's black director, Robert Taylor, planned to build much-needed public housing on vacant land in white neighborhoods; Chicago's city council overrode him, constructing almost all of the units in existing black neighborhoods.[59]

The civil rights movement in the 1950s, spurred in part by the *Brown v. Board of Education* (1954) that struck down official segregation in schools, began to gain steam. The Congress of Racial Equality (CORE) and the National Association of Interracial Officials (NAIRO) joined the NAACP in a campaign to battle housing discrimination. Following the *Brown* decision, NAACP Executive Secretary Walter White asserted that the organization would "use the courts, legislation, and public opinion to crack the iron curtain of segregation in housing."[60] The American Civil Liberties Union, the Anti-Defamation League of B'nai B'rith, the National Urban League, the Brotherhood of Sleeping-Car Porters, and the United Auto Workers all joined the fight against residential segregation. In addition, advocacy groups formed the National Committee Against Discrimination in Housing, which would become the most vigilant and persistent group documenting and protesting housing discrimination, as a directing body.

Federal housing agencies were unlikely candidates to spearhead civil rights efforts, and not only because of their record supporting segregation. The close ties of these agencies to private-sector interests also made them prone to corruption. In 1954, the Senate Banking and Currency Committee investigated agency programs involved with construction of rental apartments and loans for home repairs. The most severe abuses occurred when private builders of apartment projects made "windfall profits" by securing FHA-insured mortgage loans well in excess of actual construction costs; when the project was completed, rents were computed based on these greatly overestimated costs. The congressional committee blamed the scandals on "a few greedy, and sometimes dishonest, builders and repairmen, and incompetent, lax and sometimes dishonest FHA officials." Sen. Paul H. Douglas (D-IL) traced the scandals to the fact that FHA was "an industry-dominated agency" that was largely steered by bankers and builders. Similar scandals would emerge in the early 1970s, with adverse consequences for desegregation efforts, tangentially related as they were. The Senate panel recommended no immediate changes to existing law, noting that the recently passed Housing Act of 1954 included provisions to address some of the issues raised by the scandal.[61]

A CABINET DEPARTMENT FOR HOUSING AND URBAN ISSUES

Congress was still some distance from addressing questions of housing discrimination, but interest in the problems of metropolitan areas was increasing. The 1960 presidential campaign marked the first time that the problems of cities and suburbs became a national campaign issue. A 1959 *Architectural Forum* article noted that one million more people lived in slums than on farms; while the average farm family received three thousand dollars annually in federal benefits, the annual slum family saw a mere eighty-four dollars. Illustrated in another manner, in 1960 the shrinking farm population was represented by a cabinet department with over 100,000 employees, while urban residents were represented by HHFA, a noncabinet department with about 14,000 employees. This was due partly to the fact that Congress still reflected the rural majorities of fifty years earlier, rather than the urban majority that existed in 1960.[62]

Despite no record of writing or pushing for urban bills while a member of Congress, John F. Kennedy projected a strong urban image and supported the proposal in the 1960 Democratic platform for a cabinet-level agency devoted to metropolitan issues. Richard Nixon and the Republican Party did little to vie for urban votes. While Kennedy aimed his appeals at large urban states, Nixon sought to portray himself as the national candidate, a man of experience to guide the nation in times of "peace and prosperity." Despite Kennedy's attempts to put housing and urban issues into the spotlight, these were overshadowed by issues such as the missile gap, Fidel Castro, the recession, and Kennedy's Catholicism. Housing came up just once in the Kennedy-Nixon debates. The 1960 platforms of both parties pledged to end discrimination in federal housing programs, including federally assisted housing.[63]

During his campaign, Kennedy had promised that if elected he would end segregation in federally supported housing "by a stroke of the Presidential pen." Kennedy said President Eisenhower "could and should act now. By such action, he would toll the end of racial discrimination in all federal housing programs, including federally assisted housing."[64] After his election, Kennedy delayed the fulfillment of his promise, as the open occupancy issue threatened to cause the withdrawal of Southern Democratic support in Congress. Kennedy had another battle to fight with this faction over his appointment of Robert Weaver to head the Housing and Home Finance Agency. Since its creation in 1947, the HHFA had been headed by individuals who were closely connected to the private housing sector. In contrast, Weaver's experience was mostly in government housing construction. After working for the War Production Board and the War Manpower Commission during World War II, Weaver left the public service but still continued to emphasize the importance of public housing in his writings and other activities.

Even more troubling to Dixiecrats was that Weaver was African American. Senate Banking and Currency Committee Chair Willis Robertson (D-VA) and Sen. John Sparkman (D-AL), chair of that panel's Housing Subcommittee, did not want a firm supporter of integration running HHFA.[65] Previous administrators had blunted the drive for open occupancy by claiming that an antidiscrimination order would dampen new housing construction. Adding to their discomfort was the possibility that HHFA would be elevated to cabinet department–status, resulting in Weaver integrating the cabinet. Kennedy eventually won the confirmation battle, with Weaver sworn in as HHFA head on February 11, 1961. The White House, however, quashed Weaver's attempts to improve urban renewal's treatment of nonwhites.

Meanwhile, civil rights groups were getting impatient with Kennedy's delay in making good on his campaign promise to sign the executive order on housing. The Leadership Conference on Civil Rights asserted, "In no area of civil rights is the need for Executive action more compelling than in the field of housing. For segregation in housing virtually assures segregation in schools, in recreation and in other community facilities. At the same time, there is no area in which the policies and programs of the Federal government more clearly served to perpetuate—and indeed to extend—racial segregation."[66] In its "Ink for Jack" campaign, the National Committee Against Discrimination in Housing asked its members to implore Kennedy to sign the order and to include in their letters a pen with which to sign it.[67] The White House received thousands of pens, but civil rights backers would have to wait a bit longer. After the 1962 midterm elections, Kennedy finally redeemed his pledge, though only partially. Executive Order 11063 covered only new housing and excluded homes financed by Savings and Loans Associations that operated under the Federal Home Loan Bank Board.

The order applied to all property owned by the government or receiving government assistance and to all institutions handling loans insured by the U.S. government. Violators were subject to cancellation of federal contracts and exclusion from other federal assistance. In theory, the order covered all public housing projects and all properties that were purchased using FHA or VA insurance, but federal officials were reluctant to compel local compliance, and FHA essentially refused to apply the new requirements to its portfolio of loans. As of March 1964, the Public Housing Authority reported that of the 3,289 projects it helped to fund, 2,370 (72 percent) were entirely segregated by race.[68] Tellingly, it was not until 1980 that HUD issued the final regulations to implement the requirements of the order.[69] For enforcement, Kennedy created the President's Committee on Equal Opportunity in Housing, which subsequently concluded that EO 11063 was too limited. After passage of the Civil Rights Act of 1964, the Committee formally recommended to President Johnson that the order be strengthened.[70]

The Kennedy White House was also backing proposals for a new cabinet-level department of housing and urban affairs. A bill to accomplish such an objective had the backing of the United States Conference of Mayors, the American Municipal Association, the National Housing Conference, the National Association of Housing and Redevelopment Officials, the American Council to Improve Our Neighborhoods, the American Institute of Planners, and the AFL-CIO. Opposition was varied, and at times quite vehement. The National Association of Home Builders and the Mortgage Bankers Association of America agreed to support the legislation if it was amended to retain the operation of FHA in its existing form. The National Association of Real Estate Boards insisted that the federal government get out of public housing and urban renewal, and sell FHA to private groups.[71] Southern members of Congress demanded that Kennedy promise not to appoint an African American to head the proposed department; the president refused.

The Creation of HUD in the Civil Rights Era

With Republican candidate Barry Goldwater winning only six states in the 1964 presidential election, the American public swept Lyndon Johnson into office along with two new Democratic senators and thirty-seven new Democratic House members. As his term began, Johnson enjoyed Democratic margins of 295-140 in the House, and 68-32 in the Senate. In an era when black protests in the South were gaining support and the black vote in the North was growing in magnitude, civil rights and urban affairs assumed great prominence in national politics.

The landmark Civil Rights Act of 1964, while saying little about housing directly, included language making it illegal to discriminate on the basis of race, color, or national origin in the administration of federally assisted programs, and authorizing agencies to terminate funds in cases of noncompliance. This provision, Title VI, provided a potentially powerful weapon to fight discrimination in publicly aided housing, although the 1964 legislation specifically exempted federal mortgage insurance, including the FHA and VA loan programs, from coverage. The 1962 executive order and 1964 legislation covered an estimated 3 percent of existing housing.[72]

On the state and local levels, open housing battles continued nationwide with mixed results. In 1964, California voters passed Proposition 14, which guaranteed a homeowner the right to sell, lease, or rent property—or refuse to do so—"as he, in his absolute discretion, chooses." Voters had decided by a nearly 2-1 margin that home and building owners should be free to discriminate on any grounds they chose. The U.S. Supreme Court invalidated Proposition 14 three years later in *Reitman v. Mulkey* (387 U.S. 369), ruling that it violated the equal protection clause of the Fourteenth Amendment. On the other hand, by April 1968, twenty-three states and 130 cities, towns, and counties had some sort of fair housing law, covering an estimated 62 percent of the U.S. population.[73]

In 1965, the Housing and Urban Development Act authorized the creation of the Department of Housing and Urban Development (HUD). This time around, the legislation engendered little serious opposition. LBJ had remained silent on his choice for HUD secretary, somewhat defusing the racial issue. When the nomination of Robert Weaver was announced, even segregationist Southern senators supported his appointment. The National Association of Manufacturers, the U.S. Chamber of Commerce, and the American Farm Bureau Federation expressed some opposition, but a sense of resignation permeated their remarks. The National Association of County Officials and the National Association of Home Builders, both of which had opposed the creation of the department in 1961 and 1962, voiced support for the 1965 effort.[74]

The law also introduced rent supplements, which President Johnson had believed would markedly increase integration across income levels by enabling the residential mobility of working families. Whereas Johnson envisioned supplements being targeted largely to moderate-income people, congressional liberals said that the poor should receive them as well; conservatives emphasized the danger of "across the board economic integration." The provisions that ultimately passed directed supplements only to individuals eligible for public housing, quite the opposite of what the administration had intended, which was to allow working families to move out of ghetto housing. Congress denied funding to the program in 1965 and funded it the following year only after inclusion of a provision that granted local authorities veto power over the use of rent supplements in urban renewal projects.[75] Rent supplements represented the first attempt by the federal government to encourage racial and economic integration in a manner that would be less confrontational than construction of public housing (though selection of public housing sites was made by local authorities, and thus typically did not challenge segregation).

In the newly created HUD, the secretary was to oversee all of the previous duties and functions of the Housing and Home Finance Agency, including the Community Facilities and Urban Renewal Administrations, the Federal Housing Administration, the Federal National Mortgage Association, and the Public Housing Administration. The act did not consolidate housing and urban development functions existing in other sectors of the federal government.[76] By placing "housing" first in the new department's title, the administration had hoped to ease the anxieties of the construction industry, which had feared that their interests would be submerged in an urban department. In response to pressures from private housing groups, the law assigned special status to FHA, retaining its separate identity under a commissioner who would have assistant secretary status at HUD as well. FHA was also given responsibility for all other HUD programs relating to the private mortgage money market. Historically, FHA's popularity and budgetary friendliness "helped to make it remarkably independent of the other agencies in Washington."[77] HUD secretaries would come to find that getting FHA employees to consider themselves part of the HUD team was exceedingly difficult.

As a lifelong fighter against discrimination, HUD Secretary Robert Weaver placed a high priority on equal opportunity and fair housing. HUD's equal opportunity policy spelled out several notable measures, including FHA collection of racial data in multi-family projects and sales housing; requiring violators of EO 11063 and HUD equal opportunity requirements to implement affirmative open-occupancy programs if they were seeking reinstatement as fund recipients; site selection guidelines denying public housing funds to authorities locating projects only in areas of racial concentration (unless able to show conclusively that no other sites were available); and notice that "unimaginative site selection or bad relocation practices" in urban renewal efforts may be considered violations of Title VI (Civil Rights Act of 1964).[78]

The Federal Housing Administration dramatically altered the thrust of its operations. Throughout its first thirty years, FHA wrote off the poor and the nonwhite as too risky. The landscape was transformed by 1967, after repeated instances of urban rioting. Commissioner Phillip Brownstein told a meeting of FHA directors and chief underwriters that encouraging the private sector to provide decent housing for low- and moderate-income families, and to improve housing conditions in the inner city, was "the greatest and most urgent responsibility of FHA—its principal reason for existence" in 1967.[79] Brownstein stressed repeatedly that FHA should be aggressive in seeking sponsors and builders for inner-city projects, and "to slash through red tape, indecision, and pussyfooting." This emphasis on rapid decision-making sowed the seeds for far-reaching scandals that would devastate the program several years later (see chapter 5).

Pushing for Fair Housing Legislation

President Johnson was not finished pressing housing or civil rights matters. In 1966, he greeted Congress with open housing legislation as a high priority. From 1964 to 1966, the path to passage of civil rights legislation had become noticeably more treacherous as public support began to deteriorate. Beginning in 1965, the nation endured three consecutive summers of deadly urban riots. In August of that year, a police stop of a drunk driver in the Watts section of Los Angeles escalated into six days of chaos that left thirty-four dead, nine hundred injured, and four thousand arrested. Several thousand local police officers were joined by fourteen thousand members of the National Guard to stop the rioting. The following summer, no single riot matched the intensity of Watts, but thirty-eight "civil disorders" across the United States resulted in seven deaths, four hundred injuries, three thousand arrests, and $5 million of property burned or looted. The summer of 1967 saw more violence in the streets, culminating in the July riot in Detroit, which claimed forty-three lives and left hundreds injured, five thousand people without homes, and thirteen hundred buildings destroyed. In April 1968, riots broke out in 138 localities after the murder of the Reverend Martin Luther King, Jr.; forty-three people died. All told, "hostile outbursts" occurred in forty-four cities in 1966, seventy-one cities in 1967, and 106 cities in 1968, with many cities recording more than one outburst.[80]

On Capitol Hill, the expanded scope of legislation from blatant Southern racism to issues applicable nationwide made many non-Southern congressional members less zealous in their advocacy of civil rights. Indeed, many observers were surprised that Johnson would call in his January 1966 State of the Union address for legislation that would target discrimination "in the inner sanctum of middle-class America—housing."[81]

Johnson's advisors had been split on the political advisability of calling for open housing legislation.

While some advisors, such as Attorney General Nicholas Katzenbach, cautioned against moving too quickly on such a volatile issue, others feared the dangers of inaction. Some White House staffers worried that a failure to push open housing legislation would result in embarrassing criticism internally from the White House Conference on Civil Rights and the President's Committee on Equal Opportunity in Housing, and externally from the National Committee Against Discrimination in Housing. The NCDH's pamphlet, "How the Federal Government Builds Ghettos," first released in February 1967, painstakingly categorizes the opportunities missed by HUD and its predecessors as well as their missteps in the area of housing desegregation. The advocacy group charged that "the road to segregation is paved with weak intentions. . . . [The federal government's] sin is not bigotry (though there are still cases of bald discrimination by Federal officials) but blandness; not a lack of goodwill, but a lack of will."[82]

Domestic program coordinator Joseph Califano alerted the president in 1965 to "tremendous pressure from civil rights leaders and the President's Committee on Equal Opportunity in Housing to do something" about housing not covered by Kennedy's limited executive order. He warned that "it is only a matter of time before some Republicans (like Javits and Kuchel) recognize the importance of this [fair housing legislation] to the Negro voter and begin to ride you on it."[83] In fall 1966, Vice President Hubert Humphrey reported to Johnson that "talks with civil rights leaders have produced the strong feeling that if [the fair housing title] fails, some *positive response* by the federal government is essential."[84] While these two memos suggest that civil rights leaders were pushing hard, the NAACP's Clarence Mitchell—widely regarded as the chief lobbyist behind the passage of fair housing legislation—believed that Johnson's leadership on fair housing was "way ahead of the leadership of some of the people even in the civil rights movement."[85]

Although some scholars have argued that housing integration was at the top of the civil rights agenda by 1965, protest events did not focus on this area of the struggle. Of 181 protest events relating to segregation/integration initiated by the civil rights movement between 1966 and 1970, only twelve targeted housing.[86] The most prominent protest in favor of open housing took place in Chicago, led by Martin Luther King, Jr., and his Southern Christian Leadership Conference (SCLC). As recalled by an SCLC aide, "Open housing was not selected because it was believed to be the key problem facing the Negro community. . . . It was chosen because it offered the best opportunity for the Negro to 'stand up and be a man, to declare that he was a human being and would henceforth expect to be treated like one.' " Writing in 1967, the SCLC aide also recalled that the issue was chosen because "the problem of housing discrimination is an easy solution, compared to other types of problems. It would only take an administrative order—from the mayor, the governor, Congress, or the President—to end discrimination in housing." The reasoning was that, because realtors are licensed by the city and state, discriminatory action by them could be met with confiscation of their licenses.[87] Other participants recalled that open housing represented a clear-cut moral issue and that housing discrimination violated the city's 1963 fair housing ordinance.[88]

The SCLC organized a number of open housing marches through white neighborhoods in Chicago, stirring an intensity of opposition that left many of the leadership and marchers stunned. On August 5, King marched with over five hundred individuals through Marquette Park and Chicago Lawn. Near the end of the march, a crowd of four thousand enraged whites confronted the marchers. Thirty demonstrators were injured, including King himself, who was hit in the head with a rock early in the march. Later, King said that he had "never seen as much hatred and hostility on the part of so many people."[89] The Chicago Freedom Movement subsequently planned a march through all-white Cicero, a notoriously racist suburb that was the site of a large race riot fifteen years earlier when a black couple tried to move into an apartment there. The Cook County sheriff pleaded with the organization to cancel such a "suicidal" act.[90] The Chicago Freedom Movement canceled the march after agreeing with city leaders on a number of provisions affirming the commitment of real-estate brokers and a number of city and county government agencies to open housing.[91] Establishing no yardsticks for the achievement of this objective, the agreement achieved virtually nothing beyond the symbolic realm.

While King and his colleagues were struggling through the Chicago campaign, Congress had begun to consider fair housing legislation. It does not appear, however, that the Chicago demonstrations inspired action in Washington. During the week-long debate in the House, only six representatives mentioned the Chicago demonstrations, all in a negative manner. Lobbying for the legislation was led by the NAACP, backed by a number of labor and religious groups, including the AFL-CIO, the United Steelworkers, the United Autoworkers, the American Civil Liberties Union, the Americans for Democratic Action, and the Anti-Defamation League of B'nai B'rith.[92] The NAACP insisted that "no amount of progress in any single phase of the civil rights movement can have lasting effect so long as racially separate patterns of residency continue to be enforced."[93] The organization, though opposing weakening of the bill, continued to believe that passage was worthwhile.

The National Association of Real Estate Boards (NAREB) led opposition to the bill. At the time of the fair housing debate, the organization consisted of about 83,000 real-estate brokers, accounting for roughly 90 percent of the nation's real-estate business. The association printed a leaflet "in the millions" opposing fair housing legislation and organized an aggressive letter-writing campaign to members of Congress. The Leadership Conference on Civil Rights attempted, with little success, to provoke a countercurrent of pro-fair housing mail. NAREB contended that the 1966 Mathias compromise, which substantially weakened the bill, was "more dangerous because it uses clever language to distort meaning, knowing full well that the federal bureaucracy will take maximum advantage of every loophole."[94]

"I suppose from their point of view," Rep. James C. Corman (D-CA) remarked acidly, "that is a correct analysis because now the attention of this Congress and of the nation is focused on their role in perpetuating segregated housing."[95] Members of Congress said that their mail ran strongly against open-housing legislation. Sen. Sam J. Ervin (D-NC) reported mail running 2,000 to 5 against, while Sen. Philip A. Hart (D-MI) reported opposition of 107 to 1. Much of the opposition mail—one congressional staffer estimated it could be as high as 75 percent—was written in response to NAREB's campaign. Senate Minority Leader Everett Dirksen (R-IL), who two years later would broker the compromise that led to the passage of fair housing legislation, called the provisions "absolutely unconstitutional."[96]

The House passed fair housing legislation in August 1966, but the bill fell victim to a Senate filibuster.[97] Militant young black leaders were largely dismissive of the watered-down housing legislation. Stokely Carmichael, chair of the Student Nonviolent Coordinating Committee, called the proposed law "totally useless and totally unnecessary . . . a fraudulent bunch of words to convince the black people of this country that Congress has taken action to deal with their problems."[98] Even Martin Luther King, Jr., who said little about congressional fair housing legislation during the Chicago campaign, called the amended bill "virtually meaningless" because it was so weak.[99] King later reversed his position after the House-passed bill was sent to the Senate, reiterating his support for fair housing legislation.

As passed, the bill strikingly reflected the ambivalence of House members about the expansion of federal governmental powers. The 1966 bill—but not the 1968 bill that became law—included the creation of a Fair Housing Board to investigate complaints of discrimination. The proposed board would have heard charges filed by the HUD secretary after the investigation of a complaint. Following procedures used by the National Labor Relations Board, the fair housing panel would have been authorized to issue orders for relief and pursue enforcement orders through circuit courts of appeals.[100] The evidence in subsequent chapters suggests that aggressive pro-integrative measures in housing would have stood a substantially stronger chance had fair housing responsibilities been assigned to a stand-alone agency rather than being subsumed within HUD.

The 1966 civil rights bill also included passage of amendments to limit agency powers in enforcing the Civil Rights Act of 1964. The Whitener amendment required the attorney general to receive a written complaint of denial of equal protection of laws before instituting a suit to desegregate public schools or facilities, despite numerous reported instances of intimidation when individuals did step forward. The Callaway amendment made more specific the intention of the 1964 legislation not to require racial balance, though the original law stated this already. The House defeated another hotly debated Whitener amendment that would have prohibited cut-off of federal aid funds under the 1964 law except for violation by local authorities of the Constitution or federal law, not of agency guidelines; it was rejected by a 89-104 standing vote and again by a 127-136 teller vote, despite the reported support of a large number of Republicans, including Minority Leader Gerald Ford (R-MI).[101] Whitener contended that his amendment would insure in the future that Title VI of the 1964 Act "will be implemented according to the intention of Congress and not the whim of bureaucrats who are not answerable to the people for their sociological follies" (August 9, 1966, p. 18702). At this time, Southern school districts were under increasing pressure from HEW's Office of Civil Rights to devise school desegregation plans that produced concrete results, and Southern congressmen were livid.

Congressional Debates over Fair Housing Legislation

The 1966 debate over fair housing legislation is in several ways more instructive than the 1968 debate, which resulted in passage of legislation. First, only the 1966 legislation included the creation of a Fair Housing Board to investigate complaints of discrimination. Thus, the floor debate starkly reveals the uneasiness of many members with another group of bureaucrats going beyond congressional intent, as they felt was occurring in the area of school desegregation. Second, the 1966 House debate lasted twelve days, the longest floor fight in thirty years. In contrast, the 1968 Senate bill was introduced during floor debate without clarifying committee or conference reports. When the bill was sent to the House, no amendments were permitted. As a result, "the level of debate during the 1968 Senate discussions . . . remained at the highly generalized level of discourse that the senators thought appropriate for the public toward whom they were aiming their remarks."[102] The dearth of data on congressional intent would later spawn rancorous debates about what steps Congress intended for HUD to take in carrying out the aims of the law.

The 1966 House debate was marked by three frequently articulated objections: (1) the legislation would reward rioters; (2) it would create false hopes and satisfy no one, making it likely that Congress would seek to strengthen and expand the law in coming years; and (3) it would create another big government bureaucracy that would overstep its bounds and intrude upon local affairs.[103] As with previous civil rights bills, a number of opponents attacked fair housing as unconstitutional or communistic. The bill was widely regarded as the first Northern civil rights bill, as its scope was national rather than focused squarely on the South. Southern members still led objections to the legislation, however, warning their Northern colleagues of the overzealous enforcement by Washington bureaucrats that would ensue after passage of the legislation. Many members also asserted that the legislation destroyed the rights of property owners to dispose of their property however and to whomever they chose.

Southern members nevertheless took some pleasure in the prospect of a civil rights bill that extended beyond their region of the country. Rep. Prentiss Walker (R-MS) noted that the fair housing provision could be termed "the great equalizer." "For the first time," he noted, "many of my colleagues from north of the Mason-Dixon line have expressed concern that they feel this bill goes too far. I well understand what they mean, it goes too far north. For the first time, we have a civil rights bill that reaches home—every home in the nation" (July 29, 1966, p. 17595).

A glance at some voting tallies bears out the concern of non-Southerners with legislation that might affect their constituents directly. A comparison of voting by House members on the Civil Rights Act of 1964 (passed 290-130) and 1966 fair housing legislation (259-157) reveals that forty members (thirteen Democrats and twenty-seven Republicans) supported the 1964 legislation but voted against the 1966 bill. Nine of these "yes in 64, no in 66" votes came from California, and eight from Ohio. None came from Southern representatives, who voted overwhelmingly against both bills (with the exception of a handful of members from urban districts). Four members—two from Florida and one each from Texas and Georgia—voted against the 1964 bill but for the 1966 one.[104]

Warnings about "Rewarding" Rioters

Opponents of the bill repeatedly asserted that passage would reward and encourage rioters. Rep. Robert T. Ashmore (D-SC) challenged his colleagues: "Are you going to swallow this mess of pottage in the vain hope that it will appease or pacify or probably satisfy a few minority groups in this country in their constant, endless—and I repeat, endless—demands upon you? As for me, I refuse to prescribe such medicine as this, however sick the patient may be" (July 27, 1966, p. 17185). Echoing these sentiments, Rep. Albert W. Watson (R-SC) commented that "under the guise of civil rights Congress appears to be willing to pass a law—any law—to satisfy the demands and appetites of howling mobs and demonstrators who are storming the streets of America" (August 4, 1966, p. 18199).

A number of opponents implicitly used "rioters" as a synonym for all African Americans, while proponents drew a distinction between black rioters (generally judged harshly) and hard-working blacks, especially those fighting in Vietnam. During the 1968 congressional debate, fair housing supporters brought up riots nearly twice as often as did opponents.[105] The NCDH, for example, warned that "racial alienation and tension in the ghetto areas are reaching catastrophic proportions which can lead to unprecedented explosions." The organization's executive heads said they had been told repeatedly on ghetto streets, "We need two and a half more riots to get out of here."[106] This statement suggests that inner-city blacks had lost faith in change via mainstream political institutions, and a fair housing law would help to restore some of that faith. During the 1968 fair housing debate, Senate co-sponsors Mondale (D-MN) and Brooke (R-MA) made the same point.

Creating Illusory Hopes

Opponents also insisted that passage of the legislation would raise false hopes and satisfy no one, causing further unrest. The position articulated by many proponents is noteworthy. In contrast to the debate over civil rights bills in 1964 and 1965, in which many members had great expectations for the changes that would take place, a number of civil rights supporters in 1966 and 1968 acknowledged that such legislation might not result in noticeable changes in housing opportunities for African Americans.

Rep. William T. Cahill (R-NJ), a supporter of the 1966 bill, said that the housing title "in my judgment is nothing more than a legislative symbol" that "is not going to accomplish a great deal." He added that Congress has "taken the attitude here that this is a political issue, and we must get a housing bill through, no matter how inadequate, so all of the headlines will read, 'The Johnson Administration has passed a fair housing bill'" (July 26, 1966, p. 17119). Rep. John Anderson (R-IL), who opposed fair housing legislation in 1966 but was a pivotal figure in its passage two years later, said in the earlier floor debate that "very, very few of us" believe that the legislation would solve the housing problems of Negroes. He related a conversation with a prominent black leader in Chicago, who guessed that the bill would result in 2 percent of blacks moving out of the ghetto.

The notion that fair housing legislation was unlikely to result in far-reaching changes in living patterns may have actually increased congressional support. Fair housing proponents felt compelled to argue that passage of the law would result in some—but not "too much"—housing desegregation.[107] Contemplating passage of a law that would result in little tangible change could cause opponents to claim that such a halting measure would be futile or hypocritical, while spurring supporters to push for more far-reaching legislation. A number of opponents stressed the inevitability of Congress revisiting and strengthening the proposed legislation. Rep. Harold R. Collier (R-IL) noted that Congress strengthened provisions for fair employment practices written into the 1964 Civil Rights Act less than ten months after the law went into effect. He predicted that his congressional colleagues would do the same for this bill. (As it turned out, Congress would take two decades to strengthen fair housing law.) Collier was referring to the House passage of the Equal Employment Opportunity Act of 1966 (299-94), giving the EEOC the same authority and procedures as the Fair Housing Board would have had in housing; the EEOC bill died in the Senate.

Overzealous Washington Bureaucrats

House members, their tendency toward exaggeration notwithstanding, were clearly concerned about the proposed powers of the Fair Housing Board. Rep. Richard H. Poff (R-VA) argued that the proposed Fair Housing Board "will take on the qualities and characteristics of the investigator, the prosecutor, and the judge" (July 26, 1966, p. 17122). Rep. John J. Rhodes (R-AZ) advised his colleagues that Title IV "may create another super agency larger and more powerful than the National Labor Relations Board to investigate the thousands of complaints that are bound to arise under this title" (August 1, 1966, p. 17768).

Perhaps Rep. Howard H. Callaway (R-GA) expressed this sentiment most sharply, when he pondered, "Could there ever be any set of circumstances under which [the fair housing section] of this bill could be used by some bureaucrat to successfully force a racial balance in a given residential or housing area? Proponents, I am sure, would assure me that this is not the thrust of the bill, the intent of the congress, or the letter of the proposed law. True. But to these gentlemen, I would like to point out a close and frightening analogy" (July 27, 1966, p. 17187). Callaway related Sen. Hubert Humphrey's assurances during debate over the 1964 Civil Rights Act that the federal government would not withhold assistance from schools failing to correct racial imbalances. Nevertheless, Callaway continued, "they have drawn federal guidelines that establish percentages of racial balance, and they have cut off funds from schools that refuse to go along with the arbitrary ratios" (17187). He concluded that "just because this [fair housing] bill does not refer to racial balance, doesn't mean that in practice the bill will not operate under a bureaucratic formula of racial balance" (17189).

Rep. George W. Andrews (D-AL) speculated that because of the precedent set by the HEW guidelines for enforcement of the 1964 act,

> it seems quite possible for a regulatory agency to require a financial institution to maintain a financing portfolio in terms of race, color, religion, or national origin. . . . If the percentage of loans, say, for Chinese, was less than the percentage of Chinese who lived in the community, there might be 'reasonable grounds' for the instituting of a civil suit. . . . Such percentage discrepancies have given HEW cause to intervene in education. We would be naive not to expect the same assumption of power by another agency. (August 3, 1966, p. 18132)

Opponents of civil rights legislation in the House were unable to prevent passage of the 1966 fair housing bill, but the measure died in the Senate as midterm elections were approaching.

An Unexpected Second Life for Fair Housing Legislation

After failing to be voted out of a Senate subcommittee in 1967, fair housing legislation got another chance in 1968 due to an odd confluence of political miscalculations by civil rights opponents and external events. At the outset, the prospects for a fair housing law of 1968 seemed remote. Former Assistant Deputy Attorney General Barefoot Sanders recalled that during the 1968 fight for fair housing legislation, "the civil rights groups which could fill the galleries in '64 and '65 and flood the Congress with letters just didn't have any muscle," adding that the NAACP's Clarence Mitchell was one person who did contribute greatly to passage of the law. "I would have bet pretty heavy odds against it at the beginning of 1968," Sanders recalled.[108]

The opportunity for a fair housing law started inconspicuously when Southern senators decided to begin a filibuster against HR 2516, a fairly minor bill that sought to protect civil rights workers. After a week of this stalling, President Johnson sent a special message to Congress urging passage of HR 2516 as well as fair housing legislation. A group of civil rights lobbyists and Senate sympathizers plotted strategy. Joseph Rauh, counsel for the Leadership Conference on Civil Rights, recalled that the group reasoned, "As long as the Southerners want a filibuster, we might as well give them something to filibuster about. We can beat a filibuster for two things as easily as one, perhaps easier." In retrospect, Rauh concluded, the decision to filibuster HR 2516 was "the worst judgment the Southerners ever made," because fair housing would not have had a chance without this opportunity.

On February 6, 1968, Sen. Walter Mondale (D-MN) and Sen. Edward Brooke (R-MA) offered an amendment to prohibit discrimination in the sale or rental of housing.[109] After ten days of debate, Senate Majority Leader Mike Mansfield (D-MT) attempted to close off debate, anticipating an easy defeat for the legislation. Southern senators opposed cloture, wishing to continue the debate until liberals would be forced to suspend their effort. Two more cloture motions (on February 21 and 26) failed as well, but they revealed growing support for fair housing among moderate Republicans, who reportedly believed that blocking the legislation would make them look bad in an election year.[110]

On February 28, the Senate adopted a compromise amendment proposed by Senate Minority Leader Everett Dirksen (R-IL) that reduced coverage to 80 percent of all dwellings, from 91 percent. In agreeing to broker the compromise after blocking similar legislation two years earlier, Dirksen cited the growing racial unrest in American cities, the injustice of housing discrimination that returning black Vietnam veterans were likely to face, and the plodding pace with which states and localities were adopting their own fair housing laws.[111] The compromise excluded two major categories of housing from coverage: (1) owner-occupied dwellings of four or fewer units; and (2) owner-occupied single-family houses, provided owners did not use a real-estate agent or broker, and did not indicate racial preferences or discrimination in advertising the sale or rental of housing. More importantly, the amendment reduced HUD's authority sharply. The agency could no longer hold hearings, issue complaints, or publish cease and desist orders. Penalties for violations of the act were reduced as well.[112]

The day after the Senate compromise, the Kerner Commission released its highly anticipated report on urban riots, fueling the sense that some legislative action must take place in the area of housing. Cloture was invoked on March 4, and after consideration of more than eighty amendments, the Senate passed the bill by a 71-20 margin, with all opposing votes cast by Southern senators. Forty-two Democrats and twenty-nine Republicans voted for the legislation.

The bill still faced an uncertain fate in the House. HR 2516 was referred to the Rules Committee, which deferred action until March 28. During the first few days of April, it appeared that the legislation might die in committee. On April 4, 1968, Martin Luther King, Jr., was assassinated and riots broke out across the United States, with Washington, D.C., the hardest hit. Some members urged their colleagues not to be swayed by outside events. Rep. H. R. Gross (R-IA) insisted that "to approve this legislation today . . . means a capitulation to those who have nothing but contempt for law and order. It will be a shameful day in the nation's history if on this day the House of Representative spinelessly capitulates." Five days later, Rep. John Anderson broke with his Republican colleagues on the Rules Committee and cast the deciding vote to send the Senate amendments intact to the full House. With armed National Guardsmen continuing to provide security for the Capitol, the House passed the bill 250-71 on April 10 after one hour of debate. President Johnson signed the bill into law the following day.[113]

Reflecting Congress's "carrot and stick" attempt to prevent future unrest, the law included provisions punishing perpetrators of violence. Persons convicted of intimidating or injuring civil rights workers and African Americans exercising specific rights—such as participating in schooling, housing, voting or registering to vote, jury duty, and the use of public facilities—were subject to fines of up to $10,000, and prison terms of ten years for inflicting bodily injury or life sentences for causing death. The law also made traveling across state lines or using the facilities of interstate commerce (such as radio or television) with the intent to incite a riot punishable by up to five years in prison and a $10,000 fine.[114] The same penalties applied to individuals manufacturing, selling, or demonstrating the use of firearms, firebombs, or other explosive devices intended for use in a riot or other civil disorder.

Most observers agree that King's death was critically important in gathering sufficient support for the 1968 fair housing legislation. Also significant was the softened resistance of interest groups, such as the National Association of Home Builders and the Mortgage Bankers Association, who in earlier years had vocally opposed open-occupancy measures. Robert Weaver recalled that the Home Builders "became increasingly concerned about their image as a selfish little trade group and set out to improve the picture."[115] Builders who constructed homes using federal financing wanted to ensure that nongovernment contractors would also be bound by open-housing provisions. The Senate vote apparently surprised the National Association of Real Estate Boards, which did little to no lobbying in that chamber prior to the vote. When the bill moved to the House, NAREB picked up its 1966 strategy of encouraging a massive letter-writing campaign by individuals opposed to the legislation. This time around, NAREB's lobbying was evidently not enough to prevent passage. Three "extreme right-wing groups" also conducted anti–fair-housing campaigns. One of these groups, the Emergency Committee of One Million, warned in a letter that if the fair housing bill passed, "LBJ's bureaucrats will be swarming over every neighborhood in the United States—setting up Negro-White quotas, forcing homeowners to sell their property, and encouraging vicious gangs of rioters and looters to destroy neighborhoods which dare to resist."[116]

While most Americans presumably did not believe this scenario, passage of the fair housing bill was not due to united pressure from the badly divided civil rights movement. Nor was there a groundswell of public opinion in favor of fair housing. A 1967 Gallup Poll revealed that, between 1963 and 1965, 34 to 35 percent of whites said that they might move or definitely would move if a black family moved next door, while 69 to 71 percent said they would move if a great number of Negroes moved into the neighborhood. A memo presenting these findings to Johnson notes that "basic white attitudes toward integration in housing have not changed since 1963"; this is not quite accurate, as attitudes became notably more tolerant between 1963 and 1965. The memo adds that "close to one in three white persons now have a lower regard for Negroes because of the recent riots."[117]

The fair housing section of the 1968 Civil Rights Act built upon a pair of more limited fair-housing policies: Kennedy's 1962 Executive Order 11063 and Title VI of the 1964 Civil Rights Act. These two provisions prohibited discrimination in the sale and rental of low-rent public housing; the initial sale of newly constructed housing built with mortgages insured or guaranteed by the VA or FHA after the 1962 order (though the agencies were lax in enforcing these laws); and new housing under the urban renewal program, college housing program, senior citizens' housing program, and some of the federal rural housing programs, provided that the federal assistance was received after the applicable effective date of the 1962 order or 1964 legislation.

Title VIII of the 1968 Civil Rights Act prohibits refusing to sell, rent to, negotiate or deal with a person based on race, color, national origin, or (as amended in 1974) sex; discriminating in terms of the conditions for buying or renting; advertisements indicating racial preferences; or denying that housing is available when it actually is. The title also contains specific provisions against "blockbusting," in which real-estate brokers promote racial transition for profit. The law directs the HUD Secretary "to administer the programs and activities relating to housing and urban development in a manner affirmatively to further the policies of this title." Congress did not specify its expectations of agencies charged with carrying out this mandate. However, the 1968 fair housing debate suggests that even supporters of the legislation did not expect to see a major reshuffling of housing patterns as a result of passage.[118]

Only two months after passage of the 1968 Act, the Supreme Court ruled in *Jones v. Mayer* (392 U.S. 409) that an 1866 civil rights law barring "*all* racial discrimination, private as well as public, in the sale or rental of property" guaranteed the right to nondiscrimination virtually without exception. The Supreme Court ruling did not render the 1968 Civil Rights Act moot. The *Jones v. Mayer* decision addresses only racial discrimination (not discrimination on the grounds of religion or national origin); does not specifically cover discrimination in the provision of services or facilities related to sale or rental of a dwelling; does not forbid advertising including discriminatory preferences; does not refer explicitly to discrimination in financing arrangements or brokerage services; does not authorize a federal administrative agency to aid aggrieved parties; and makes no express provision authorizing a federal court to order payment of damages.[119]

The year also saw the passage of the Housing and Urban Development Act of 1968, which set a national goal to build or rehabilitate twenty-six million housing units between 1969 and 1978. Six million units would be constructed or rehabilitated with federal assistance, a huge increase over previous levels of federal assistance. Subsidized housing starts numbered around seventy-two thousand in 1966 and ninety-one thousand the following year; an annual average of 600,000 subsidized starts would be needed to reach the goal stated in the new legislation.[120] The private sector would build the remaining 20 million units without federal assistance. Two new programs, Section 235 and Section 236, would account for most of the subsidized housing. Section 235 was designed to aid low-income families in purchasing homes by authorizing HUD payments to commercial mortgage lenders that would decrease the borrower's interest payments to as low as 1 percent. Section 236 gave similar breaks on interest rates to cooperative, nonprofit, or limited-profit private developers building multi-unit rental or cooperative dwellings; these developers were then required to pass on these benefits to lower-income tenants through reduced rents.

The two programs increased the market for subsidized housing in the suburbs by targeting families with higher incomes than those in public housing.[121] Because these federally aided developments would be mixed-income and privately owned, the hope among fair-housing sympathizers was that subsidized housing would be a less contentious means of encouraging racial and economic integration than standard public housing was. The law also included Section 223(e), which extended FHA guarantees to "older, declining urban area(s)" that could not meet standard eligibility requirements. While Congress intended this provision to help revive inner-city neighborhoods, in practice many of these loans financed "white flight" from older inner cities.

The Section 235 and 236 programs represented an attempt to bridge the chasm between respected FHA programs and their stigmatized public-housing counterparts. Section 235 attempted to help low- and moderate-income families purchase homes, as their middle-class counterparts did. This program, when combined with efforts to break down suburban housing barriers, could have led to some racial and economic desegregation. Section 236 attempted to enable low- and moderate-income families to pay reduced rents while avoiding the stigma of public housing and the social problems that can result from concentrations of the poor.

PROSPECTS FOR CHANGE

The unlikely passage of a fair housing law, coupled with an ambitious federal commitment to address the housing shortage, set the stage for HUD to act swiftly and boldly in the area of civil rights. Questions remained, however. Would the housing agency be constrained by prior policies encouraging or tolerating segregation, or derailed by continuing its symbiotic relationship with the private sector? Could the HUD leadership create a cohesive agency culture from formerly independent agencies? Of particular concern was FHA, which had new responsibilities related to the massive increases in federal housing production subsidies and the new focus on inner-city mortgage insurance. How would employees carry out this reconstituted mission, and how would they interact with other offices, some of whom were also grappling with newly assigned tasks? Also unclear at this point was the degree of leverage that HUD's equal opportunity staff would have with other parts of the agency, and with HUD's clients. Would increasingly aggressive civil rights policies in education and employment embolden HUD's equal opportunity staff? If HUD did begin to act with force and resolve, how would the incoming presidential administration respond to these actions? The foggy future of integrated housing mirrored a larger uncertainty about civil rights policies generally, as substantial numbers of African Americans felt that the federal government must move more quickly and forcefully in battling black disadvantage, many whites felt that the government should ease its enforcement zeal, and newly vocal groups—among them, Latinos, women, and white ethnics—began to demand government attention to the issues that concerned them.

Chapter Four

Conviction and Controversy

HUD Formulates Its Fair Housing Policies

NOT LONG BEFORE UGLY, violent clashes broke out in New York City between antiwar protestors and construction workers, Mayor John V. Lindsay remarked that the United States "is virtually on the edge of a spiritual—and perhaps physical—breakdown. For the first time, we are not sure there is a future for America."[1] This uncertainty revolved around continued American involvement in Vietnam, signs of economic trouble, and the perpetual dilemma of race. A number of political analysts interpreted the election of Richard Nixon—as well as the respectable showing of George Wallace—as symptomatic of a voter backlash against rioting, militant blacks, and dirty, disruptive, unpatriotic youths (mostly white) protesting the war. A 1969 *Newsweek* report described this backlash in largely sympathetic terms:

> All through the skittish 1960s, America has been almost obsessed with its alienated minorities—the incendiary black militant and the welfare mother, the hedonistic hippie and the campus revolutionary. But now the pendulum of public attention is in the midst of one of those great swings that profoundly change the way the nation thinks about itself. Suddenly, the focus is on the citizen who outnumbers, outvotes and could, if he chose to, outgun the fringe rebel. After years of feeling himself a besieged minority, the man in the middle—representing America's vast white middle-class majority—is giving vent to his frustration, his disillusionment—and his anger.[2]

The *Newsweek* story conflated whites' fears about their own vulnerability with their fears about African Americans. The "Middle American," according to the report, "is in a financial vise, with inflation and rising taxes threatening what precarious security he has—and to make this threat worse, black Americans are demanding an ever-greater economic share." A forty-four-year-old factory worker in Milwaukee, watching picketers lobbying for the hiring of more minorities, grumbled, "Bastards don't want jobs. If you offered them jobs now, 90 per cent of them would run like hell. . . . We're just peons. And if you don't like it, there's always somebody waiting for your job."[3] These vulnerable white workers felt angry that blacks did not want to work and, paradoxically, fearful that blacks were ready to take their jobs.

The standard narrative about black social and political advances is that white backlash had set in by 1968, if not a couple of years prior to that. In this view, the Civil Rights Act of 1968 (when it is even remembered) is the last gasp of the pro–civil rights coalition in Congress, or an anomalous event attributable only to the aftermath of Martin Luther King's assassination. Four consecutive years of multiple riots, coupled with the increasingly harsh rhetoric of black militants, made large numbers of whites want to reverse the gains made by African Americans. This story, while pointing to important drifts in cultural currents, makes white backlash seem more absolute and decisive than it actually was.

George Wallace was, in many respects, the vessel for the discontent of white voters, especially those from the working class. Despite his skill in speaking to the fears of white middle- and working-class voters, Wallace lost substantial support by Election Day in 1968. As Wallace biographer Dan T. Carter observed, "Polls as late as October 3 had showed Wallace winning more than one of every five voters. But in the end, only the Deep South remained steadfast. His support had weakened in the border states and had plummeted from 13 percent to less than 8 percent in the North in the last month of the campaign." On Election Day, Wallace received 13.5 percent of the popular vote and 46 electoral votes, carrying Alabama, Georgia, Mississippi, Arkansas, and Louisiana. Outside of the southern and border states, Wallace made his most notable showings in Ohio, with 11.8 percent of the vote, and in Michigan, with 10 percent. The 1970 midterm results also suggest that voters were not moving to the GOP in droves because of the party's more conservative policies on race. The Republicans picked up two Senate seats, leaving the Democrats in control; Democrats picked up nine seats in the House, and 11 governorships.[4]

The well-respected journalist Samuel Lubell conducted extensive interviews of voters during the 1968 presidential campaign. Among whites, he found that the "desire to halt racial violence was the strongest single sentiment voiced by the voters throughout the whole campaign. But most of those advocating stiffer law enforcement did not want to stop Negro advances." One interview subject, a sixty-year-old textile mill supervisor in Greensboro, North Carolina, told Lubell, "Wallace says he would shoot the looters but I'd go further. If anyone tried to put fire to my house, why—I'd tie them up in the street and burn them!" Given a list of current civil rights programs, and asked which ones he would keep and which ones he would abandon, the supervisor responded, "I'd keep them all. I ain't for holding the colored down." Lubell observed that "the strength of this desire for a middle-ground racial policy has never been generally appreciated, even though it has been the majority feeling in the nation."[5] Of course, one person's middle-ground policy is another's extremist governmental intrusion.

Wallace tapped into the fears and resentments of those who felt that their economic situation and, indeed, their way of life were imperiled by uncontrollable social change. The economic fears of workers were well founded. The sharpest economic downturn occurred in 1973 and 1974; however, inflation was proving worrisome prior to this time, leading President Nixon, quite uncharacteristically, to impose a ninety-day freeze on wages and prices in 1971. The freeze continued in various forms for almost three years, until April 1974. Between 1968 and 1970, the unemployment rate increased by more than one-third, from 3.6 to 4.9 percent. Employment prospects for blue-collar workers dimmed as the 1960s ended and the 1970s began. By the late 1960s, white, male baby boomers were competing for jobs with increasing numbers of women, racial minorities, and immigrants (as a result of 1965 legislation liberalizing immigration policies).[6]

In the North particularly, Wallace supporters were concentrated heavily in white neighborhoods that abutted predominantly black districts. These were the whites who felt the impact of housing and school desegregation, and probably employment desegregation, most directly. Politicians from the national to the local level feared the intensity of white backlash, but also the continued frustrations of black Americans, and the potential for further violence that these frustrations signified. The politics of race during this period defy easy explanation. For the most part, employees of civil rights agencies were more concerned with black gains than with white anger. The fact that these agency employees did not face election and thus were well insulated from public pressures emboldened them to push forcefully for desegregation, which they believed was a moral and legal obligation, even in the face of white resistance.

Fair housing advocates were unsure what 1969 would bring. Civil rights agencies in education and employment were discovering ways of using governmental powers to chip away at the racial caste system. Courts were largely enthusiastic in backing these agency efforts. Two new laws—the Civil Rights Act of 1968 and the Housing and Urban Development Act of 1968—charged HUD with policing housing discrimination and overseeing major increases in housing production. It was unclear exactly how the Nixon Administration would handle civil rights enforcement. As a presidential candidate, Richard Nixon published a collection of positions he had staked out on 167 issues; not included in this group were positions on civil rights, the cities, and Vietnam. At the 1968 Republican Convention in Miami, Nixon secured the backing of influential Southern conservatives, who expected a relaxation in school desegregation requirements as payback once he assumed the presidency. Nixon had told Southern delegates at a private meeting, secretly tape-recorded by the *Miami Herald*, that he had supported passage of fair housing legislation earlier that year "to get the civil rights and open housing issues out of our sight so we didn't have a split party over the platform when we came down here."[7] He shared his feeling that open housing was best handled at the state rather than the federal level.

But Nixon had other debts within the Republican party. Seeking to avoid the intraparty factionalism that helped bring about the 1964 Democratic landslide, Nixon repeatedly stressed the need for party unity as the 1968 election neared. Nixon's courting of Southern conservatives angered progressives within the GOP, and the nomination of Maryland Governor Spiro Agnew as vice presidential candidate sparked a mini-revolt on the floor of the 1968 Republican convention. Liberals drafted Michigan Governor George Romney—the future head of the Department of Housing and Urban Development—as their vice presidential nominee. Agnew won a floor vote for the vice presidential nomination over-whelmingly. Romney subsequently released a statement claiming that "the poison [of intra-party division] that was spreading was lanced and the party leaves Miami united."[8] When party progressives campaigned for Nixon in the fall, the future president said he would give them im-portant roles in his administration. Nixon made good on his promise, mainly tapping progressives and moderates to head domestic service de-partments and his foreign policy team; his economic policy team was largely moderate.[9]

The confusion about how to read Nixon also swirled because he was a known micro-manager, yet one with very little interest in domestic pol-icy. Nixon later reflected, "I've always thought this country could run it-self, without a president. All you need is a competent Cabinet to run the country at home."[10] As fate would have it, Nixon assumed the presi-dency at a time when knotty domestic policy issues competed insistently for his attention with foreign policy issues, most prominently the ongo-ing war in Vietnam. With respect to civil rights, Nixon would discover that getting activist bureaucracies to perform in accordance with his wishes was not easy. With courts increasingly deferring to the expertise of civil rights agencies, and civil rights bureaucrats opposing dismantle-ment of their efforts, the Nixon White House would encounter deter-mined resistance each time it attempted to dilute federal antidiscrimina-tion initiatives. The ways that the Nixon White House guided and responded to civil rights enforcement activities have been a focus of in-creasing scholarly attention. This topic has drawn interest because the idiosyncratic zigs and zags of Nixon-era civil rights policies are a rich, complex story to unravel, and because much of the "action" occurred at this time. While most prominent civil rights laws were passed during the Johnson Administration (in the Civil Rights Acts of 1964 and 1968 and the Voting Rights Act of 1965), the specific policies that would carry out the aims of these laws took form under Nixon. During his presidency, unrivaled levels of southern school desegregation took place, and affirmative action in employment became entrenched.

Scholars have accorded considerably less attention to civil rights efforts in housing, largely because these initiatives brought about few changes in segregated residential patterns. To be sure, HUD faced formidable hurdles in its attempts to move the nation toward economically and racially desegregated residential patterns, due to such factors as the lagging momentum of the civil rights movement, public antipathy toward residential integration efforts, and the fact that such changes would leave virtually no area of the country untouched, rather than targeting the South. These factors alone were not sufficient to prevent implementation of forceful desegregation policies: civil rights bureaucracies in employment and education overcame similar obstacles, and HUD came close to doing the same.

Nevertheless, housing did present difficulties that did not exist or were not as severe in other areas. First was deciding precisely what "fair housing" would entail. Did it mean merely the elimination of blatantly discriminatory practices, or some level of actual desegregation? The education and employment bureaucracies had concluded that schools and businesses should be required to show not just the elimination of discriminatory intent but also actual statistical progress in desegregation. If HUD were to define a similar "effects" standard for housing, what parts of the industry would the agency monitor? In education, one could examine changes at the level of school districts, and in employment, the racial makeup of a company's work force.

The numerous moving parts in the housing industry made it less clear what policy approaches would be wisest to follow. Should HUD focus on real-estate brokers or developers, savings and loan institutions or builders, localities or metropolitan areas? While taking some stabs in all of these areas, HUD chose to focus primarily on localities receiving federal funds, with an eye toward a more encompassing regional approach. In retrospect, despite HUD's ultimate failure, this appears to have been a sensible decision, since it offered the best hope for a comprehensive attack on segregation.

HUD staffers did not throw up their hands in futility at the prospect of attempting to decrease racial isolation in housing; they believed they could provoke considerable desegregation, and tried to do so, though at times in ham-handed ways. The fact that fair-housing responsibilities were placed within HUD—a weak institutional home for civil rights—made a difficult task a Herculean one. Designing and administering civil rights policies is never simple. Doing so in a department with intimate historical ties to the housing industry, no cohesive culture, no shared sense of mission, and multiple points of potential political vulnerability due to this bureaucratic setup is bound to be a baffling, frustrating endeavor. It does not appear, however, that this endeavor was impossible. Aided by favorable federal court rulings, HUD came surprisingly close to establishing a workable policy that probably would have led to measurable decreases in residential segregation.

HUD's civil rights prospects were bright in the early days of the Nixon Administration, though political fallout from its Open Communities program, and the White House's growing involvement in the agency's fair housing activities, later shrunk these possibilities for change. HUD faced a complex tapestry of opportunities and constraints that were influenced by external political forces such as business elites, advocacy groups, and the public at large. Without question, public resistance to housing desegregation presented problems for HUD. Yet the trajectory of school desegregation policies—in which HEW continued to act aggressively despite White House resistance and widespread public opposition—suggests that this explanation by itself fails to account for what happened at HUD, whose desegregation attempts were much less prominent than those in education. HUD felt pressure in the opposite direction from advocacy groups, which were exerting constant pressure on the agency to step up its activities.

Within the agency, tensions and vulnerabilities grew, as equal opportunity and housing production staffers butted heads, and scandals at FHA destroyed the agency's legitimacy. The weak institutional home for civil rights in housing made HUD a more inviting target for the White House to decimate than civil rights agencies in employment and education. Because the Administration could dismantle its civil rights efforts indirectly, and the agency had few weapons with which to defend itself, HUD presented few of the political risks that attacks on other civil rights bureaucracies would have entailed.

An Ambitious HUD Gets to Work

Despite the obstacles that HUD faced, there was ample reason for optimism early in the Nixon Administration. At several junctures between 1969 and 1972, HUD appeared to be building the momentum to help forge elementary changes in segregated residential patterns. In fact, it was not until Nixon took the drastic step of freezing all federal housing funds that the door shut completely. In addition to the newly passed fair housing law, prospects for advances in residential desegregation were buoyed by huge increases in federally subsidized housing, which gave HUD leverage in its fair-housing efforts (though the two goals could come into conflict as well); by judicial support for forceful race-conscious actions by government; by a HUD secretary who was a strong integration advocate and a top-notch salesman; and by early support for residential desegregation efforts by several key White House aides, most prominently domestic policy advisor Daniel Patrick Moynihan.

To direct HUD's efforts, Nixon tapped liberal Republican George Romney, a three-time governor of Michigan (elected in 1962, 1964, and 1966) who briefly sought the GOP presidential nomination in 1968.[11] The vibrant, sixty-one-year old Romney had been considered an early front-runner, but suffered irrevocable political damage after claiming in August 1967 that U.S. government officials in Vietnam had "brainwashed" him into supporting American involvement in the conflict.[12] Romney first ran for governor as an independent Republican, barely mentioning the party by name and declining a chance to have former President Dwight Eisenhower campaign for him. Romney was governor when riots rocked Detroit in the summer of 1967. Always looking for innovative solutions, Governor Romney proposed that clouds over the ghetto be seeded to bring forth rain; his suggestion was not executed.

After failing to earn his bachelor's degree at three different colleges, Romney moved to Washington to work as a lobbyist, first for Alcoa and later for the automobile industry. Later on, Romney became president of American Motors Corporation, where he led the development and mass production of the first American compact car, "The Rambler." This experience in mass production was probably a major factor in Nixon's selection of the former auto executive.[13]

Romney had very little background in housing, especially compared to his predecessor, Robert Weaver. Agency wide, HUD faced the problem of housing desegregation with very little accumulated expertise. In employment, the EEOC clearly reached beyond congressional intent by instituting affirmative action procedures, rather than only investigating individual complaints of discrimination. The agency, however, drew from the legacy of the federal government collecting racial data from employers, though on a voluntary basis. Federal bureaucrats had no such experience in school desegregation, but their task—at least when their efforts were confined to the South—was relatively straightforward: ensure that school districts moved to a unitary system, rather than having two racially separate ones. Civil rights staffers within HUD did not have the relatively strong institutional legacy to draw upon that the employment bureaucracies did, nor the relatively clear path of action that HEW's Office for Civil Rights did.

Federal housing agencies never did much to address segregation in public housing, and FHA historically looked to aid the housing industry, not make demands of it. Agency staffers viewed subsidized housing—

government aid to private developers building mixed-income developments—as a less contentious vehicle than bricks-and-mortar public housing for promoting racial and socioeconomic integration. Yet many families faced with the prospect of nearby subsidized housing either did not consider the distinction between mixed-income, privately owned subsidized housing and government-owned public housing to be meaningful, or they were unaware that such a difference existed.

Before HUD could tease out the best way to tackle desegregation, scandals in FHA's inner-city programs destroyed HUD's legitimacy, and the subsequent freeze on federal housing funds destroyed its capability to effect change. In this sense, then, the late adoption of fair-housing legislation put HUD at a disadvantage compared to other civil rights bureaucracies. In employment and education, the most far-reaching action did not take place until the Nixon Administration. School desegregation, however, became a plausible scenario in 1954, and desegregation in both employment and education a genuine possibility beginning in 1964; though the actual gains were relatively modest during the Johnson Administration, it is probably the case that the employment and education bureaucracies were more ready to act confidently at the dawn of the Nixon Administration than was HUD, a recently created agency lacking a civil rights legacy and a sense of shared mission. By the time HUD began devising desegregation plans, Congress and the White House had become more wary of agency activism in civil rights, having witnessed such activism as it began to take root in employment and education.

While Romney lacked knowledge of housing, he was quite proud of his civil rights credentials, noting in congressional testimony that he had publicly opposed segregated war housing and public housing in the 1940s and had urged delegates at the 1964 Republican National Convention to strengthen the party's civil rights platform. In February 1968, he sent telegrams to Republican senators urging them to support cloture on the fair housing bill.[14] The newly elected Nixon stressed that each of his appointees was "an independent thinker," telling the public that "I don't want a Cabinet of 'Yes' men and I don't think you want a Cabinet of 'Yes' men."[15] By the end of his first term, Nixon would clearly see the benefits of having "Yes" men—rather than independent men such as Romney—in his corner.

Romney was a man of complex and sometimes conflicting convictions. For example, he was a long-time supporter of civil rights and a devout member of the Mormon Church, which until the 1970s did not permit blacks to become members of the priesthood, as they were believed to be members of a cursed race. As HUD Secretary, convinced that the Nixon Administration's fiscal 1971 budget was several billion dollars too high, he offered in a cabinet meeting to take 5 percent fewer funds for his department, a move that other agency heads followed, resulting in the total budget being cut by $3 billion. At a congressional hearing in December 1971, the HUD chief partially blamed inadequate congressional funding in defending the limited scope of HUD's fair housing activities. Romney was also torn between his conviction about the urgent need to address residential segregation and his long-held belief that local officials were best suited to solve local problems.[16]

The former Michigan governor never lacked enthusiasm. When Nixon introduced his cabinet, he applauded Romney for his "tremendous missionary zeal about the need to do something about the problems of cities."[17] One congressional staffer later commented that "when it comes to proselytizing, no one is better at it than George Romney. He's a super-salesman and he's the perfect kind of guy to be selling something as controversial as [suburban integration]—even if you disagree with what George Romney might be telling you, you would never think that he was anything other than a solid all-America type. The message might strike some listener as radical but Romney himself never comes over as a radical."[18]

Given the momentous tasks that he faced in his new position, Romney would need all of the verve and salesmanship he could muster. Congress had coupled HUD's new fair housing responsibilities with an unprecedented commitment to federally subsidized housing construction. As spelled out in the 1968 Housing and Urban Development Act, the federal government set a ten-year goal of six million subsidized housing units, in addition to encouraging the private construction of an additional twenty million units over the same period. This was a wildly optimistic goal, as the industry had never built as many as two million units in a single year, and had averaged less than 1.5 million new units in the prior decade. The housing industry had produced only 634,000 federally subsidized units in the previous ten years, and only 938,000 assisted housing units since passage of the Housing Act of 1949.[19]

The 1968 housing legislation created several housing programs with the potential to aid economic and racial desegregation efforts. The Section 235 program subsidized interest payments for home buyers by paying all mortgage interest above 1 percent. The Section 236 program gave similar breaks on interest rates to cooperative, nonprofit, or limited-profit private developers building multi-unit rental or cooperative dwellings; these developers were then required to offer a specified number of apartments to lower-income tenants, who would pay no more than 25 percent of their income toward rent. Section 235 subsidies were available for new, rehabilitated, or existing single-family units, while 236 subsidies were available only for new or rehabilitated multi-family units. The two programs quickly became the most widely used subsidized housing programs in the United States. By 1970, subsidized housing accounted for 29.3 percent (429,800) of total housing starts (1.47 million), up from 6.9 percent (91,400 of 1.32 million) in 1967. This increased federal involvement was especially dramatic in light of the fact that traditional public housing units constituted a mere 1.5 percent of the nation's housing stock at the end of 1972.[20]

To complicate Romney's endeavor, he inherited an agency known as one of the most lethargic in Washington, and rife with structural flaws. The secretary's initial evaluation of the agency, prepared for President Nixon, stresses that the department's creation from formerly independent agencies had resulted in "a marked tendency to organize along lines relating more to historical status and/or the administration of particular statutory programs (such as public housing, urban renewal, FHA, etc.) than to a realistic appraisal of Departmental functions and objectives."[21] By HUD's count, the federal government administered 20 subsidized and 46 unsubsidized housing programs.

Early on, Romney set about trying to improve HUD's complex organizational structure by redefining the job responsibilities of four assistant secretaries and decentralizing the agency's operations "to the lowest administrative level practicable."[22] (HUD would continue its attempts to make its operations more efficient, with little success, throughout Romney's tenure.) In Washington, program managers were left with few resources and little authority to carry out their responsibilities. Under the reshuffling, final decision-making responsibility for approving project applications was vested primarily in field and area offices, with substantially reduced supervision by higher-level regional offices or HUD headquarters in Washington. One of the main motivations for this change was to increase the speed with which proposed projects were approved. The trade-off was less oversight with regard to proper program functioning and other agency objectives, such as equal opportunity in housing.[23] Down the road, this drive for production above all else would lead to crippling effects on HUD's legitimacy and viability.[24]

Romney initially saw potential in the convergence between the equal opportunity and production objectives, commenting that "this housing shortage provides an opportunity to begin to penetrate these barriers and open up these metropolitan districts."[25] Because of the shrinking availability of land in inner cities for housing, Romney pressed suburban localities to accept subsidized housing or risk loss of federal aid in other areas. As neither the term "fair housing" nor the requirement that agencies act "affirmatively" is clarified in the Civil Rights Act of 1968, opinions ranged broadly about HUD's responsibilities under the law, and the tools it could use to carry them out.

In contrast to the backtracking that would ensue midway through

Nixon's first term, members of the administration widely shared the goal of residential desegregation early on. Indeed, this belief in the need for residential desegregation had entered into the mainstream of political thought. The Kerner Commission, a panel filled by President Johnson with political moderates, opined in its 1968 report that "federal housing programs must be given a new thrust aimed at overcoming the prevailing patterns of racial segregation. . . . Residential segregation prevents equal access to employment opportunities and obstructs efforts to achieve integrated education. A single society cannot be achieved as long as this cornerstone of segregation stands."[26] Proponents of the fair housing bill, including many congressional supporters and advocacy groups such as the NAACP, had warned that failure to pass the legislation might result in more riots. Private-sector experts such as Anthony Downs testified on Capitol Hill that suburban integration efforts could take place in a measured fashion that respected the views and desires of both whites in the suburbs and less affluent blacks who wished to escape harsh inner-city living conditions. One important tactic, Downs argued, was to locate "many new low-and-moderate income housing units in suburban areas both in relatively small clusters and in individual scatteration in middle-income neighborhoods through rent subsidies and public housing rent allowances extended to individual households."[27]

In the White House, residential desegregation had a particularly strong backer in Presidential Counselor Daniel Patrick Moynihan, who told an interviewer, "I'm a dispersal man. To the extent that a society has problems due to concentrations of race, that society would minimize those problems by spreading them out."[28] In July 1970, the White House let Romney use the Camp David presidential retreat to convene a two-day planning session on suburban integration, and acceded to Romney's wishes by successfully demanding the resignation of HUD General Counsel Sherman Unger, who had clashed with HUD civil rights chief Samuel Simmons over suburban integration efforts.[29]

Implementation, however, presented some political problems for Richard Nixon, who risked alienating white suburban supporters already angry about school busing initiatives. In broad terms, HUD had three primary options to carry out its fair housing mandate.[30] The first—probably the minimum effort required by the law—would have involved federal intervention only in cases of individual discrimination. In awarding federal monies, HUD would not consider the racial and economic impacts of a proposed project seeking agency assistance. Like its counterparts at the EEOC, HUD quickly discovered that pursuing individual complaints of discrimination consumed considerable resources, resulted in ever-growing backlogs, and produced few measurable results. A middle road, which is what HUD largely stuck to, entailed Justice Department intervention in clear cases of official, as well as individual, discrimination and gave some weight to anticipated racial and economic impact in approving sites for subsidized housing and grant awards. Justice secured court orders against several large housing developers, which were required to take steps such as giving preferential notification of vacancies to African Americans (or members of other victimized groups), encouraging blacks to fill openings in white buildings from which they had been turned away, and targeting marketing and advertising efforts to non-whites.[31] The third option—the one urged by fair housing and civil rights groups—would have followed the employment bureaucracies and initiated government action in cases where zoning or other provisions had the *effect* (even in the absence of intent) of limiting housing opportunities for minorities. Staffers in HUD's Office of Equal Opportunity clearly wanted the agency to pursue this third option. The Supreme Court has never ruled on whether fair housing cases could rely exclusively on disparate impact theory, and appeals courts have been divided on this issue.[32]

HUD carried out its desegregation efforts through five primary programs: (1) urban renewal, used mainly by cities and older suburbs, running at $1.4 billion annually in 1971; (2) Model Cities, a $725 million per year program operating in all major cities but Houston; (3) a range of housing subsidy programs (including Section 235 and 236), with federal spending around $2 billion; (4) water and sewer grants (for expansion or improvement of such facilities), a $700 million program that was becoming quite popular among suburban communities; and (5) the open space program, running at around $100 million and also appealing to many suburbs. Applications for water and sewer grants exceeded appropriations by over 4-1; urban renewal grants, roughly 3-1.[33] As a result, HUD could give preference to applications from localities or developers that would fulfill other agency objectives, such as providing low- and moderate-income housing, or promoting fair housing. HUD was obligated to ensure that recipients of grants related to the construction of housing did not use these funds in ways that perpetuated residential segregation. With grants not directly related to housing production—such as water and sewer grants, Model Cities funding, and planning grants—HUD had the authority to require adequate provision of low- and moderate-income housing. In certain non-housing programs, such as urban renewal and open space grants, HUD had been directed by Congress to condition grants on local willingness to provide low- and moderate-income housing.[34]

The workable program requirement mandated that cities and suburbs receiving urban renewal funds acquire HUD approval for community improvement plans ensuring that reasonable provision of low- and moderate-income housing was available. Grants for comprehensive planning were required to have a housing element to insure that "the housing needs of both the region and the local communities studied in the planning will be adequately covered in terms of existing and prospective inmigrant population growth."[35] Communities often used these grants to formulate area-wide plans, which were a prerequisite for HUD funding under the water and sewer, open space, and new community programs. More often than not, the metropolitan agencies created by state legislatures to devise these plans were vested with little authority to ensure that the stated objectives were carried out.[36]

CREATING OPEN COMMUNITIES

Almost immediately after Romney took office, the agency began formulating its strategies for increasing racial and economic integration. Romney's first focus of attention as HUD chief was Operation Breakthrough, which was intended to spur volume production of factory-built housing by large corporations. As part of this effort, the program sought ways around local zoning and building codes. While HUD required Breakthrough developers to use affirmative fair-marketing practices to assure maximum housing opportunities for minorities, the agency consciously downplayed the potential for the program to foster racial integration. When local residents discovered that Breakthrough would involve subsidized housing, sometimes occupied by blacks, initial enthusiasm to participate in the program dampened quickly. Ultimately, only one suburban site was developed through Operation Breakthrough. The struggle to gain local acceptance of Breakthrough projects foreshadowed the difficulties the agency would confront in trying to move toward racial and economic integration in suburbia.[37] HUD's more direct effort at attacking residential segregation was its Open Communities program. When it began in 1969, the media paid little attention, despite some vivid public pronouncements from Romney. The HUD secretary insisted that the nation could not survive the persistence of "a run-down, festering black core, surrounded by a well-to-do, indifferent white ring."[38] HUD's stated policy aim was the creation of "open communities which will provide an opportunity for individuals to live within a reasonable distance of their job and daily activities by increasing housing options for low-income and minority families."[39]

One of HUD's biggest hurdles, which it never really cleared, was communicating the depth and scope of the problem of residential segregation. "This problem is as complex and sensitive domestically as Vietnam is internationally," Romney remarked, "and I might add that it has been burdened by the same lack of accurate reporting."[40] The fact that HUD had a number of other messages to convey to the public—for example, about its efforts to increase housing production and revitalize inner cities—was a hindrance to the agency articulating a clear message about segregation.

Moreover, HUD seemed unsure about what specific message it should convey. In employment, reduction in black unemployment rates was the relatively uncontroversial goal that helped to justify the contested strategy of affirmative action.[41] It is easy to measure and understand unemployment rates. The same is true of statistics reporting, for example, the percentage of black students in segregated schools, or the percentage of schools that are racially segregated. With residential desegregation, the ultimate goals may take a longer time to realize (e.g., better life outcomes for children, greater appreciation in home value), and short-term progress (decreases in segregation) may seem less urgent and more difficult to convey to a larger audience. Quite simply, the index of dissimilarity and other measures of segregation do not convey the same rhetorical weight as do unemployment rates. Moreover, whereas a steep decline in unemployment rates or segregated schools would be greeted mostly with enthusiasm, rapid changes in the racial composition of neighborhoods are less likely to signify laudable progress than "white flight" and neighborhood decline.[42] The most sensible way of communicating progress in housing desegregation would be to note changes in the number of localities that are considered integrated by some standard (i.e., white population between 30 and 90 percent); this is similar to the way changes in school and public housing desegregation are reported.

Another issue in housing is that the trade-offs necessitated by a push for desegregation may be more severe and more complex than those in other policy areas. To use Wilson's terms, welfare and status ends clash most forcefully in housing when civil rights groups face the choice of supporting the construction of low- and moderate-income housing in locations that would increase segregation, or only supporting construction in locations that would increase integration, which in many cases reduces the number of units that are built.[43]

All of these considerations notwithstanding, HUD believed it could develop policies that would increase residential integration. Notably, a 1969 Gallup/*Newsweek* poll found that 70 percent of white Americans believed that they would be living in integrated housing within five years. These findings do not indicate that most whites would have welcomed this change. Nonetheless, the fact that nearly three of four whites were willing to accept such a reality, even if grudgingly, suggests that some level of housing desegregation was not unrealistic.[44]

HUD staffers needed to convey the urgency of desegregation to the public, while paradoxically assuring nervous whites that the change would be peaceful and deliberately paced. Unsurprisingly, they were unable to do so. Within the agency, Romney clearly conveyed the centrality of equal opportunity to HUD's mission in a proposed departmental circular: "In the administration of all of the programs in our Department, we should take affirmative steps to counteract discrimination against and the social isolation of low income families and minority groups."[45] HUD's Open Communities task force was aware that this area of policy was littered with political minefields. The staff deliberated over how explicit it should be in announcing the goals of the program, reasoning that a subtle, relatively nonconfrontational approach might be the best strategy.[46] In trying to pinpoint suburbs that would make good candidates for subsidized housing, the task force considered criteria such as a sufficient tax base, adequate transportation, the volume of HUD grants, the availability and price of vacant land, and job opportunities (especially in areas where a labor deficit existed). Particularly appealing were communities that had a sizable need for low- and moderate-income housing, especially for individuals who worked in that locality.[47] HUD data about Detroit and its surrounding suburbs, presumably used to select Open Communities targets, examined factors such as total population, the density and increase/decrease of the population, percentage nonwhite, and income distribution.

Early on, the agency cut off the funding of several jurisdictions that refused to accept subsidized housing. Stoughton, Massachusetts, a Boston suburb, approved a housing project despite local objections after HUD held up the town's water and sewer grant application. The agency also withheld a $1.4 million sewer grant from Baltimore County when it refused to accept subsidized housing. After the Toledo, Ohio, city council canceled three public housing sites located outside of the ghetto, HUD cut off $15 million of the city's urban renewal, open space, and water and sewer funds.[48]

Having gained some confidence from its initial efforts, HUD was unprepared for its confrontation with Warren, Michigan, which had received agency funds since 1967. A working-class suburb of 180,000 residents, Warren was home to only twenty-eight minority families (twenty-two of whom lived on a military reservation), despite a labor force that was nearly one-third black. Internal agency deliberations reveal tension over whether to focus on blatant offenders, which risked causing an uproar from town residents, or on towns less likely to object strongly to prointegrative efforts. Warren was clearly in the former category. When a black man moved in with his white wife and their young daughter in 1967, agitated residents burned crosses on their lawn, threw rocks through their windows, and shouted obscenities as they passed the family's home.

HUD cut off Warren's urban renewal funds in May 1970, citing a policy of racial discrimination in housing. The town had received an initial
federal grant of $1.3 million to rehabilitate aging sections of the commu-
nity; in exchange, it agreed to accept 100 units of low-income housing.
When town officials went to collect their second installment of $2.8 mil-
lion in 1970, HUD informed the town that it must first alter housing
policies that discriminated against blacks. After the two sides failed to
agree on the steps that would satisfy this requirement, Warren officials
traveled to Washington to meet with Romney and Undersecretary
Richard Van Dusen. Romney tried to be conciliatory, but he turned com-
bative when Warren Mayor Ted Bates insisted that Warren was "an
open city" free of racial problems. "Mr. Mayor, you do have a problem
or you would not be here," Romney insisted, banging his hand on the
conference table. Bates told Romney that the town had spent $75,000 to
protect the racially mixed couple's right to live in Warren peacefully. "I
was Governor of Michigan when the Bailey family moved in," Romney
reminded him, "and I had to send the state police in there to protect
them because the local officials would not fulfill their responsibilities."[49]

Following the meeting, the Warren city council agreed with HUD's
Chicago office to take several, largely innocuous integration measures.
This may have been the end of the story, had it not been for a week-long
series in the *Detroit News* that began with the front-page banner head-
line: "U.S. Picks Warren as Prime Target in Move to Integrate All Suburbs." The story was based on an internal memo from a staffer in
HUD's Chicago office that read, in part, "Detroit suburbs represent an
unparalleled opportunity to the application of fair housing strategy.
Nowhere else in the Midwest, perhaps nowhere else in the country, is
there a combination of a large central city with a substantial black population, more than forty percent, surrounded by large white suburbs
which may use HUD programs and in which suburbs there is extensive
black employment and a great deal of middle income housing."[50]

Mayor Bates, who later recalled that town residents "were about to
secede from the Union," threatened to renege on the city's agreement
with HUD, saying he would not "tolerate Warren being used as a guinea
pig for integration experiments."[51] (Also on the purported list of targets
were South St. Paul, Minn.; Fairborne, Ohio; and Waterloo, Iowa.) Attempting to quell the uproar caused by the stories, Romney traveled to
Warren in late July to meet with representatives of that town and thirty-
nine other suburbs. In front of a testy crowd, Romney expressed outrage
at the *Detroit News* story, contending that "it is completely misleading
to indicate that a memorandum written by a subordinate in the Chicago
regional office is establishing policy for the whole Department." Romney
explained that he opposed "forced integration," but favored "affirmative

action" by the community as a condition of receiving federal urban renewal grants.[52] Asked if Warren would have to show that increasing numbers of blacks were moving to the town, Romney explained, "Look, we're not going to bring any people here. . . . We're not going to ask you to provide housing for anyone other than those who want to live in Warren."[53] By saying "for those who want to live in Warren," rather than "for those who live in Warren," the scope of the change Romney was demanding was unclear, perhaps intentionally so.

At one point, city council members complained that seeking their support for integration was asking them to give up their jobs. If tensions ran high inside the meeting, they were worse outside, where three to four hundred angry demonstrators jeered and pounded the car of their former governor as he left. Some carried signs with messages such as "Get rid of the dud at HUD" and "Romney is a HUDache." The crowd cheered Dearborn Mayor Orville Hubbard, a vocal segregationist, as he departed.[54]

HUD was clearly anxious to salvage something positive from the meeting. At first, it proposed a dozen steps that Warren could take to show a good-faith effort in open housing. This was cut to five steps, and later to two: passage of an open housing ordinance and appointment of a human relations commission. Warren voters eventually decided to forgo the $10 million in proposed renewal funds rather than making such an effort.[55]

In the wake of Warren, the White House instructed all federal agencies to hold off on pro-residential integration policies until the administration had settled on a uniform policy.[56] Even prior to the Warren incident, the White House was beginning to feel discomfort with Romney's aggressive statements in favor of integrated housing. As early as March 1970, Nixon Chief of Staff H. R. Haldeman recorded the desire of the White House to get rid of Romney. By November 1970, Haldeman concluded in his diary that "George won't leave quickly, will have to be fired. So we have to set him up on the integrated housing issue and fire him on that basis to be sure we get the credit." Top Nixon domestic policy aide John Ehrlichman warned the president in October 1970 of "a serious Romney problem." Ehrlichman noted that "there is no approved *program* [on suburban integration] as such, nor has the White House approved such a *policy*. But [Romney] keeps loudly talking about it in spite of our efforts to shut him up. And he is beginning some administrative maneuvers in that direction." "Stop this one," Nixon scribbled in response. The president predicted that same month that "Romney will go . . . *if* we can find a good black to replace him." Romney did not help his standing in the White House when he criticized its 1970 midterm campaign for being too negative, suggesting instead that the administration might have placed greater emphasis on its successes in housing and school desegregation.[57]

After the blow-up in Michigan, HUD began to pursue fair housing aims in quieter fashion by denying applications for agency funding rather than withholding monies already granted. Nevertheless, HUD aides continued to talk confidently of a full-scale assault on suburban segregation that would kick into high gear after the November 1970 midterm elections. HUD staffers informed Romney that their developing policy on tenant assignment in federally funded housing "does contain the proposal that good faith efforts be exercised to achieve predetermined quotas" according to race. Romney responded, "OK—I do not consider possible goals as quotas."[58] HUD Assistant Secretary for Equal Opportunity Samuel J. Simmons argued persistently for the collection of racial data and the creation of goals and timetables to foster integration.

Tensions escalated between the White House and HUD. Assistant Secretary Eugene A. Gulledge told a reporter that agency staffers could not tolerate constant litmus tests, in which the White House tells the agency, "Now if there's too much flack out there, don't do it." Gulledge wondered, "How much flack is too much?"[59] Romney declined Nixon's suggestion (via Attorney General John Mitchell) that the HUD Secretary accept an appointment as ambassador to Mexico (Romney's birthplace), professing puzzlement at the president's feeling that the two were on a "collision course." "How is it possible," Romney asked in a letter to Nixon, "to know with certainty that we are on a collision course when the Department's policies have not yet been determined?"[60] According to media reports, Romney was less deferential at his meeting with Mitchell, who told the secretary that he should resign if he was unwilling to follow administration policies. "What the hell is Administration policy?" Romney reportedly shot back. "It changes from day to day and hour to hour."[61] As an experienced politician with well-honed survival instincts, Romney did begin to temper his remarks and directives on suburban integration.

Nixon Restrains HUD

In November 1970, Nixon began to hint at the direction administration policy would take. Asked at a press conference about the extent to which the federal government should use its leverage to promote racial integration in suburban housing, the president replied, "Only to the extent that the law requires—in two cases, as a result of acts passed by the Congress that the Federal Government not provide aid to housing, or to urban renewal where a community has a policy of discrimination and has taken no steps to remove it." He added that "it is not the policy of this Government to use the power of the Federal Government or Federal funds in any other way, in ways not required by the law for forced integration of the suburbs. I believe that forced integration of the suburbs is not in the national interest." The use of the term "forced integration" struck many observers, including Romney, as an inflammatory appeal to suburban whites.[62] Nixon later amended his statement to say that he opposed forced integration on economic rather than racial grounds, presumably meaning that localities should not be compelled to change zoning laws or accept subsidized housing if they did not wish to do so. This was misleading: he clearly opposed "forced integration" on racial grounds as well.

Finally, in June 1971, the White House released Nixon's tepid and ambiguous, eight-thousand-word Statement of Equal Housing Opportunity.[63] "By 'equal housing opportunity,'" Nixon said, "I mean the achievement of a condition in which individuals of similar income levels in the same housing market area have a like range of housing choices available to them regardless of their race, color, religion or national origin." The president stated that housing officials should, in their evaluation of applications for aid, consider the extent to which the proposed project would open up new, nonsegregated housing opportunities. Housing officials would also consider a number of other factors and would not necessarily deny aid to a project that would increase or maintain segregation. Romney publicly supported this relatively narrow reading of HUD's affirmative action mandate, which Nixon insisted applied only to the specific housing program in question and could not be used to justify withholding other kinds of aid; others within HUD and the White House, along with fair-housing groups, had interpreted the mandate to permit broad authority to withhold federal funds.[64]

In characteristic fashion, the Nixon statement eluded easy interpretation, which allowed him to avoid some potential blame from conservatives who felt he was caving into civil rights supporters, and vice versa.[65] The president pounded home his assertion that federal authority was limited in the area of economic and racial integration of housing, and expressed sympathy for those communities fearing that subsidized housing would bring with it lowered property values and "a contagion of crime, violence [and] drugs." Nixon asserted, "We will not seek to impose economic integration upon an existing local jurisdiction: at the same time, we will not countenance any use of economic measures as a subterfuge for racial discrimination."

The statement also suggested the use of a broader "effects" standard (as opposed to a "treatment" standard): "If the effect of the action is to exclude Americans from equal housing opportunity on the basis of their race, religion, or ethnic background, we will vigorously oppose it by whatever means are most appropriate—regardless of the rationale which may have cloaked the discriminatory act." The president indicated that the federal government was prepared to sue suburbs in which racial considerations led to rezoning designed to block subsidized housing.[66] At a follow-up press conference, Attorney General John Mitchell suggested that the federal government would act only in cases where it could show not just a racially discriminatory effect, but discriminatory intent as well—a much higher threshold of proof. Romney stated that the government would not "assume the role of omnipotent hero righting all wrongs, knocking down all barriers with a flourish and redrawing the crazy-quilt map of our metropolitan areas." The *Milwaukee Journal* judged Nixon's conception of fair housing to be "a narrow, cautious and profoundly disappointing view, plump with legalistic phrases and thin on moral leadership." Reflecting much of the media reaction, the *Detroit Free Press* labeled the housing statement "as ambiguous as earlier pronouncements on school desegregation."[67] As in the case of school desegregation, Nixon was mistaken if he believed that a presidential statement—especially one that left so much open to interpretation—would cause civil rights staffers to defer to the executive branch's idea of how antidiscrimination laws should be enforced.

Nipped in the Bud?

Consequently, one must look beyond the simple explanation that the department's failure was a direct result of the White House stopping the agency before it had a chance to establish momentum in housing desegregation. Given the greater prominence of school desegregation efforts and the intense backlash against these initiatives, it is implausible to argue that public resistance to housing desegregation alone explains the weakness of civil rights policies in this area. The claim that the White House neatly dispatched of HUD's desegregation drive does not do justice to the difficulty an administration encounters when trying to restrain federal agencies, nor does it account for the countervailing pressures pushing HUD in the direction of more forceful action on the desegregation front. Most importantly, this account cannot explain why HUD came closest to achieving its desegregation goals *after* the White House increased its scrutiny of the agency.

As noted earlier, the executive and legislative branches often find it hard to stop an agency, especially a civil rights agency, from acting against the wishes of its staffers. Regarding HUD's attempts to foster suburban integration, a House member observed that the agency was trying to reach its objectives via program regulation rather than legislation. "HUD could not get enough votes to pass open communities amendments," the Democratic congressman said, ". . . but it's a whole new ball game [for Congress] to try to round up enough votes to negate something."[68] In highlighting the political dangers that a president faces in attacking civil rights bureaucracies, Glazer explains that "when a civil rights official resigns in protest against the Executive—this happened a number of times during the first Nixon Administration—the major news media uniformly handle it as a case of noble and unselfish men and women truly committed to justice committing an act of self-sacrifice against a politically minded Executive seeking to sell out the blacks and the minorities to gain the support of the most backward and reactionary elements."[69]

White House battles with OCR illustrate the difficulties in restraining bureaucracies even in cases where public opinion appears to be firmly on the side of the president. While a substantial number of school districts desegregated with relatively minimal upheaval (and subsequently minimal media attention), the issue of busing drew determined opposition in many communities. More prominent displays of opposition occurred in Pontiac, Michigan, where ten empty school buses were bombed; Richmond, Virginia, where parents drove 110 miles through snow in a 3,300-car motorcade to Washington in a busing protest; and Lamar, South Carolina, where about a hundred whites attacked two school buses carrying black children to Lamar High School.[70] Between 1972 and 1984, rarely did more than one in ten whites support mandatory busing to achieve integration over keeping children in neighborhood schools. During this same span, in only one year—1976—did more than 50 percent of black respondents express support for the former alternative.[71] As one Urban League strategy paper observed, "Any strategy that attempts to reverse the rising tide of anti-busing hysteria now given respectability by [President Nixon], has to deal with the unpalatable reality that the position has wide-spread support."[72]

Advocacy groups contended that politicians and the media deliberately distorted school desegregation issues. The Leadership Conference on Civil Rights argued in a media release that the oft-used phrases "massive busing" and "busing for racial balance" both distorted reality: the former by ignoring that only 3 percent of American schoolchildren were being bused for desegregation, and the latter by implying incorrectly that courts were ordering busing for "racial balance," rather than desegregation.[73] Public opinion surveys supported the notion that attitudes toward school desegregation varied widely, depending on precisely what question was being asked. For example, the National Opinion Research Center's 1972 General Social Survey found that 84 percent of nonblack respondents agreed that white and black students should go to the same schools, but 83 percent opposed busing of students across school districts.[74]

In Washington, the president railed to his advisors about keeping HEW employees in line. "More than once I was given instructions to 'tell [HEW Secretary Robert] Finch to keep that goddamned [OCR head Leon] Panetta out of Atlanta' or some other Congressman's district," John Ehrlichman recalled. Nixon's liaison to the South, Harry Dent, complained that "the basic tenet" of Nixon's 1970 school desegregation statement "is being flouted at the working level" by HEW.[75] Nixon and numerous congressional members made plenty of noise about the evils of busing, but were never able to translate their opposition into legislation that slowed this practice substantially.[76]

While much of the public opposed integration in both education and housing, comparing the magnitude of opposition between these two areas is somewhat difficult. Directly comparable survey questions from this era do not exist. Perhaps the most similar questions were asked in a 1972 Institute for Social Research survey, which asked people to respond to the statement, "White people have a right to keep black people out of their neighborhoods if they want to, or, black people have a right to live wherever they can afford to, just like anybody else?" Four in five whites agreed with the "black rights" option, with the remainder choosing "keep blacks out." Asked if "you think the government in Washington should see to it that white and black children go to the same schools, or stay out of this area, as it is not its business?" 35 percent of whites chose "see to it," 54 percent chose "stay out," and 12 percent chose neither.[77] The responses tell us little about the relative intensity of white opposition to desegregation in housing and education.

The school busing differed in character from housing because policies in the former area were carried out in a more comprehensive fashion and received substantially more public attention. *Congressional Quarterly* observed early in 1972 that residential "dispersion . . . has attracted little attention nationally, perhaps because the major presidential candidates see busing as the major race problem."[78] This relative lack of public attention is probably advantageous to an agency attempting to carry out unpopular policies. Even if we had more directly comparable public opinion data on housing versus educational desegregation, "what opinion surveys can never tell us is how people would respond if they confronted a new reality." For example, 81 percent of white Southerners opposed the 1954 *Brown v. Board of Education* decision at the time, but only 15 percent did forty years later. On a similar note, a 1978 Louis Harris poll found that 88 percent of black parents and 79 percent of white parents whose children were bused to school for racial reasons found the experience to be "very satisfactory" or "partly satisfactory."[79]

Despite the ambiguous role of public opinion, few would argue that, all else being equal, unpopular policies are no less vulnerable than popular ones. But the unpopularity of housing desegregation alone does not explain its failure, given that school desegregation produced tangible results (for the period during which it was actually attempted) in the face of intense opposition. Even unpopular policies—once they are in the hands of administrative agencies—can be surprisingly difficult for Congress and the White House to dismantle.

THE ROLE OF BUSINESS ELITES

While public opinion is often diffuse and difficult to link directly to policy outcomes (especially in cases where courts back agency actions), a number of scholars have claimed that business elites or other powerful interest groups steer public policy. The National Association of Real Estate Boards was the most vocal opponent of fair housing. The trade group led the opposition to fair housing legislation in 1966, when it passed the House before stalling in the Senate, and again in 1968. At the time of the fair housing debate, the organization consisted of about 83,000 real-estate brokers, accounting for roughly 90 percent of the nation's real-estate business.[80] Reflecting its great reluctance to involve itself with social issues, NAREB asserted in a 1966 meeting with religious groups that "the prime responsibility" in the area of race and housing lies with the clergy, which must accept leadership "in paving the way for the Realtor to conduct his business on an open occupancy basis—without losing his business."[81] After passage of the 1968 Act, NAREB adopted a policy statement supporting the principle of open housing, though the association remained firmly opposed to attempts by the federal government to dismantle racial and economic segregation.[82]

NAREB criticized Nixon-era HUD policies for overemphasizing subsidized housing starts at the expense of existing housing, which presumably could be turned over more quickly by brokers. The White House considered NAREB to be a "very effective lobby" whose leadership had been strongly Republican for many years.[83] However, NAREB did not appear to be a major influence on the housing agency. HUD production staffers were unsympathetic to NAREB's contention that housing policies focused too much on new production, and civil rights staffers accorded little weight to the views of the association, which had historically embraced segregation and still was considered no friend of open housing.

Other business groups had a self-interest in easing racial and economic exclusion in suburbia. In particular, employers who contracted with the government and were required to abide by affirmative action guidelines often found their efforts to hire workers of color hamstrung by the inability of these individuals to find housing within reasonable commuting distance. Some large employers took an active role in the fight against housing discrimination. For example, in 1958, black IBM employees at the firm's new Louisville typewriter plant found that their housing prospects improved markedly after the company specified that it would use only realtors that did not discriminate.[84] While other companies have also exerted successful pressure on localities and real-estate brokers to help house their lower-income and/or nonwhite workers, the U.S. Commission on Civil Rights found that firms typically were unwilling to take part in fights over housing in the absence of governmental pressure or severe economic necessity.[85]

With respect to trade groups, the National Association of Home Builders (NAHB) was perhaps the strongest voice, boasting more than 51,000 members, an operating budget of over $4 million, and a well-respected lobbying organization. The builders served as a legitimate counterweight to the antigovernment posture of NAREB. NAHB viewed HUD's attempts to encourage subsidized housing in suburbia as beneficial to builders. "Our motivation is pretty straightforward: If a guy can build all types of housing, he can make more dollars," one lobbyist noted. NAHB, which claimed that its members built two-thirds of all homes and apartments constructed by professional builders, enthusiastically supported HUD's racial and economic desegregation initiatives. In 1970, NAHB President Louis R. Barba advocated passage of a HUD proposal that would have prevented local governments from blocking subsidized housing construction in predominantly or completely undeveloped areas. He went on to urge that the legislation not be limited only to underdeveloped areas, and that HUD assistance be conditioned upon a community having building codes that were not more restrictive than a nationally recognized model code.[86]

Also supporting the spread of subsidized housing were large housing producers, who risked losing money if disputes over site selection were not resolved. For example, the chairman and CEO of National Homes Corp., which was the nation's largest and most successful producer of factory-built houses (over half of which were federally subsidized), argued that "somebody in the federal government has got to get some guts on this issue [of suburban exclusion]. Everyone has to be forced to take their fair share."[87] Large builders such as NHC brought suits on their own, and joined with civil rights groups in other suits, to permit the construction of subsidized housing in the suburbs.

Big-city mayors also wanted suburban localities to take their "fair share" of low- and moderate-income housing. Chicago Mayor Richard

Daley complained that Chicago and other major cities "are caught in the middle of conflicting policies. The position of the national administration is to resist efforts to use the legal and financial leverage of the federal government to compel suburbs to accept low and moderate income housing against their wishes. It holds that the law does not require that the federal government step in and provide in a neighborhood the type of housing that an individual could afford to move into. On the other hand, the Department of Housing and Urban Development is pursuing the exact opposite policy in the cities," where it had more leverage due to greater reliance on HUD programs than in the suburbs.[88] When the U.S. Conference of Mayors met the day after Nixon's Statement of Equal Housing Opportunity, unhappiness prevailed. The largely Democratic group of mayors may not have been the Nixon Administration's most cherished constituency, but they apparently mattered enough to provoke an angry speech by Romney at the meeting.[89] After being chastised by the HUD secretary, the mayors dropped a clause in their housing resolution that accused Nixon of retreating from equal housing opportunity, but they continued to advocate that *all* federal funding to communities be made contingent upon their willingness to provide low- and moderate-income housing opportunities.[90]

Advocacy Groups Press for Fair Housing

If business elites were not responsible for blocking suburban integration efforts, another possibility is that advocacy groups did too little to prompt assertive civil rights initiatives in housing, or that civil rights groups did not capture HUD as they did the enforcement agencies in employment and education. Nixon's housing statement seemed to puzzle civil rights and housing groups initially. For example, National Committee Against Discrimination in Housing (NCDH) president Robert L. Carter attacked the statement at a Civil Rights Commission hearing as "nothing less than an open endorsement of apartheid in the United States." He reconsidered his position in a subsequent interview: "Either I've misread the full import of the statement or these principles may not mean what I thought they meant. I'm now adopting a wait-and-see attitude."[91]

The Leadership Conference on Civil Rights, in a statement co-signed by other groups, including the NAACP Legal Defense Fund, the NCDH, and the Center for National Policy Review, argued that Nixon's statement attempts "to maintain an artificial distinction between 'economic' and 'racial' discrimination." While agreeing with Nixon that "poor" and "black" are not interchangeable, the LCCR maintained that exclusionary zoning ordinances affected nonwhite citizens most severely.[92] As a result, the Leadership Conference reasoned, drawing this distinction between economic and racial discrimination could only cause confusion. (That may have been Nixon's intention.) The National Urban Coalition dismissed the statement as "an 8,000-word essay on the practical problems of public administration."[93]

Even before the statement, advocacy groups increasingly were turning their attention to fair housing during the Nixon Administration. At its 1970 convention, the NAACP released an in-depth statement of housing resolutions, asserting that "the all-inclusive scope of federal housing activities and its far-reaching effect upon housing conditions and living environment make it perhaps the most significant of all national activities."[94] Among other recommendations, the organization urged federal preemption power over local zoning decisions, the collection of racial data by federal agencies involved in housing, and measures to foster "much greater movement of blacks into predominantly white residential areas." NAACP General Counsel Nathaniel R. Jones, citing the fact that 80 percent of all new jobs had been in the suburbs during the past decade, declared in 1971 that "the NAACP is placing absolute top priority on breaking the white noose surrounding the cities. The school situation, unemployment, welfare, everything—they all tie into this."[95]

The National Urban League, the National Urban Coalition, and the NCDH also undertook legal battles against residential segregation. The NCDH, an umbrella organization of fifty affiliated religious, civil rights, labor, and civic groups, was a particularly vehement advocate for residential desegregation, as housing was its sole civil rights focus. The NCDH recommended on several occasions that an independent agency with the power to hold hearings and issue cease-and-desist orders be created to police housing discrimination.[96] In addition to continually pushing HUD to act more aggressively in its fair housing activities, the housing organization assisted local groups in combating discrimination, and received a HUD grant to help the San Francisco Bay Area plan for regional growth without perpetuating segregated living patterns.[97]

Pro-desegregation groups pushed repeatedly for HUD to adopt a "goals and timetables" approach (as in employment), as they found the case-by-case approach to be largely ineffective. The NCDH asserted that "the individual complaint system, even in pattern and practice suits, is at best a mere palliative which fails to respond effectively to the fundamental problem, opening up the previously existing patterns of lily white suburbs and city neighborhoods to the minorities confined in local ghettoes."[98] HUD's Office of Equal Opportunity itself acknowledged that complaint processing would not begin to get at "the real problem" of institutional racism, which could only be addressed through community-wide investigations.[99] Because the first step in a more systemic attack against discrimination is to gather data, HUD critics were especially annoyed by the agency's delay in collecting racial data, particularly that pertaining to the racial composition of neighborhoods where subsidized housing was placed. The Civil Rights Act of 1968 explicitly authorizes the agency to collect this information.

Civil rights groups were disappointed with Secretary Romney for asserting that HUD did not have the authority under existing law to impose across-the-board funding cut-offs to localities found to be discriminating in a particular program. Thus, these groups alleged, suburban localities could benefit from HUD aid such as water and sewer grants while rejecting programs such as subsidized or public housing that would foster economic and racial integration. These groups also recommended that HUD cut off all aid to communities that refused to revise their zoning laws to allow for the provision of low- and moderate-income housing. Whether the agency rightfully should have exercised this authority is a matter of debate, but it is clear that other agencies granted similar powers by Congress were able to take such steps. The U.S. Commission on Civil Rights argued that HUD's Office of Equal Opportunity had inadequate staff to investigate Title VIII complaints, urging instead that the unit concentrate on "community compliance reviews which would uncover the total range of discriminatory housing practices occurring in an investigated community rather than the exact facts of the individual discriminatory act."[100]

The agency argued that it did not have the authority to conduct a compliance review of a nonrecipient of HUD assistance unless a complaint had been filed against that party. This position was at odds with that of the EEOC, which regularly undertook investigations without having received a complaint. HUD did conduct these reviews for respondents who had entered into conciliation agreements under Title VIII of the 1968 Civil Rights Act, and it said that it might examine evidence of past compliance by current applicants for HUD program funding.[101] In fiscal year 1972, HUD started 158 compliance reviews of single agencies, thirteen community-wide reviews, and thirty-seven FHA developer/sponsor reviews; HUD funded twelve-thousand agencies that year. The Civil Rights Commission complained that HUD failed to monitor whether involved parties were adhering to their compliance agreements.[102]

The Equal Opportunity Office was also weakened by a provision in fair housing law that required HUD to defer its authority in states and localities with fair housing laws at least as strong as the federal law. Groups such as the NCDH argued that many state agencies were underfunded and that a good portion operated under state administrations that were unsympathetic to fair housing laws. By the end of 1971, twenty-six states and eight localities were determined to have "substantially equivalent" fair housing laws.[103]

Within the federal government, the presidentially appointed U.S. Commission on Civil Rights applied consistent pressure on HUD to step up its antidiscrimination activities. In a 1971 report, the commission criticized HUD for having "regressed" the most in its civil rights enforcement efforts over the prior seven months. The White House became quite irritated with the panel, eventually asking the chair, Father Theodore Hesburgh, to resign. In a memo recommending against a proposal to expand the USCCR's authority, Nixon speechwriter and right-wing firebrand Pat Buchanan labeled the commission "a thorn in the side of the Nixon Administration; it has recognized that the way to get good media is to attack the Administration, and preferably the President, for foot-dragging in the area of Civil Rights."[104]

While staffers in HUD's Office of Equal Opportunity largely shared the views of social movement organizations, housing production staffers did not. Romney, though believing strongly that desegregation was imperative, often seemed confused and overwhelmed in his attempts to achieve the multiple objectives of the agency. While largely failing to heed the advice of advocacy groups, Romney characteristically bristled at those who criticized him. In a June 1971 speech, HUD Secretary Romney appeared to take a shot at civil rights and fair-housing organizations, asserting, "If only a fraction of the citizen energy poured into the advocacy of legislation could be applied to the vital implementation and enforcement of legislation, we would be much closer today to the reality of fair housing than we in fact are."[105]

Cause for Guarded Optimism

Despite the frustrations of civil rights groups with HUD and the mixed messages of the presidential housing statement, a flurry of governmental activity after the announcement seemed to offer some prospects for progress. Most prominently, Attorney General John Mitchell announced that the federal government would, after wavering for nearly seven months, sue Black Jack, Missouri. The town, a white working-class suburb of St. Louis with a population of 4,000, had changed its zoning laws in a thinly disguised attempt to stop construction of an integrated apartment development.[106] When a group of churches in Black Jack planned a racially mixed, middle-income housing project using HUD Section 236 funding, residents mobilized quickly to stop the development. The Black Jack Improvement Association circulated an information sheet to residents warning of declining property values and the beginning of "a process that completely changes the economic character of the community," an increased tax burden due to more school-age children, and the possibility of "disturbances" resulting from "crowding low income families into such a close space."[107] Pressured by residents, the Black Jack City Council incorporated the town, which transferred zoning authority from the county to the new municipality, and passed a zoning ordinance that excluded multiple dwellings. St. Louis County had originally zoned sixty-seven acres of land to permit multi-family dwellings, and private developers had already constructed over three hundred apartments on part of this land. Earlier, an apartment development with only white tenants was constructed without major problems. Romney labeled Black Jack's actions "a blatant violation of the Constitution and the law."[108]

Also in the wake of Nixon's statement, HUD issued guidelines for the award of water, sewer, and other community-development grants in which provision of low-income housing accounted for 10 percent of the application's ranking in the funding queue; signed an agreement with the General Services Administration to ensure the availability of low-cost housing for federal employees in the vicinity of new federal installations; published affirmative marketing guidelines for housing developers requiring that the availability of housing be publicized in a nondiscriminatory manner; and issued new site-selection criteria for subsidized housing that gave preference to applications that would foster racial and economic integration. The marketing guidelines required builders, developers, and sponsors applying for HUD aid to solicit buyers and tenants affirmatively. Equal opportunity staff monitored compliance with plans. In many other aspects of HUD operations, that staff mainly aided in tasks such as designing implementation instructions. The regulations did not apply to FHA-insured or subsidized projects.[109]

The site selection guidelines instructed HUD officials to judge applications under several subsidy programs in terms of eight broad objectives. The objectives listed under "minority housing opportunities" were "to provide minority families with opportunities for housing in a wide range of locations; [and] to open up nonsegregated housing opportunities that will contribute to decreasing the effects of past housing discrimination." A proposed project would receive a superior rating if it would be located to house minorities in areas outside of existing minority concentration, in a racially mixed area that would not be expected to change its racial proportions with the proposed project, or in or near an area of minority concentration that was part of an urban renewal, model cities, or other local redevelopment plan expected to foster racial and economic integration. A project located in an area of minority concentration, but that met overriding housing needs that could not realistically be met otherwise in that housing market, would receive an adequate rating. Applications that would not meet any of the previously mentioned conditions and would cause a substantially mixed area to become one of minority concentration would receive a poor rating, which would result in automatic rejection of the application.[110]

The Leadership Conference on Civil Rights argued that under the rating system, a site receiving a superior rating on these criteria "may be at a disadvantage under criteria for 'neighborhood environment' and 'employment and utilization of employees and business in project areas' "; as a result, pro-integrative plans effectively might be penalized.[111] Site selection issues were dicey for civil rights groups. While agreeing on the need for sites to be developed in suburban areas, many groups feared that inner-city sites would not be approved and suburban sites would not be proposed, thus resulting in no low- and moderate-income housing construction.

The agency's leverage in site selection was modest, as HUD remained completely dependent on applications from local governments and developers. As Romney later conceded, "The fact is the HUD programs are of marginal interest to most well-established suburbs, and it is therefore sheer illusion to think that HUD can bring about overnight changes in the entire existing suburban physical and social landscape by turning Federal money on or off."[112] This was true to the extent that HUD, in contrast to the other civil rights bureaucracies, interpreted its authority as being limited to cases where it was providing funding. (Whereas Title VI of the 1964 Civil Rights Act applies only to entities receiving federal funding, Title VIII of the 1968 Civil Rights Act applies to virtually all housing.)

In mid-1971, the prospects for progress in residential desegregation remained murky. A pessimistic observer could point to the public relations debacle in Warren, public opposition, White House pressure on HUD to ease its enforcement zeal, and resistance of influential business elites as factors making suburban desegregation doubtful. On the other hand, the White House had staked out a middle ground on the issue, and advocacy groups were applying pressure on HUD to step up its civil rights activities. The threat of funding withdrawal had convinced some localities to change their discriminatory practices. As will be explored in chapter 5, courts were starting to rule in favor of residential desegregation remedies. It would be the challenge of HUD's civil rights team to parlay this mixed bag of opportunities and impediments into firm policies of residential desegregation.

Chapter Five

Indirect Attack

A Housing Freeze Kills Civil Rights Efforts

BY THE EARLY 1970s, government bureaucracies had gotten a bad name. In his 1968 and 1972 presidential campaigns, George Wallace aimed much of his venom at federal bureaucrats for their ineptitude, their insensitivity, and their interference with matters that were, in his view, none of their business. This was a clever way of attacking programs that ostensibly favored blacks without resorting to explicitly racist appeals; Ronald Reagan later used this tactic with cynical effectiveness by spinning apocryphal tales of "welfare queens" getting rich off of government largesse. Wallace relished tearing into the "intellectual snobs who don't know the difference between smut and great literature," and "the hypocrites who send your kids half-way across town while they have their chauffeurs drop their children off at private schools."[1] He seemed to derive the greatest satisfaction from taunting the "thousands of bureaucrats toting briefcases in Washington who don't know why they're there. . . . I'll bet if you opened half of their briefcases all you'd find would be a peanut butter and jelly sandwich." When Nixon tried a similar tactic in trolling for Republican votes in the 1970 midterm election, it failed, since he was the putative boss of those bureaucrats.[2]

Federal housing programs were notorious for their complexity. The frank but defensive George Romney told a congressional committee in 1971 that "housing subsidy programs are so complicated that they are practically impossible of administration."[3] Consider, for example, the perverse incentive system used in the Section 236 program. With the approval of HUD, a builder-developer could acquire an FHA-insured mortgage covering 90 percent of the estimated construction cost for a rental housing project with some low-income tenants. The builder-developer would sell shares in the project, amounting to around 15 percent of the mortgage, to buyers who were often interested mainly in the tax write-off for owners of rental property. These buyers usually would earn after-tax returns in the 15 to 20 percent range. This administrative arrangement meant that builders had an incentive to increase construction costs, which would allow them to sell shares for higher prices, and entitle buyers to bigger tax write-offs. Because the developer's interest in the project normally ended after selling his or her shares, and investors were concerned mostly with taking paper depreciation losses (which expired after ten years), only the tenants had a stake in the long-term viability of the project.[4]

Desegregation in private housing was also a highly complex task (see chapter 4), and civil rights staffers had little policy experience on which to draw. Nevertheless, employees of civil rights agencies—including HUD's civil rights staffers—still largely retained the faith that the federal government can and should lead the way in promoting racial equality in America. Substantial numbers of former civil rights movement participants now held posts in bureaucracies assigned to carry out antidiscrimination laws. A sense of mission prevailed in agencies exclusively devoted to fighting discrimination, such as the EEOC. In multi-mission agencies, however, some staffers—particularly longtime employees of the agency—were indifferent or even hostile to relatively recent civil rights mandates. According to the institutional homes approach presented here, the structure and mission of an agency have important direct effects on the actions and effectiveness of government agencies. In addition, the institutional home of a policy shapes the ways in which prior policies and external political actors—such as interest and advocacy groups, other branches of government, and the public—affect policy development in specific cases.

HUD's weak institutional home was a major factor in its ultimate failure to implement policies that attacked residential segregation on a comprehensive basis, acting to alter broad patterns of residential concentration rather than investigating individual complaints of discrimination. This failure occurred despite substantial activity by advocacy groups in support of affirmative action, a significant faction of institutional activists within the agency, little sustained opposition from interest groups, and a favorable policy legacy from prior race-conscious civil rights policies, among other factors.

As explained in chapter 2, the Equal Employment Opportunity Commission (EEOC), the Office of Federal Contract Compliance (OFCC), and HEW's Office for Civil Rights (OCR) all faced formidable political obstacles in acting forcefully. For the EEOC, meager enforcement authority and funding, unstable leadership, early skepticism from civil rights groups, and actions that appeared to fly in the face of congressional intent all made its chances for success seem slim. The OFCC's Philadelphia Plan, compelling construction contractors to specify minority hiring goals, had been declared illegal by the comptroller general during the Johnson Administration. There was little reason to believe that the more conservative Nixon Administration would support its revival. In education, OCR battled with a White House that purged several backers of aggressive desegregation efforts, and even disavowed a HEW desegregation plan in court. Large sectors of Congress and the public were hostile to school desegregation efforts, particularly as they involved busing of students.

What these three agencies had in their favor were strong institutional homes. The EEOC was a stand-alone agency with the singular mission to fight discrimination. Its legitimacy would hinge upon achievement of that objective alone. The OFCC had the strong support of its parent agency, the Department of Labor, and a very specific mission: to ensure that federal contractors fulfilled the terms of their agreements with the federal government. OCR's school desegregation efforts became the most visible activity at HEW, and thus the one on which political actors evaluated the agency. Other missions such as civil rights enforcement in health care received virtually no attention after 1967; that year, HEW's operational structure was shifted from having separate civil rights shops in each of the component agencies to a centralized civil rights operation.

With respect to its institutional home, HUD stood in clear contrast to those other agencies. As a conglomerate of formerly independent agencies (some of which had promoted segregation) with numerous missions and complex measures of success, HUD was in a relatively weak position to fulfill these multiple missions, particularly secondary ones such as fair housing enforcement. A HUD undersecretary explained the bureaucratic bifurcation that existed within the recently created agency:

> HUD is really still two departments, not one. The 'Department of Housing' and the 'Department of Urban Development' operate under different basic philosophies. For those responsible for housing, production is the goal—production at almost any cost. For those responsible for community planning and community development, the emphasis is on building local capacity to improve the total living environment. Housing and, in fact, all physical development are but one component of this overall effort. . . . The 'Department of Housing' operates primarily through the private sector almost without regard for the impact of its actions on the plans and priorities of affected communities.[5]

More harmfully, this obsession with creation of housing units and quick processing of applications led to scandals that destroyed the legitimacy of the entire agency. Consequently, President Nixon gained the necessary political cover to declare a housing freeze, which saved large sums of money and prevented court-driven integration plans from taking hold. As in other areas of civil rights, Nixon used available opportunities to practice blame avoidance, where the onus of controversial actions would fall on other political actors.

Despite considerable public opposition to open housing, it is not as if Nixon could kill these initiatives without a fight. As examined in chapter 4, advocacy groups such as the National Committee Against Discrimination in Housing (NCDH), the Leadership Conference on Civil Rights (LCCR), the NAACP, and the U.S. Commission on Civil Rights (USCCR) exerted considerable pressure on HUD to fulfill the "affirmative action" mandate of the 1968 Fair Housing Act. Moreover, HUD did not lack institutional activists, social movement participants (or sympathizers) who hold positions within governments and seek to attain movement goals through normal bureaucratic channels.[6]

CIVIL RIGHTS ENFORCEMENT VERSUS HOUSING PRODUCTION

These institutional activists did not let the agency's fixation on production, to the exclusion of other missions, go unchallenged. In principle, if not always in practice, HUD acknowledged that antidiscrimination efforts were central to its responsibilities. In communication with the White House, HUD identified its three basic missions as helping to ensure "a decent home in a suitable living environment for every American family" (the stated goal of the Housing Act of 1949); aiding community development; and assisting "in the advancement of equal opportunity for minority group citizens."[7] Assistant Secretaries Samuel J. Simmons (equal opportunity) and Samuel C. Jackson (metropolitan planning and development), HUD's two highest-ranking black employees, were particularly passionate advocates for aggressive affirmative action remedies. In 1969, Simmons stressed to Secretary Romney that HUD should more actively seek the advice and assistance of advocacy groups such as the NCDH and the NAACP Legal Defense and Educational Fund: "Too often at present we tend to act as though these organizations are attempting to achieve goals others than those which we are interested in. We must realize that these groups are attempting to achieve the same goals that we espouse." Further into Nixon's first term, Simmons worried about "the accelerating negative image HUD is acquiring in regard to equal housing opportunities."[8]

The equal opportunity chief publicly expressed his desire for more aggressive actions, including the use of goals and timetables to monitor progress in residential desegregation. "If we don't have some kind of quantifiable criteria," Simmons told a reporter, "no one knows what the heck you're talking about. . . . When we got ready to send a man to the moon, we didn't do it in general terms. We said we'd do it in so many years and for so much money. It was something to shoot for."[9] The first step in doing this was the collection of racial data for HUD programs, an activity that Simmons (and advocacy groups) pleaded for persistently to no avail. The 1968 Civil Rights Act directs HUD to collect and disseminate "data on the race, color, religion, sex, national origin, age, handicap, and family characteristics of persons and households who are applicants for, participants in, or beneficiaries or potential beneficiaries of, programs administered by the Department." In one specific proposal to Under Secretary Richard C. Van Dusen, Simmons suggested that the agency prepare maps of the one hundred largest standard metropolitan areas (populations of at least 250,000), "showing the distribution of minority group populations (Negro, Spanish, Oriental, and Indian) and the location and ethnic occupancy of HUD-assisted housing developments, model city areas and urban renewal areas, plus the location of other HUD-assisted projects such as open space projects, water and sewer projects and the like." HUD still was unable to provide such data, which was essential to developing a goals-and-timetables approach, as late as fall 1972.[10]

Undersecretary Richard Van Dusen and Romney himself were convinced of the need to address residential segregation. The HUD Secretary insisted publicly that "the future of our country depends upon our success in finding more effective solutions to our problems of poverty, race, housing and the cities." He called the confrontation between poor, minority central-city residents and middle- and upper-class people in the segregated suburbs "the most explosive threat to our nation."[11] As HUD's integration effort kicked into gear, Romney was ambivalent about trying to override local officials, who he had long insisted were best suited to spearhead social change. By late 1971, he apparently resolved this dilemma by trying to convince local officials to collaborate on residential desegregation remedies in order to avoid the prospect of considerably more stringent court requirements to develop these policies.[12]

Internal dissatisfaction with the agency's hesitancy in the area of equal opportunity sometimes made headlines, most notably in the very public resignation of Robert Affeldt, the director of the Equal Opportunity office's conciliation division. Affeldt asserted at a news conference that

> the program directors are production oriented and they regard any form of quality control in the form of equal opportunity as an infringement upon their feudal domains. It is a tragedy that program directors and not the assistant secretary for equal opportunity possess the power to withhold or cut off funds. . . . This is comparable to a person being a judge, jury, and prosecutor in his own case. It is seldom that such a person or program director will act against his own self-interest. . . . I thought the Nixon Administration was serious about enforcing the law not enforcing it in a radical and ultra-liberal manner but simply enforcing it. . . . [However] when it disagrees with the law it takes a different view of [its emphasis on] "law and order" under its present policy of funding without any form of social or legal accountability for adverse racial effects.[13]

As Affeldt pointed out, production staffers largely found civil rights concerns to go against their interest in self-preservation. Some high-ranking career officials feared that programs that had become unpopular due to their linkages to the Open Communities program would be transferred to other agencies; for example, it was rumored that the water and sewer grant program would be handed over to the newly created Environmental Protection Agency. They were also concerned that the addition of even more federal criteria would make HUD programs (particularly FHA ones) less attractive to local communities and developers, thus affecting grant processing and production figures. FHA Commissioner Eugene Gulledge pleaded with Romney to relax a number of regulations, including several related to equal opportunity, that he felt constrained production.[14]

The equal opportunity staff had little power to increase the priority given to civil rights concerns, since it lacked veto power over agency programs. In contrast to HEW, where OCR could order termination of funding to institutions refusing to correct discriminatory practices, project approval power in HUD was left to the production staff, which predictably was more concerned with getting homes built than with enforcing civil rights objectives. Consequently, the agency never used its authority under Title VI of the 1964 Civil Rights Act to cut off funds to a local housing authority, private developer, or landlord operating a federally subsidized development.[15] This lack of power existed despite the fact that HUD was the only federal department other than Justice with an assistant secretary whose sole responsibility was civil rights.

In many ways, the Warren, Michigan, incident discussed in the previous chapter crystallized HUD's dilemma in fulfilling two of its primary missions. Former Housing and Home Finance Agency General Counsel Milton P. Semer (1961–65) observed in 1970 that "you probably have enough statutory and constitutional authority to have an active program in the racial-integration-of-housing field. But," he wondered, "can you have that and housing production also?"[16] He pointed to Warren and Chicago, where public housing construction had been continually delayed because courts had ordered public housing on scattered sites in white neighborhoods, which resisted fiercely. Because HUD exerted pressure only where it had the leverage of funding, its efforts could appear more expedient than principled. The agency's attempts to secure token measures of good will from Warren reflected the agency's fear of bad publicity and its desperation to get housing built.

Romney was aware that the distribution of power within the agency would weaken civil rights efforts. In a 1969 letter to President Nixon recommending ways to address shortages of labor for housing construction, the secretary asserted that "the primary responsibility for enforcement or compliance [with HUD's equal employment opportunity requirements] should rest with equal opportunity personnel. The past practice of relying on those with program responsibilities has not worked, for in many cases they have lacked the necessary expertise and, understandably, have often felt that their first duty is to implement their program rather than enforce non-discrimination or affirmative action requirements."[17] Yet, for all his concern with discrimination, Romney was apparently unwilling to gum up the production process by vesting real compliance power with his own civil rights staff at HUD. Equal opportunity staffers knew the dimensions of this dilemma all too well. When his office was able to act, as with the release of HUD's Affirmative Fair Housing Regulations, Simmons was concerned that the Equal Opportunity office "not end up being held responsible for *slowing up production*."[18]

From the outset, advocacy groups had feared that HUD's civil rights initiatives would be timid. In 1971 congressional testimony, an NCDH representative recalled that the organization initially had "grave reservations" about HUD enforcing fair housing law. "What we were concerned about," she explained, "was that the old people who had been there twenty years ago, who were the Federal bureaucrats at that time, were still in HUD and were still basically following the kinds of concepts that they had followed in those earlier days."[19] For most of its life FHA and other housing agencies had no interest in upsetting the status quo. Historically, FHA staffers believed that racial homogeneity was absolutely necessary for residential areas to remain stable and desirable. It was not until the 1950s that FHA, prodded by the Supreme Court's *Shelly v. Kraemer* (1948) decision declaring restrictive covenants to be unenforceable, began to take halting steps away from its segregationist policies. Even after this time, civil rights groups often criticized the agency for continuing to tolerate discrimination and segregation, despite its more principled rhetoric.

Open housing supporters in the late 1960s had reason to be concerned about FHA's influence, since an estimated 60 percent of HUD's full-time personnel were part of the Federal Housing Administration.[20] Sen. Edward Brooke (R-MA), an original co-sponsor of fair housing legislation in the Senate, elicited laughter during a congressional hearing when he asked HUD Secretary Romney, "Does FHA finally realize it is under HUD?" Assuring Brooke that FHA did in fact realize this, Romney noted that he had taken over a "bureaucratic conglomerate" of previously separate agencies that Congress had assembled under a single roof without changing. It was not until fiscal 1973 that FHA's thirty-eight insuring offices, where most of the funding decisions were made, had equal opportunity staff.[21]

Looking to the Courts for Leadership

In the aftermath of Nixon's June 1971 statement and with mounting frustration over HUD's ineffectiveness, a number of fair housing supporters grew pessimistic about the prospects for suburban racial and economic integration. Some observers, however, continued to foresee revolutionary progress in this area. In this view, federal courts would be the primary instigators of change. President Nixon's statement on equal opportunity in housing identified two cases as representing the outer bounds of judicial opinion on civil rights in housing. In *Kennedy Park Homes Association v. City of Lackawanna, N.Y.* (1971) (436 F2d 108), a Circuit Court of Appeals struck down a town's zoning and other municipal restrictions after it was shown that these provisions were racially motivated actions to prevent construction of a low-income housing development in an all-white neighborhood; the Supreme Court refused to review the decision (401 U.S. 1010). The other case, *James v. Valtierra* (1971) (402 U.S. 137), was cited as embodying the limits of the law. In this decision, the Supreme Court upheld a California law requiring a referendum to approve publicly built low-income housing in a locality. While the White House and others used this case to argue that the Fourteenth Amendment does not protect the poor, as such, against housing discrimination, the scope of the decision is relatively narrow, concerning itself largely with the referendum procedure and local governmental involvement in public housing construction. The decision did not cover federal housing subsidy programs.[22] Consequently, one cannot identify *James v. Valtierra* as the death blow to open housing efforts.

In *HUD v. Shannon* (1970) (436 F.2d 809), the U.S. Court of Appeals (Third Circuit) ruled that HUD's decisions on approving proposed housing projects must consider whether they would perpetuate racial concentration. Judge John H. Gibbons wrote, "Increase or maintenance of racial concentration is *prima facie* likely to lead to urban blight and is thus *prima facie* at variance with the national housing policy." The decision said only that HUD must consider racial concentration, allowing that the agency could weigh other factors as well. An internal White House memo regarding *Shannon* notes,

> Under the unanimous and accelerating trend of federal and state decisions HUD's policies are essentially what the courts require. . . . The hydraulic principle that was operative in the school desegregation area is now clearly at work in housing—a vacuum of governmental policy in a Fourteenth Amendment area producing energetic "affirmative action" policy on the part of the courts. The judicial surge in the housing area is particularly rapid because of preconditioning of courts and litigants by a decade of civil rights legislation.[23]

Shannon was one of several cases that suggested the possibility of a real transformation in housing patterns. Such a shift would take shape through several vehicles: (1) court-ordered metropolitan-wide housing plans; (2) court-ordered re-zoning of racially and economically exclusionary residential areas; (3) legislation imposing low-income housing quotas for suburban communities that attracted a large manufacturing firm from the city; and (4) legislation conditioning federal housing subsidies on participation in metropolitan-wide housing plans. Under this scenario, federal court decisions demanding that subsidized housing be spread beyond the city limits of Atlanta, Chicago, and Philadelphia would be the main engines to bring about such a change.[24] The Atlanta case, *Crow v. Fulton County, Ga. Commissioners* (1971) (332 F.Supp. 382), was the most sweeping at the time. After Fulton County rejected a building permit and sewer hookup for a subsidized, multi-family development that the Atlanta Housing Authority had proposed in the suburb of Red Oak, the District Court ordered suburban officials to devise a plan that would disperse subsidized housing into the suburbs. Noting that HUD policy clearly "requires that public housing be dispersed outside racially compacted areas," the court ruled, "In absence of supervening necessity, any county action or inaction intended to perpetuate or which in effect does perpetuate concentration of blacks in compacted areas cannot stand, nor can county action or inaction which would thwart correction of conditions be permitted to continue."[25]

The best known of these cases, *Hills v. Gautreaux* (425 U.S. 284), was not resolved until 1976, a full decade after the filing of the original suit alleging discrimination by the Chicago Housing Authority (CHA) in its site selection for public housing, and by HUD for approving and funding the sites. A 1969 ruling by Judge Richard B. Austin instructed the CHA to build three out of every four future housing units in white neighborhoods. The CHA responded by building no housing at all from 1969 to 1974. HUD, which had been absolved of responsibility in Austin's original decision, was deemed guilty of aiding and abetting segregation in the Chicago area in a 1971 U.S. Court of Appeals ruling. The 1976 Supreme Court decision resulted in a far-reaching, metropolitan-level desegregation plan that enabled more than 7,100 families to leave public housing and move into private rentals; more than half of the families moved into middle-income white suburbs, while the others moved into lower-income, predominantly black neighborhoods in the city of Chicago. On average, suburban movers did better than city movers in adult employment patterns and children's educational outcomes. The court consent decree expired in 1998, ending the program.[26]

In addition to the cases discussed earlier, courts in seven states overturned local zoning ordinances and building codes that discriminated

against low- and moderate-income housing. While a number of observers pointed with pessimism to the refusal of the Supreme Court to
address such questions, a competing view was that the high court's refusal to grant certiorari to these cases signaled its support for the rulings
of the federal courts. HUD attempted to convince communities that their
agreement to accept a reasonable share of low- and moderate-income
housing voluntarily would forestall stringent, court-mandated requirements. Romney predicted that "if the courts start ordering housing dispersal across metropolitan areas, it will provoke a far greater social crisis
than the school busing one." He insisted that courts would, nevertheless,
force these housing opportunities to be created if localities did not do it
themselves. "And if that happens," Romney warned, "the local communities will have to suffer the consequences. I can tell you right now that
they won't like them. We have been trying to tell communities that. And
so has the President."[27] Romney was referring to Nixon's June 1971
statement on housing, in which the president said it would be unwise for
courts to make these policies, "[b]ut they no doubt will end up in the
courts if they are not satisfactorily dealt with outside the courts through
timely and enlightened local action."

Foreseeing the move toward suburban integration as inevitable, several members of the administration became interested in legislation that
would create agencies to oversee housing allocation on a regional basis.[28] These agencies would have the power to overrule local objections
to subsidized housing. Using an explicit rationale of blame avoidance,
one White House staffer argued that the metropolitan housing agencies
"would serve as devices to relieve the pressures of suburban integration
from the President" if they had authority in the areas of site selection,
project selection, and approval, and the power to enforce and manage
such decisions. The memo stresses that these agencies must bear responsibility for their decisions, thus taking the heat off of the federal government. In response, speechwriter Pat Buchanan objected that "there is no
guarantee that it will surely diminish the ultimate political responsibility,
which will fall . . . on the President—as many Court decisions on busing
have hurt the President." Instead, Buchanan suggested that the White
House "tie the hands of HUD, and prevent them from the kind of social
outrage they attempted to perpetrate upon the folks of Warren, Michigan." He expressed pessimism that his view would win out, given "our
desire to 'split the difference' on the issue of forced integration. . . . I am
sure there are those within the White House here who are determined
that Richard Nixon is to be the last worshiper in the Church of Integration before it closes down for good."[29]

Congress also flirted with the idea of creating metropolitan-wide agencies, funded by federal block grants, to plan and construct low- and

moderate-income housing throughout an area's cities and suburbs. Support for the House bill, which was at one time believed to be broad and bipartisan, dissipated by April 1972, as skittish northern Democrats feared the electoral consequences come fall. HUD supported the measure behind the scenes, though it was sponsored by Democrats, but did not attempt to save the proposal when it began losing support.[30]

Romney insisted repeatedly that many urban problems could be addressed effectively only on a metropolitan basis, which he dubbed a "Real City" approach. It had become clear to HUD officials that metropolitan-level plans were the only rational and just means to get communities to accept their "fair share" of low- and moderate-housing.[31] Without such plans, isolated communities willing to accept such housing were likely to be inundated with it, as subsidized housing is difficult to stop after zoning and other regulations are changed to clear the way for initial construction. Predictably, persuading metropolitan areas and individual communities to accept HUD's line of reasoning would take some time.[32] When word first began to leak in fall 1972 that the administration was considering a cut-off of all federal housing funds, towns and regional planning boards typically chose to wait and see whether the White House would in fact take this step. The rumors proved true in January 1973. As a result, communities had no subsidized housing to refuse and thus no judicial decisions to fear.

Scandals at HUD Give Nixon an Escape Hatch

Nixon could not use his objection to affirmative action in housing to justify the housing moratorium publicly, since the United States remained mired in a housing shortage. The president found his justification in the scandals that emerged in FHA's central-city programs. The U.S. Commission on Civil Rights reported that, in a sample of HUD programs from July 1971, residential segregation remained quite prevalent. Under HUD's basic home mortgage program, Section 203(b), black families comprised a mere 3.5 percent of new homeowners, the same percentage as was found in a 1967 survey of FHA-insured subdivisions. Under Section 235 (interest subsidies for homeownership), all new homes built in "blighted" areas were purchased by blacks, while 70 percent outside these areas were purchased by non-Hispanic whites.[33] Under Section 236 (interest subsidies for rental housing), two-thirds of the units were occupied by non-Hispanic white families. Nearly one-third (120 out of 380) of the projects reporting were entirely segregated by race and ethnic group: eighty all white, thirty-eight all black, and two all Hispanic. Of the remaining 269 projects, only one hundred were more than 15 percent integrated; that is, 142 were more than 85 percent white, and twenty-seven were more than 85 percent black.[34]

At the end of 1971, Romney admitted that the increase in black families living in the suburbs was modest, and that a large portion of the uptick was the result of families moving just across city borders to expand existing areas of black settlement. The situation in individual metropolitan areas told a more vivid story. Between 1950 and 1970, the population in the St. Louis region swelled by 600,000, while the city itself lost 250,000 residents. During that period, the black population in the city almost doubled, while the white city population was halved. All but 5 percent of new housing was built in the suburbs, and less than 1 percent of housing built in suburban subdivisions was sold to blacks from 1962 to 1970.[35]

More damaging to HUD's reputation than meager progress in the area of desegregation were the scandals in FHA programs that began to come to light as early as 1970. Several new programs enacted by Congress in the 1960s led FHA to do business in "risky" locales that it had historically avoided. Section 221(d)(2), an unsubsidized program enacted in 1961, liberalized down-payment rules and lengthened maturities to enable inner-city residents to use the insurance programs. The Housing and Urban Development Act of 1968, in addition to initiating the Section 235 and 236 mortgage subsidy programs, established Section 223(e), which created a special risk pool to back mortgages in areas that were traditionally redlined. The former program enabled real-estate speculators to sell to the poor, while the latter led FHA and the private lending industry to underwrite high-risk mortgages.

These well-intentioned changes created an environment that invited corruption, with unscrupulous individuals finding an easy path to quick profit. The scam would typically begin with a team of realtors (often one white and one black) warning white residents in a declining neighborhood of impending racial transition and social problems. In turn, the realtors would convince families to sell their homes cheaply, then make small cosmetic improvements to the property (which often left serious problems), and secure an FHA mortgage guarantee. Key to the generation of quick profits was the cooperation of FHA appraisers, who were often local realtors working for fees and, in a number of cases, were willing to submit inflated appraisals in exchange for under-the-table payments. At that point, it was relatively easy to find a lender, which under FHA guarantees assumed no risk. Likewise, finding a buyer usually presented little problem, as the relaxed down-payment and mortgage-repayment terms, perceived security of FHA approval, and relative scarcity of housing for sale to low-income individuals created strong demand. The speculators would walk away with a healthy profit in little time.

The buyers were often not so fortunate. In many cases, the new home owners were unable to afford essential repairs to the home. Eventually, the mortgage would go into serious default, the private lender would foreclose on the property, and HUD would be required to pay the lender and take possession of a property with no willing buyers. From January 1968 to June 1971, the agency foreclosed on over 2800 properties, exceeding the cumulative total for the prior thirty-three years of FHA activity. HUD was thought to be the largest owner of single-family dwellings in cities such as Detroit and Philadelphia. Some Detroit neighborhoods came to resemble ghost towns as families abandoned dilapidated FHA-financed homes. The Detroit media documented collusion between FHA appraisers who inflated their figures, HUD officials who accepted bribes, and the real-estate operators and agents who reaped great profits. In one St. Louis neighborhood where crime had risen sharply, block busters bought twenty-three houses for an average price of $5,000 each. After making minor, cosmetic repairs, the buyers got FHA appraisers to estimate the houses to be worth $10,000 and good for twenty- to thirty-year mortgages. Unsuspecting families purchased the homes. By early 1972, every one of the twenty-three houses had been demolished.[36]

Romney's bluntness regarding the FHA scandals may have made a bad situation worse. He admitted plainly that FHA had been unprepared for the "speculators and fast-buck artists" who swooped down on central cities after Congress relaxed procedures in those areas to help people secure adequate housing. The HUD chief told a Senate appropriations subcommittee that "there was practically no preparation for this fundamental change. As a matter of fact, it occurred when FHA was least prepared for it. Shady, get-rich-quick schemes have involved some real-estate salesmen, some builders, some developers, and even some housing authorities who lined their pockets with the food money of unsophisticated home buyers and renters." Romney had reacted to early reports of corruption quite differently. At a December 1970 hearing before the House Banking and Currency Committee, he dismissed suggestions from several committee members that Section 235 approvals be slowed until additional staff could be hired to handle increased volumes of applications.[37] The next month, he suspended Section 235 approvals for existing housing but insisted that the program was not suffering from a scandal. In 1972, twenty-eight HUD officials were indicted for illegal activities. The agency referred over 1,300 cases of possible corruption to the Justice Department for investigation.[38]

By early 1972, Romney sounded defeated. In a March 1972 speech, he said of inner-city blight, "The truth is—none of us are now sure what are the right things to do." Ultimately, what George Romney lacked as HUD secretary was not the desire to foster change, particularly in the urgent area of desegregation. Instead, it was Romney's inability to steer this "hastily merged conglomerate of antiquated government agencies and divergent special interest programs" that helped to assure that the dual goals of desegregation and massive housing production would remain unfulfilled.[39] This task would have been extremely difficult even for someone who had entered the job with some background in housing, or in running a massive federal bureaucracy. Romney, with neither of these experiences to draw upon, was in over his head.[40]

HUD during the Nixon era did little to inspire confidence in its abilities, in many ways shooting itself in the foot. From the start, the Office of Equal Opportunity was in a disadvantaged position, and not only because its mission was secondary in the agency. It was also part of an agency that was ripe for scandal: a large organization of formerly separate agencies in the highly complex field of housing. The agency might have avoided these scandals if production goals had been balanced by other objectives. As of April 1972, over half of HUD's single-family inventory of units (totaling 22,918) that had been acquired following foreclosure and that were not yet resold came from seven cities: Detroit, Seattle, Dallas, Los Angeles, Lubbock (Tex.), Hempstead (N.Y.), and Philadelphia. Detroit alone accounted for one-third of the inventory.[41]

In other locales, the inner-city programs seemed to work well. For example, safeguards in Milwaukee's inner-city program resulted in only nine foreclosures for 8500 mortgages insured in Wisconsin in 1972. The Milwaukee program, which targeted mothers receiving Aid to Dependent Children (ADC), required applicants to take classes in home buying, inspect the property personally, and have representation by a Legal Aid lawyer at the closing. Among other safeguards, the county department of social services screened all ADC mothers wishing to buy a home; religious, charitable, and civil groups helped to provide down payments on homes; FHA and the county agencies inspected homes rigorously; and real-estate and mortgage banking firms abided by the conditions set by FHA and the county agency. During that time, the FHA director in Detroit—where the worst scandals would occur—"was the hero of the whole Department," Romney recalled. "He was used to hit Milwaukee over the head . . . to say, you go out and do more."[42] The Milwaukee FHA director, Lawrence S. Katz, was fired in the summer of 1971 to make room for a Republican appointee.[43]

The fact that FHA scandals essentially closed an unparalleled window of opportunity for the implementation of aggressive, race-conscious policies on housing discrimination is rich with irony. Open-housing supporters questioned the commitment of long-time FHA employees to recent fair-housing objectives, as their careers had developed in an agency that tolerated and in earlier times encouraged segregation.[44] What is more, the FHA program to promote home ownership in largely segregated inner-city areas represented an approach that was the antithesis of "opening up the suburbs."[45] That HUD's Office of Equal Opportunity could be tarred by the brush of the scandals at FHA starkly illustrates the vulnerability of a weak institutional home.

Romney Bows Out

In 1972, Romney was a weary, frustrated man with little political capital to spend within the administration. Although the HUD chief had tried to be a good soldier since Nixon's June 1971 housing policy statement, the White House still viewed him with suspicion. Presidential advisor Ken Cole complained that HUD's actions in a dispute over the construction of low-income housing in Hempstead, N.Y., were "such a clear-cut example of how HUD is thwarting the President's policy objectives that I think we ought to give strong consideration to taking them on." The following month, Romney surprised many observers by making strong denunciations of urban renewal programs before Congress. Cole noted in an internal memo that he agreed with the HUD secretary's criticisms, "but it is so unlike [Romney] to be [taking] on this program that I wonder if there isn't a hidden trap for us somewhere."[46]

The former Michigan governor chafed at his inability to meet with the president personally so he could request greater hiring authority for HUD, a move he felt would increase program oversight and avoid further scandals. By the summer of 1972, the White House tried to appease Romney to avoid any signs of friction during the president's reelection campaign. These attempts, however, were short-lived. When the administration was criticized for inadequate attention to flood victims in Wilkes-Barre, Pa., Nixon made Romney the scapegoat, instructing the secretary to go there himself in a tersely worded order released to the media.[47]

Romney had had enough. On August 10, 1972, he wrote to the president, "Developments in recent months and days have convinced me that you are no longer interested in my counsel and advice before making policy and operating decisions directly affecting the activities of the Department I head. Consequently, I have concluded more can be accomplished in the future if the Department is headed by someone whose counsel and advice you want." Recommending that his resignation be made effective immediately, Romney suggested that he could make a greater contribution in the private sector "because national domestic problems are so controversial that their real character and solution will again be largely ignored by the parties and candidates in this year's election."[48]

Romney eventually agreed to stay until sometime after the November election, when the administration would name a replacement. During the fall, he spoke numerous times as a surrogate for Nixon in the president's reelection campaign. Some reporters expressed surprise that Romney had lasted as long as he had, given that other appointees such as HEW's Robert Finch and Interior's Walter Hickle were replaced during Nixon's first term. In Romney's November 9 letter of resignation to President Nixon, he wrote that candidates avoid significant issues in political campaigns "for fear of offending uninformed voters and thus losing votes." That is, politicians avoid important issues to avoid blame. Thus, he concluded, reform is nearly impossible without a crisis. While intending his remarks to be taken about American politics generally, Romney acknowledged in response to a reporter's question that he did not believe Nixon and Democratic candidate George McGovern had discussed the important issues in the 1972 Presidential campaign.[49]

In an editorial mixing disappointment and admiration, the *Washington Post* concluded that Romney left HUD "in no better shape than he found it—which wasn't very good." The editorial made this judgement "reluctantly of a forthright man who has our admiration for making a hard and honest effort to put the nation's urban house in order." Unfortunately, according to the *Post*, Romney faced daunting odds. For such an entity to gain the backing of Congress and localities as well as attend to the housing shortage, urban problems and the like, "a climate of national resolve" is required. Such a climate did not exist in 1972, the editorial concluded.[50] For all of his conviction about the need for desegregation, Romney was a man whose background as an auto executive and primary mandate as secretary was in production. When, in 1970, members of Congress first started to suggest that production might be slowed to afford better oversight of the programs, Romney resisted. This delay in acknowledging the severity of existing problems proved devastating to the agency.

Freezing Housing Funds

In fall 1972, the White House began to consider a moratorium on all federal housing subsidies for 1973. The following January, the outgoing HUD secretary announced that the eighteen-month moratorium would indeed take effect for all housing not already approved by HUD. As out-lined by Romney, the housing freeze consisted of a moratorium on all new commitments for subsidized housing programs (including Section 235 and 236); no new commitments for water and sewer grants, open-space land programs, and public facilities loans until Congress established a program of community development special revenue sharing under which these programs would be subsumed; and a hold (effective July 1, 1973) on all new commitments for urban renewal and Model Cities funding, as well as smaller Farmers Home Administration programs in the Agriculture Department.[51]

Romney said he was "personally delighted that the administration has decided to stop doing business as usual in these programs." Yet, one week prior to the announcement, Romney worried privately to Nixon that "the actions proposed will only be taken by the American people— and especially those in the central city—as further evidence of a hard-headed, cold-hearted indifference to the poor and racial minorities. This, in my opinion, could inflame the central cities and could contribute to eventually bringing Belfast to the streets of our cities." The White House labeled the nation's subsidized housing programs "inequitable, wasteful, and ineffective in meeting housing needs."[52] By early 1973, according to Nixon, the federal government was the outright owner of ninety thou-sand federally subsidized housing units.[53]

Prior to the moratorium, HUD made no effort to fix problems in the Section 235 and 236 programs. In fact, the agency did not develop for-mal justification for the decision until after the freeze was announced, and HUD's rationale was criticized in a March departmental memo as "paper-thin, highly subjective, and totally unsupported by any back-up data." William Lilley III, who was named deputy assistant secretary for policy development in 1973 (after covering HUD for the *National Jour-nal*), admitted that HUD's decision on the freeze had been "impressionis-tic," rather than one based on rigorous data analysis.[54]

A Congressional Research Service report criticized the methodology and findings of the HUD report at length. The economist Anthony Downs argued that criticisms of the basic designs of the Section 235 and 236 programs were often unjustified, and that the federal government could address existing problems without drastic alterations to the pro-grams or severe cutbacks in the volume of units produced under them. Critics of the moratorium noted that the highest default termination rates in multi-family programs were in Section 221(d)(2) unsubsidized loans, high default rates in the Section 235 program were confined to a few cities, and most of the 235 defaults were believed to be in older units, not newly built ones.[55]

Some members of Congress angrily accused Nixon of overstepping his

authority as president. Sen. Edward Brooke (R-MA) said that the freeze
brought forth the serious issues of "the right of the executive to refuse to
carry out programs that have been enacted into law" and "the right of
the executive to refuse to spend funds appropriated by Congress." Sen.
Harrison Williams (D-NJ) called the moratorium "blackmail" intended
to force congressional passage of the President's special revenue-sharing
proposal, which was designed to increase state and local autonomy in
spending federal funds. The president's $2.6 billion special revenue–
sharing package for community development had died in Congress in
1972.[56]

Continuing controversies over suburban integration and the spiraling
costs of building subsidized housing were clear incentives for the president to declare the freeze. In retrospect, Samuel Simmons, HUD's Equal
Opportunity chief during the first Nixon Administration, believes that
the White House declared the freeze so it would have "one less little nit-
picking headache to deal with."[57] During Nixon's first term, housing
subsidy outlays increased five-fold, with nearly $2 billion allocated in fis-
cal 1973, as federal subsidized housing starts jumped from 91,400 in
1967 to a peak of approximately 430,000 in both 1970 and 1971. By
the middle of Nixon's first term, Ambrose recounts, "the economy was
drowning. The causes were continued inflation, continued high unemployment, a looming trade imbalance, and an international monetary
crisis, featuring a dollar under attack by speculators because of inflation,
unemployment, and the trade imbalance."[58] The scandals in the mortgage subsidy programs gave Nixon the justification for decimating the
agency's controversial and expensive efforts to aid private housing construction and push for desegregation.

To replace Romney, Nixon named Undersecretary of Commerce
James T. Lynn, a Republican loyalist. Senator William Proxmire, one of
three Senators on the fifteen-member Banking, Housing, and Urban
Affairs Committee to vote against the nomination, criticized Lynn as
"unqualified, having no understanding of cities' problems, and being appointed to carry out the President's plan to gut the subsidized housing
programs."[59] Most of HUD's institutional activists had departed by the
time Lynn took over. When Nixon rescinded the moratorium in the summer of 1974, the window of opportunity for substantial progress in residential integration had closed. Congress passed the Housing and Community Development Act of 1974 under new President Gerald Ford. The
legislation emphasized local prerogatives in the use of federal funds and
did not reflect a serious attempt to address racial and economic segregation in suburbia. Ford himself certainly felt no compunction to do so.
When asked about his views on "open housing," Ford responded, "I
would not use that term to describe any of my policies, period. I do feel

that an ethnic heritage is a great treasure of this country, and I don't think that Federal action should be used to destroy that ethnic treasure."[60] The 1974 law continued Sections 235 and 236 at drastically reduced levels of funding, and relied heavily on the Section 8 program, which provided direct subsidies to tenants for rent. Users of Section 8 infrequently made pro-integrative moves. (See chapter 6 for a more detailed discussion.)[61]

WHY DID NIXON GO AFTER HOUSING?

The weak institutional home for civil rights did not *cause* the housing moratorium and resulting end to suburban integration initiatives. Yet if civil rights enforcement had been situated in a stand-alone agency—as envisioned in the 1966 Fair Housing Act that passed the House before stalling in the Senate—aggressive desegregation efforts would have been considerably more likely. This fair-housing board would have had a lessened risk of losing legitimacy, since scandals in other agencies presumably could not have been used to tarnish its own reputation. Moreover, Nixon would have faced a higher-stakes political gamble had he chosen to attack the fair housing agency directly. In fact, even if the Office of Equal Opportunity remained within HUD but had funding cut-off authority, it might have developed its own separate identity, and this may well have resulted in a different sequence of agency actions and White House responses. One might have seen the Office of Equal Opportunity acting in similar fashion to HEW's Office for Civil Rights, battling publicly with the White House as agency employees tried to carry out desegregation plans. In the case of school desegregation, the Nixon White House appeared to be most concerned with publicizing its opposition to busing and with shifting the political burden of desegregation to Congress or the courts. It is a good guess that Nixon would have attempted a similar strategy in housing, had the position of HUD's civil rights office within the agency more closely resembled that of OCR.

The actual historical circumstances provoke reconsideration of Nixon's actions in civil rights. Nixon had the image of a politician playing to white racial resentment amidst rapid civil rights gains and increasing violence in urban areas. At the same time, he oversaw the greatest increases in school desegregation and was a central figure in the entrenchment of affirmative action in employment. Presidential speechwriter Pat Buchanan wrote that Nixon "is viewed as the quintessential political pragmatist, standing before an ideological buffet, picking some from this tray and some from that. On both sides he is seen as the textbook political transient, here today, gone tomorrow, shuttling back and forth, as weather permits, between liberal programs and conservative rhetoric."[62]

In terms of political strategy, the Philadelphia Plan to integrate the construction trades was his masterstroke. The original version of the plan, put forward during the Johnson Administration, was declared illegal by the comptroller general in the General Accounting Office, because it did not include specific minimum standards for affirmative action set forth prior to bidding. The Nixon Administration revived the Philadelphia Plan, requiring prospective construction contractors to select a specific minority hiring goal within ranges provided in the invitation for bids. The administration described these percentages as targets rather than quotas; employers who did not reach their targets would have to show that they had made a "good faith" effort to reach the target.[63] Civil rights skeptics might accept this initiative as a narrowly targeted effort aimed at the notoriously discriminatory construction industry that would widen the pool of potential workers and thus lower construction costs and housing prices. As recalled by domestic policy advisor John Ehrlichman and noted by many scholars, Nixon viewed the Philadelphia Plan as a means of causing rifts between African Americans and labor, two core constituencies of the Democratic Party.[64] In early 1970, the Labor Department expanded affirmative action requirements to all federal contractors, and affirmative action in employment received judicial backing in the Supreme Court's *Griggs v. Duke Power Co.* (1971) decision.

Despite his pivotal role in establishing racial goals and timetables in employment, Nixon was able to label Democrats as the party of race and quotas in his 1972 reelection campaign.[65] In an October 1972 radio address, Nixon offered reassurances to whites who were tagged racist. "When a mother sees her child taken away from a neighborhood school and transported miles away, and she objects to that, I don't think it is right to charge her with bigotry. When young people apply for jobs—in politics or in industry—and find the door closed because they don't fit into some numerical quota, despite their ability, and they object, I do not think it is right to condemn these young people as insensitive or racist."[66]

For all of Nixon's inflammatory rhetoric, the White House only intervened once to delay busing. The administration shifted its enforcement emphasis from funding cut-offs to suits in federal court, so that the judiciary, rather than the executive branch, would receive blame for continued busing orders. When the Supreme Court's *Alexander v. Holmes County* decision ordered that dual school systems must be abandoned "at once," rather than granting the "reasonable" delay that the administration had originally requested, the president and his aides had no problems with the verdict, since it made the courts responsible for integration.[67]

While Nixon's primary objective was to avoid political damage from school desegregation initiatives, he raged at the Supreme Court's decisions on this issue and tried to change the political stance of the court through the appointment process. To replace the departing Abe Fortas in 1969, Nixon nominated Clement Haynsworth, a federal judge from South Carolina who fulfilled Nixon's desire for a conservative, strict constructionist from the South. Civil rights and labor groups lobbied strongly against the nomination, and Senate probes revealed financial conflicts of interests in several of Haynsworth's cases. The Senate rejected the nomination, 55 to 45. Nixon then proceeded to nominate G. Harrold Carswell, "almost out of spite," Nixon speechwriter William Safire recalled.[68] Another strict constructionist Southerner, Carswell had a record marred by racism and incompetence. The Senate defeated his nomination as well. Nixon blamed bias against Southerners for the dual rejections.[69] At least with respect to school busing, Nixon may have had the last laugh: all four of his Supreme Court appointees (Justices Burger, Rehnquist, Powell, and Blackmun) voted with the majority in 1974's *Milliken v. Bradley*, often seen as the decision signaling the end of aggressive desegregation. (Nixon was probably not, in fact, laughing, as the decision was handed down less than a month prior to his resignation as president.) In some sense, court appointments are the epitome of presidential blame avoidance: one stands a good chance of affecting political outcomes but is unlikely to receive blame for unpopular court decisions.

Concerns with blame avoidance also appear in White House deliberations over open housing policies. Laying out administration options in a March 1971 memo on housing, civil rights advisor Len Garment noted that there is "gathering momentum toward indiscriminate zoning invalidation (i.e., on economic as well as racial grounds)." John Ehrlichman scribbled in the margin, "If courts so rule ok—but the Admin. [should] not be party to this."[70] The interest in the creation of metropolitan housing agencies also reflected the paramount interest in avoiding blame and lowering political risk. Nixon's indirect halt to civil rights efforts suggests the same motive. The administration had a scandal to justify the housing moratorium, though it did not even try to address problems in the subsidized housing programs before freezing them. Nixon did not point to the controversial suburban integration policies in justifying the moratorium, despite being "fixated" (in John Ehrlichman's recollection) during his reelection campaign on publicizing his opposition to "forced integration" in housing and education.[71]

Nixon's great caution was exemplified by his decision to wait until after his reelection to enact the freeze. With the political playing field as it was, Nixon did not need to take that gamble in the fall of 1972. In May 1972, after having finished second in the Wisconsin Democratic primaries,

George Wallace was paralyzed by an assassin's bullet. He won the Maryland and Michigan primaries the day after being shot, but his days of being a real threat to Nixon's right flank were over.[72] Thus, Nixon probably saw little benefit in risking attacks from the McGovern camp for a housing freeze, given the imposing housing shortages that still existed and the array of interests that benefited from the infusion of federal funds. For example, a December 1971 HUD memo warned against substantial cutbacks to the Section 235 program: "This program is bread and butter for the builders. As such a sharp reduction from 1972 levels could have severe political repercussions among builders and allied groups."[73]

Finally, the freeze strategy itself bears mention. Nixon attempted the same strategy in education, asking Congress in March 1972 to place a moratorium (until July 1973) on new busing orders by the courts while it considered legislative approaches to the busing issue.[74] The proposed legislation would have let existing orders stand. Congress did not enact the freeze, but as John Ehrlichman recalled, "Whether Congress passed the busing moratorium was not as important as that the American people understood that Richard Nixon opposed busing as much as they did."[75] A freeze appears less extreme than declaring a permanent end to school busing or housing aid. It is a temporary halt, a time-out, rather than a seemingly permanent change in course. This maneuver, too, can be viewed as a means of diminishing blame that might accrue to the president.

How does the case of housing add to our understanding of Nixon's civil rights policies? According to Kotlowski, Nixon crafted a record of "moderate deeds matched against reactionary words."[76] Nixon seemed to flip this formula on its head with the housing freeze, a case in which the deeds reached considerably beyond the words. While the historical record does not show conclusively that suburban integration controversies drove the decision to declare the freeze, the continued concern in the White House over HUD's initiatives in this area suggests that it was an important consideration. If the White House was only concerned about scandals in inner-city housing programs, it could have acted in a targeted manner in this area, rather than indiscriminately halting virtually all federal involvement in housing.

Graham argues that Nixon, free from the sorts of ideological boundaries that a Goldwater or Rockefeller faced and "little interested in the substance of domestic policy beyond its political repercussions, . . . was free to tailor his policies on civil rights to maximize their political payoff."[77] Taking into consideration his actions in the three main areas of civil rights (housing, education, and employment), it becomes apparent that Nixon was not concerned with maximizing his political payoff so much as hedging his bets. More important to him than receiving credit was avoiding blame. It is in this context that one can understand that Nixon saved his harshest treatment for housing integration efforts, though they were less publicized and less aggressive than attempts in employment and education. Because of the weak institutional home for civil rights within HUD, and the scandals that plagued the agency, Nixon found a target that was susceptible in ways that other civil rights bureaucracies were not.

To be sure, political pragmatism, rather than ideology, primarily motivated Nixon. But his decision to freeze housing funds and indirectly stall desegregation efforts *after* his reelection begs for an explanation that goes further than one emphasizing "the primacy of reelection politics."[78] In terms of vote-seeking, the controversial housing moratorium offered little in the way of political dividends. It did, however, allow him to forestall blame in at least two ways. With the timing of the freeze, Nixon did not risk losing votes from constituencies that benefited from federal housing funds (builders, the mortgage industry, and so on). At the same time, he was able to avoid a repeat of the school busing scenario, in which the judiciary fueled highly unpopular desegregation efforts. While Nixon was able to deflect enough blame from these controversies to ensure his reelection, he engendered considerable public animosity from his failure to stop the imposition of busing plans.

As courts began to back residential desegregation remedies, Nixon certainly did not relish undergoing similar political damage—to his legacy, if not to any future election prospects—in the area of housing. With HUD ill-equipped to offer much resistance, the housing freeze gave Nixon a means of evading this potential damage without enduring attacks for reversing civil rights gains. In retrospect, the Nixon Administration squandered a prime opportunity to chip away at the cornerstone of racial inequality, residential segregation. With federal housing funds dwindling and courts tempering their support for civil rights agencies in the post-Nixon era, an opportunity of that magnitude has not arisen since the 1973 housing freeze.

Chapter Six

The Recent Past, Present, and Future
of Residential Desegregation

OVER THE PAST three decades, federal efforts encouraging housing desegregation have been scattershot and lacking in ambition. HUD's continued problems with legitimacy, fueled by numerous scandals in the 1980s, have not helped the chances for a greater federal commitment to desegregation. The agency's inability to administer its programs effectively was exacerbated by congressional actions during this decade, when it dramatically expanded the number of HUD-administered programs—from fifty-four in 1980 to over two hundred in 1992—while cutting funding from $35 billion in 1980 to $25 billion in 1990. In 1994, a National Academy of Public Administration study commissioned by Congress recommended that if HUD was not running "in an effective, accountable manner" within five years, "the president and Congress should seriously consider dismantling [the agency] and moving its core programs elsewhere."[1] While the agency survived that threat, it steps lightly in contentious areas such as residential integration.

One reason for this timidity is that the political landscape has changed to reflect a steep decline in national concern about racial issues, particularly with regard to residential desegregation. In the years since the Nixon Administration, courts have been substantially less supportive of bold civil rights policies. Federal policy on low-income housing has evolved to rely on vouchers, block grants, and credits, rather than on subsidized housing production.[2] It is certainly possible to encourage some residential desegregation through these policy tools. The Moving to Opportunity demonstration project, discussed later, is one example of using vouchers to promote integration. Metropolitan-level block grants, with requirements to encourage economic and racial desegregation, continue to represent a promising strategy.

On the whole, federal initiatives have been far less extensive than what is necessary to combat this ongoing problem. The inadequacy of these efforts is particularly important because continued inattention to residential segregation exacerbates racial disadvantage in employment and education as well as in neighborhoods. While civil rights efforts in all three areas have become more difficult due to declining resources, proliferating missions, and a less sympathetic judiciary, the weak institu-

tional home for civil rights in housing continues to place especially serious obstacles in the way of residential desegregation efforts.

The Fair Housing Amendments Act of 1988

Soon after passage of the Civil Rights Act of 1968, fair housing supporters were calling for upgraded enforcement machinery. One housing consultant compared the original 1968 legislation to "a no-parking zone
with a $2 ticket. I don't know anybody who would hesitate to park un-
der those circumstances."[3] This much-needed strengthening of fair housing laws was a long time in coming, as the congressional push for
amendments to the Fair Housing Act began in 1977. The House passed
strengthening amendments in 1980, but that legislation died in the Senate.[4] Finally, in 1988, Congress passed the Fair Housing Amendments
Act. Because both the House and Senate overwhelmingly voted for the
bill, President Reagan realized the futility of a veto and signed it into
law.

The law patched up some of the major gaps in the original Fair Housing Act of 1968. Among other provisions, the amendments permitted
complaints of discrimination to be filed up to two years after the alleged
occurrence, rather than the 180-day limit specified in the original law;
allowed prevailing plaintiffs to recover attorney's fees and court costs;
created a streamlined hearing process for trying cases before an administrative law judge; and empowered these judges to order full compensation for damages, in addition to civil fines of up to $10,000 for the first
offense and $50,000 for the third offense.[5] Moreover, the legislation au-
thorized the attorney general to seek monetary damages on an individual's behalf (to "vindicate the public interest") and to seek penalties of
$50,000 for a first conviction and $100,000 for subsequent convictions
in "pattern and practice" cases.

HUD investigations and complaint resolutions became subject to
strict time limits under the 1988 amendments. In addition, Congress
gave HUD secretaries the ability to begin investigations even in the absence of private suits and file complaints with the attorney general, who
was required to act promptly. The attorney general was also authorized
to file a civil action for breaches of conciliation agreements, and was required to prosecute cases of aggrieved parties when defendants elected
to try their cases in federal district court rather than before an administrative law judge. After the 1988 act went into effect, the Justice Department began to file far more civil fair housing cases, from roughly
fifteen in the years before the act to a peak of 194 in 1994.[6] The legislation also added two protected classes, based on family status (those

with children) and disability, to fair housing law; states and localities with "substantially equivalent" laws to enforce fair housing protection were given forty months to change their laws to comply.[7] While the 1988 amendments were much needed, and added to the arsenal of weapons for the federal government to fight residential discrimination, the law mainly benefited individual victims, rather than helping to root out systemic patterns of discrimination. More importantly, other essential elements remain absent: namely, political will, and desegregation becoming a top priority at the Office of Fair Housing and Equal Opportunity (FHEO, formerly the Office of Equal Opportunity) and in HUD agency-wide.

PRO-INTEGRATIVE MOBILITY PROGRAMS

Small-scale attempts to encourage integration have yielded some promising signs. Perhaps the best known governmental effort to encourage residential racial integration was the Gautreaux program in the Chicago area. The program was the result of a 1976 Supreme Court consent decree springing from a 1969 lawsuit brought by public housing residents against HUD and the Chicago Housing Authority, charging the agencies with racial discrimination in the administration of the city's public housing program. The Chicago Housing Authority was found to have used separate public housing waiting lists for black and white families so that they could be steered to same-race neighborhoods. From 1954 to 1966, 99.4 percent of the CHA's 10,256 family units were sited in predominantly black neighborhoods.[8] The Gautreaux ruling defined the relevant housing market as the Chicago metropolitan area, rather than stopping at city limits. This logic ran counter to the Supreme Court's reasoning in *Milliken v. Bradley* (418 U.S. 717), in which the high court overturned a federal court order that Detroit-area school desegregation be carried out on a metropolitan (city-suburb) basis.[9]

The nonprofit Leadership Council for Metropolitan Open Communities, a pro-integrative group that formed in the wake of Martin Luther King's 1966 open-housing protests in Chicago, ran the Gautreaux program, which gave Section 8 housing vouchers to public housing residents and people on the waiting list. The key departure from the standard Section 8 program was that Gautreaux participants received extensive counseling services that informed them of a range of housing options. Housing placement counselors notified families as apartments became available, discussed the advantages and disadvantages of moving to specific locations, and took them to visit housing units and localities. From 1976 to 1998, the program helped more than 7,100 families move from public housing or avoid being placed in it. More than half of the families moved to middle-income suburbs with an average population that was 96 percent white, while others moved to low-income, predominantly black neighborhoods within Chicago city limits.[10]

The program provided revealing evidence of the effects of neighborhood environment on life outcomes, since families who moved to white suburbs were selected in an essentially random manner. While the program did exclude families with more than four children or histories of large debts or unacceptable housekeeping, eliminating roughly 30 percent of eligible families, participants were not a highly selective group: all were very low-income African Americans who currently or formerly received welfare benefits and had lived most of their lives in poor inner-city neighborhoods.[11]

In several studies of this program, Rosenbaum and his colleagues examined adult employment patterns and children's school experiences among suburban movers and city movers. In employment, suburban and city movers started from roughly the same baseline, with 64.3 percent and 60.2 percent employment prior to moving, respectively. Among previously employed movers, suburban residents were 14 percent more likely to hold a job after moving. For individuals who had never held a job previously, 46.2 percent found employment after moving to the suburbs, compared to 30.2 percent of city movers. Both city and suburban movers experienced wage gains of roughly 20 percent after moving out of public housing projects.[12]

Children moving to the suburbs typically had difficulty in their social and academic adjustment to their new schools, and their grades slipped somewhat in their first few years there.[13] By the time they reached age eighteen, however, the suburban children had pronounced advantages over their city counterparts. Suburban movers had significantly better outcomes than city movers on a number of measures, including taking a college preparatory curriculum (40 versus 24 percent), attending college (54 versus 21 percent), and attending a four-year college (27 versus 4 percent). For those not in college, 75 percent of suburban movers were employed full-time, compared to 41 percent of city movers, and over four times as likely to earn more than $6.50 per hour. The Gautreaux program ended in September 1998 when the consent decree expired.

THE MOVING TO OPPORTUNITY EXPERIMENT

In an attempt to replicate the successes of the Gautreaux program in other cities, the 1992 Housing and Community Development Act provided funding for tenant-based rental assistance and supportive counseling services to "assist very low-income families with children who reside in public housing or housing receiving project-based assistance under Section 8 of the Housing and Community Development Act of 1937 to move out of areas with high concentrations of persons in poverty to areas with low concentrations of such persons."[14]

Most observers agree that the Section 8 program represents an improvement over public housing in that less than 15 percent of Section 8 recipients live in high-poverty neighborhoods (more than 30 percent poor), compared to nearly 54 percent of public housing residents. Margery Turner, the director of the Metropolitan Housing and Communities Policy Center at the Urban Institute, notes that Section 8 has "tremendous potential to be a positive force, but also to be ineffective and harmful." If Section 8 is to encourage integration and promote real mobility choices for recipients, "we can't leave it to its own devices."[15] Instead, these mobility vouchers must be accompanied by counseling to inform recipients of the range of housing options they have at their disposal. In the absence of such counseling, families tend to remain close to their former homes, often in high-poverty neighborhoods.

To establish the Moving to Opportunity (MTO) demonstration, Congress appropriated roughly $70 million for about 1,300 Section 8 rental assistance payments, and a small additional amount for housing counseling. Of sixteen potential sites that submitted applications to take part in the MTO program, HUD selected five—Baltimore, Boston, Chicago, Los Angeles, and New York City—to participate in March 1994. In 1995, Congress rescinded a second year of funding. Nevertheless, Section 8 rental assistance payments and counseling resources grew because housing authorities in Los Angeles, Boston, and later New York voluntarily added Section 8 certificates and vouchers from their own Section 8 programs to the MTO demonstration. The MTO programs established partnerships between local public housing authorities (which administer Section 8 rental assistance) and one or more local, nonprofit counseling organizations, which help participating families find appropriate units and encourage landlords to participate in the program.

Family enrollment began in fall 1994. Participants came from neighborhoods in which at least 40 percent of the population was poor; they had to have at least one child, and be income-eligible for the Section 8 program. The program specified that at least 90 percent of families in the MTO treatment group move into low-poverty areas, defined as those with less than 10 percent of the population below the poverty line in 1989. The program also tracked a comparison group of individuals who received geographically unrestricted Section 8 vouchers and no special counseling assistance from the housing authority, and an in-place control group who continued to receive project-based assistance rather than certificates or vouchers. The demonstration ended in spring 1999, with 1,820 families assigned to the MTO treatment group, 1,350 to the Section 8 comparison group, and 1,440 to the in-place control group. With regard to the eligible populations of the first two groups, 860 families in the treatment group and 816 in the comparison group moved into new homes under the program. According to HUD, except for some initial resistance in Baltimore, lease-ups by MTO families did not provoke any indications of community concern or opposition. None of the MTO families reported experiencing racial violence or hostility after moving to one of the sites.[16]

HUD data reveal that the MTO treatment group was not a "creamed" population, as this cohort had lower initial employment rates and median income than non-MTO households in the study. Three-quarters of the families in the treatment group moved to areas with less than 10 percent of the population in poverty; in comparison, only 14.5 percent of the Section 8 group did so. Early interview data indicated that respondents most often cited increased safety as their motivation for moving to suburban neighborhoods. The majority of movers—both in the experimental and Section 8 comparison group—believe that leaving public housing has improved their quality of life and life chances.[17]

The results of several preliminary site studies are promising. In Los Angeles, 27.5 percent of MTO movers felt very safe in their neighborhood, compared to 10.1 percent in the control group. In Boston, rates of severe asthma attacks for MTO children were half those for non-movers. There is also some evidence from the Baltimore site that MTO children's reading and math scores on standardized tests improved to a statistically significant degree.[18] Assuming that further research also reveals measurable improvements in the lives of MTO families, this voucher-based strategy, if practiced on a modest scale, represents a politically feasible means of encouraging some level of economic and racial integration. Voucher programs rely to a lesser degree on centralized administration than programs such as the federal housing subsidies examined in this book. As a result, a weak institutional home presumably would present less of an impediment to effective implementation of a voucher program.

STATE AND LOCAL DESEGREGATION EFFORTS

State governments, given the increasing dominance of suburban members in their legislatures, have been reluctant to promote suburban integration. When they have, their focus has been on economic rather than racial integration. In 1969, Massachusetts adopted its "anti-snob" law, which allows developers of low- and moderate-income housing to appeal to a state board if a town has denied a building permit. This board has the power to override the locality and issue the permit. California and Oregon both have a "fair-share" requirement for localities to provide housing options for lower-income households; neither state addresses racial patterns. New York had an ambitious plan that attempted to override local zoning exclusions and encourage production of below-market housing on a major scale. The Urban Development Corporation, created in 1968 to pursue these goals, was weakened substantially by the state legislature in 1973 and went bankrupt two years later.[19]

New Jersey has addressed the shortage of low- and moderate-income housing most prominently. New Jersey's Fair Housing Act of 1985, which was the legislature's response to the body of state Supreme Court decisions known as the Mount Laurel cases, created the Council on Affordable Housing (COAH). In these decisions, the New Jersey Supreme Court established a constitutional obligation for each of the state's 566 municipalities to create a realistic opportunity for the provision of fair-share low- and moderate-income housing obligations, typically via land use and zoning powers. According to COAH estimates in September 2004, the opportunity for roughly 66,600 housing units has been put in place, including 34,900 units that have been built or are under construction. Under the state Fair Housing Act, municipalities can sell off up to half of their fair housing obligations to other municipalities. Because of this provision, and because issues of race have not been a primary consideration, the state has not experienced significant increases in racial integration of towns and neighborhoods as a result of this policy.[20]

On the local level, a very small fraction of suburban towns facing racial change have enacted policies to maintain residential racial diversity. There are formidable obstacles to the successful enactment of these policies. Some of the elected officials who have espoused such policies "have found their political careers threatened or actually ended by white voter backlash."[21] Moreover, the issue is vulnerable to attack from numerous constituencies across the political spectrum, including realtors, black residents, and civil rights groups. Those supporting these policies must act quickly, as the policy windows for adoption are open only for brief periods of time, after which the initiatives will be unlikely to forestall resegregation. In addition, success is difficult to maintain if nearby towns are unwilling to adopt pro-integrative policies as well. Nevertheless, towns have good reasons for adopting pro-integrative policies. After families of color have moved in, localities may face two alternatives: do nothing and watch the town resegregate as whites move out, or attempt to create a multiracial community that remains an attractive place to live for residents of all races.

Yet only a small number of urban neighborhoods and suburban towns have attempted to promote stable racial balance in their communities. These residential diversity efforts (formerly called integration mainte-nance schemes) typically involve the following: regulatory ordinances, such as bans on "for sale" signs, close monitoring of real-estate firms for racial steering and other illegal activities, and strict enforcement of hous-ing codes; financial incentives, such as mortgage incentives for pro-integrative moves, loans for housing rehabilitation, and equity assurance guarantees to protect against decreasing property values; and civic pro-motion, including creation of municipal housing offices, support for fair-housing groups, and advertising to attract potential home buyers. Neighborhood groups in Brooklyn, Denver, Philadelphia, Washington, Milwaukee, Indianapolis, New Haven, Akron, and Rochester have acted to maintain racial diversity.[22] Municipally run efforts have been attempted in, among other towns, Park Forest, Ill., Oak Park, Ill., Cleveland Heights, Ohio; Shaker Heights, Ohio; Teaneck, N.J.; Maplewood/South Orange, N.J.; Freeport, N.Y.; Oak Park, Mich.; Southfield, Mich.; University City, Mo.; Willingboro, N.J.; and Bloomfield, Conn.[23]

Suburban towns have typically been more successful than urban neighborhoods, for several likely reasons: the age of housing, which is correlated with segregation levels, is typically younger in suburbs than in cities; governmental resources and authority are helpful; a greater por-tion of homes tend to be owner-occupied, thus preserving more class sta-bility and permitting easier monitoring of real-estate practices; families in suburban towns may be more reluctant to move if they own their own homes; and a number of families may have already moved once from a changing city neighborhood, and do not wish to move a second time. Keating's study of the ways in which Cleveland suburbs have addressed (or failed to address) residential integration, and the prospect of resegre-gation, attempts to account for variation in local responses. He argues, "Key factors that determine whether or not suburbs accept or resist racial transition and whether they adopt affirmative fair housing practices in-clude the rate and pace of racial transition, the type of housing stock available and its price, the attitudes of the population toward open hous-ing, the position of the local government and the public schools, the role of civic leaders and community organizations, support for fair housing organizations, and the activities of the real estate industry."

The federal government has been reluctant to intervene at the local level, though it has occasionally chosen to sue municipalities or to condi-tion or cut off aid for violations of fair-housing law. Federal intervention has taken place "only when violations have been both overt and prov-able, and even then action has often been taken only after intense lobby-ing by fair-housing organizations demanding federal intervention."[24]

Such blatant violations led the federal government to intervene in Parma, Ohio, a Cleveland suburb with a long history of resistance to nonwhite residents. The Department of Justice's Civil Rights Division reached a settlement with Parma in which the town agreed to open a new housing office staffed by two employees of a local fair housing organization, implement an affirmative marketing program for minorities, and provide approximately $1 million in mortgage aid and apartment renovation loans to attract nonwhite families to the town.[25] In 1980, U.S. District Court Judge Frank J. Battisti found the city guilty of violating the Fair Housing Act. At the time, African Americans comprised an estimated 0.4 percent of the town's population, or 370 black individuals out of a total population of 92,548. Eighteen years later, estimates from a national market-research firm pegged the black population at 1,046, or 1.2 percent of town residents. Despite inducements, African Americans are still largely reluctant to move to this historically hostile town.[26] In recent years, the Justice Department has also reached settlements with the Illinois towns of Addison, Cicero, and Waukegan, as well as Fresno, California.

The news on the local level is not entirely discouraging, however. Some recent scholarship has questioned the conventional wisdom that racially integrated neighborhoods are very rare and, where they exist, prone to rapid resegregation. Ellen finds that nearly one-fifth of all U.S. neighborhoods were racially mixed in 1990, and that over three-quarters of the neighborhoods that were integrated in 1980 remained so a decade later. Roughly 15 percent of non-Hispanic whites and almost one-third of blacks live in racially mixed neighborhoods (defined as being 10 to 50 percent black). The percentage of whites who live in neighborhoods with virtually no blacks (less than 1 percent) declined from 62.6 in 1970, to 48.5 in 1980, and 35.6 in 1990.[27]

Ellen argues that white avoidance of mixed neighborhoods cannot be reduced to racial or class prejudice, or even a combination of the two. Instead, she proposes a "race-based neighborhood stereotyping hypothesis," which asserts that when whites are convinced that mixed neighborhoods will remain racially stable and maintain high neighborhood quality, they are typically willing to live with black neighbors. (The inferior quality of black neighborhoods in comparison with white ones largely disappears when socioeconomic factors are controlled.) This research indicates that whites ultimately care less about the racial composition of their neighborhood than about various quality of life indicators, such as public safety, school quality, community stability, and property value accumulation (in the case of homeowners). Whites, however, often use the racial composition of a neighborhood as a proxy for its quality.

Neighborhoods that remain stably integrated tend to be ones that have been stable for a relatively long period, are not very close to an area's center of black population concentration, and have a high proportion of rental housing. In addition, these neighborhoods are typically part of a thriving housing market, offer a secure set of neighborhood amenities, and are located in a metropolitan area that lacks a history of intense racial competition for housing.[28] Metropolitan areas that have relatively smaller black populations and lower levels of segregation, and do not have a legacy of widespread neighborhood change, are more likely to contain stably integrated neighborhoods. Despite these findings, the fact remains that progress in residential integration has been painfully slow. For African Americans in particular, it is unlikely that segregation levels will drop substantially without more ambitious governmental action to battle discrimination and greater incentives for localities to encourage racially and economically integrated housing.

The Effects of Residential Segregation on Education and Employment

The impact of the segmented housing market on employment and education increases the costs of residential segregation for African Americans. Gary Orfield, the premier authority on school desegregation, argues that it is impossible to understand the issues involved with school desegregation efforts without close attention to the dynamics of residential segregation. The task of creating integrated schools is considerably more complex in the face of intensely segregated neighborhoods and, even more importantly, the common situation of largely nonwhite cities ringed by overwhelmingly white suburbs.[29]

In Atlanta, Chicago, New Orleans, Newark, and Washington, D.C., fewer than 5 percent of the schoolmates of black students are white. Between 1968 and 1988, the proportion of white students declined more than 35 percentage points in Birmingham, Boston, Dallas, Houston, Long Beach, Los Angeles, Milwaukee, and Seattle, and by at least 25 percentage points in an additional ten cities. Whereas the potential for racial integration within school districts in 1968 was great, "further efforts by districts can at best achieve marginal improvement today. Only the movement of students across district boundaries, either through interdistrict integration or changes in housing patterns, can significantly reduce the racial isolation of Black students" in any of the regions in the United States. Because the Supreme Court's 1974 *Milliken v. Bradley* decision made these interdistrict remedies very difficult to enact, in Rivkin's widely shared view, the easing of housing segregation is "the only viable way to integrate the schools."[30]

The residential segregation and confinement of large chunks of the African American population to central cities has serious consequences for employment prospects as well. After World War II, more than 80 percent of new employment in manufacturing, retail and wholesale trade, and selected services was located in suburban areas. Central-city residents have greater difficulty in discovering existing job opportunities than do suburban residents. When they do acquire jobs in the suburbs, their effective wages decline due to increased transportation time and expenses.[31] While some scholars have questioned the importance of the "spatial mismatch" between the location of jobs and one's place of residence, there is little dispute that social networks—which may be severely limited by a racially and economically isolated living environment—are an important determinant of one's job prospects, especially for low-skilled workers.[32]

ANTIDISCRIMINATION POLICIES IN EMPLOYMENT AND EDUCATION AFTER NIXON

Whereas residential desegregation never really got off the ground, affirmative action in employment has survived its share of political scuffles. School desegregation initiatives have lagged in the face of judicial backpedaling, the atrophied political will of Congress and the White House, and often-demoralized agency staffers lacking in resources and saddled with widely divergent responsibilities.[33] While school desegregation battles played out, sometimes in agonizing fashion, in numerous localities across the nation, the decade after the 1974 *Milliken* decision saw little action at the federal level. With Ronald Reagan in the presidency, the Civil Rights Division in the Department of Justice began attempts to end busing plans in a number of localities, including Norfolk, Va.; Savannah, Ga.; Seattle; and Oklahoma City. In 1986, Norfolk became the first school district to be freed from court desegregation orders.[34]

The Supreme Court came down with three major decisions in the 1990s that "undermined the legal apparatus underpinning court-ordered desegregation plans."[35] In 1991's *Board of Education of Oklahoma City v. Dowell* (498 U.S. 237), the Supreme Court ruled that a school district could be released from court oversight if there was sufficient evidence to show that "the vestiges of past discrimination had been eliminated to the extent practicable." One year later, the High Court decided in *Freeman v. Pitts* (503 U.S. 467) that individual elements of school desegregation plans could be evaluated and eliminated separately, and that school boards are not obligated to address racial disparities that exist after they have removed all vestiges of legal segregation. In 1995's *Missouri v. Jenkins* (515 U.S. 70), the Supreme Court rejected a lower court decision finding that desegregation remedies must continue until they produce beneficial results for black students. School segregation hits its low point in 1988, and has been rising since then. This trend of school resegregation coincided with the Supreme Court adopting a markedly more conservative viewpoint, and the absence of any new initiatives to encourage school desegregation over the past thirty years.[36]

A symbolic punctuation to the withdrawal of the judiciary from mandated school desegregation occurred in spring 2002, when the Supreme Court declined without comment any further review of school desegregation efforts in the Charlotte-Mecklenburg County (North Carolina) school system. The Supreme Court's 1971 *Swann v. Charlotte-Mecklenburg* was a watershed in school desegregation history. That decision approved a federal district judge's order for an extensive busing program throughout a 550-square-mile school district in North Carolina, and upheld the permissibility of using busing, alteration of school attendance zones, and pairing of noncontiguous zones as remedies to end segregation (see chapter 2). Thirty years later, the more conservative court evinced little taste for such judicial activism.[37]

Reversing the tide of race-conscious policies directly (rather than indirectly through court appointments) has proven quite a bit more difficult for the executive branch. As the Reagan Administration discovered, undoing affirmative action policies in employment is no simple task. William French Smith, Reagan's appointee as attorney general, advocated a view of equal employment law that afforded relief only to individual victims of proven intentional discrimination. Within the Justice Department's Civil Rights Division, seventy-five division attorneys—over half of its lawyers—signed a statement opposing the policies of William Bradford Reynolds, the assistant attorney general for civil rights. One attorney in the division reported, "When we—that is, the division—lose in court, all the attorneys go up and down the hall cheering because we feel we really won."[38] Civil rights advocacy groups, which had historically sought support from the Civil Rights Division, became so incensed that NAACP general counsel Thomas I. Atkins suggested at a congressional hearing that the division be dismantled and its responsibilities dispersed to other federal agencies.

The Reagan Administration substantially reduced funding and staffing for the EEOC and the Office of Federal Contract Compliance Programs (its name had been amended during the Carter era). At the OFCCP, the Reagan Administration proposed that the threshold for a mandatory affirmative action plan be changed from contractors with at least fifty employees and contracts worth at least $50,000, to firms with at least 250

employees and $1 million or more in contracts. Such a change, if imple-
mented, would have covered only 4,000 of the 17,000 firms that were
doing business with the government at the time. This proposed change
came after a period during which the OFCCP had become more aggressive. Between 1965 and 1980, the agency had debarred twenty-seven
companies from contracting with the federal government; thirteen of
those debarments took place under the Carter Administration.[39]

In formulating its proposals to change civil rights enforcement in employment, the administration did not consult with the EEOC. In the first
half of the 1980s, the EEOC reached settlements with large corporations
that the agency had begun investigating during the prior decade for discriminating against racial minorities and women. Among the most high-
profile cases were a $23 million conciliation agreement with Ford Motor
Company, a $2 million settlement with the Associated Press, and a $42.4
million settlement with General Motors and the United Auto Workers;
the latter settlement was the largest nonlitigated EEOC settlement to
date. All of these settlements included the implementation of significant
affirmative action programs. During this decade, the agency also began
to focus more attention on discrimination against older and immigrant
workers.[40]

At the same time, internal conflicts became more pronounced. A 1984
story in the *Washington Post* describes heated battles between two
groups of employees. The group devoted to "compliance" focused on investigating and resolving the roughly 75,000 job discrimination complaints that came in annually by closing them, negotiating settlements,
or referring them to agency attorneys. The agency's more aggressive staff
of attorneys pursued the separate mission of developing far-reaching discrimination cases to bring to court. Compared to other agencies, the
EEOC's general counsel has substantial autonomy, making the agency "a
bureaucratic powder keg waiting to explode if personalities or politics
are hot."[41] Moreover, the change of EEOC chairs from the aggressive,
proactive Eleanor Holmes Norton under Carter, to the markedly more
conservative Clarence Thomas under Reagan, angered many civil rights
groups. Thomas had instructed the agency's general counsel not to approve conciliation agreements including goals and timetables. The future
Supreme Court Justice argued that corporations should not be compelled to prove they were hiring enough minorities and women: "Title
VII [of the Civil Rights Act of 1964] says you can't consider race or sex
in hiring, period."[42]

By the time that the Reagan Administration tried to drop affirmative
action requirements, many large companies embraced affirmative action
as being good for business. The consulting firm Organization Resources
Counselors found in a 1985 survey that 122 of 128 CEOs of large

corporations said they would "continue to use numerical objectives to track the progress of women and minorities . . . regardless of government requirements." Some firms filed amicus briefs and sent correspondence to the Reagan White House opposing efforts to scale back affirmative action.[43]

In 1989, the Supreme Court decided two cases that cast existing precedents of employment law into doubt. In *Price Waterhouse v. Hopkins* (490 U.S. 228), the court ruled that, even in cases where a plaintiff proves that an employer's actions were motivated by discrimination, the employer can avoid liability by showing that it would have made the same employment decision based on lawful motives. *Wards Cove Packing Co. v. Atonio* (490 U.S. 642), which addressed the hiring practices of two salmon canneries in Alaska, substantially increased the burden of proof on plaintiffs in making disparate impact claims. The decision specified that in establishing a prima facie disparate impact case, plaintiffs must identify a specific employment practice (or practices) that results in statistical racial disparities in an employer's work force. The court ruled that the burden of persuasion in such cases lies with the plaintiff, and businesses need only show business justification—not business necessity—for practices that have a disproportionate racial effect.[44]

Congress responded to these decisions by passing the Civil Rights Act of 1991, which codified the disparate impact theory of discrimination as it existed prior to *Wards Cove*. In addition, the law provided for injunctive relief, attorney's fees and costs (though not individual monetary or affirmative relief) in cases where the plaintiff proved discrimination as a motivating factor for an employment decision, even when the employer proved that the same decision would have been reached without a discriminatory motive.

Despite the Reagan Administration's clear hostility toward the affirmative action model, and its laxity in enforcing affirmative action requirements, it was nevertheless unable to forge a change in employment antidiscrimination enforcement that reverted back to an individual complaint model. That large corporations came to accept—even embrace—affirmative action practices slowed the momentum of the Reagan team's effort. This example illustrates the ways in which policy legacies can have major effects on subsequent policy development, as public and private institutions form and expand in response to existing arrangements. It also shows that an agency that Congress originally intended to be relatively weak can, at least in some cases, expand its authority to become a powerful player in the political world. In its early years, the EEOC was faced with weak enforcement authority, unsteady leadership, and legal provisions that arguably precluded its use of aggressive, race-conscious remedies to attack discrimination. Nevertheless, through a creative use of the tools at its disposal, the EEOC, in conjunction with the OFCC, developed the most far-reaching antidiscrimination approach of any major civil rights policy area. Contract compliance responsibilities had served to increase the Labor Department's status. As a result, when the Reagan White House tried to do away with the "goals and timetables" approach of the contract office, top Labor officials and long-time bureaucrats zealously defended the affirmative action approach.[45] This occurrence suggests that larger agencies may fight attempts to undermine their civil rights missions, if the civil rights sector is in good stead with the agency leadership.

Why did the Reagan Administration fail in its attempts at civil rights retrenchment? The Reagan White House did, after all, devise several methods of limiting bureaucratic activism. The primary focus of this "administrative presidency" lies in appointments, where ideological compatibility with the president is given greater priority than traditional considerations such as ties to interest groups or agency clients, or other constituencies within the president's party. Other tools of the administrative presidency include requiring clearance from the Office of Management and Budget before agencies propose regulations, and cutting agency budgets.[46]

Graham points to three developments that steeled the civil rights coalition against the Reagan attack. First is the expansion of public law litigation, in which private-sector, public-interest organizations like the NAACP sue government agencies on behalf of class-action clients so that courts will mandate that the agencies take specific actions in enforcement; the *Adams* orders in school desegregation illustrate the fruits of this strategy. Second, clientele groups have largely captured civil rights agencies. Third, we have witnessed a "legislative cloning process" in which civil rights protections originally intended to benefit African Americans were extended to other constituencies (for example, other racial and ethnic groups, women, and the disabled).[47]

The addition of new, protected groups tends to bolster the civil rights coalition's resistance to far-reaching retrenchment. The price, in many cases, is that civil rights agencies are faced with multiplying responsibilities—some quite different in nature—without corresponding increases in resources. This makes it extremely difficult for any civil rights agency to set priorities and sustain bureaucratic momentum, especially as political leadership changes. The problem intensifies in multiple-mission agencies such as HUD, where there is an additional layer of competing priorities. Not only must specific civil rights responsibilities compete with each other for attention and resources, but the civil rights missions collectively must compete with numerous other tasks that are far removed from—or even opposed to—civil rights goals.

Sara Pratt, the director of the Office of Enforcement in HUD's Office of Fair Housing and Equal Opportunity (FHEO) from 1993 to 1999, maintains that the most viable long-term solution to developing adequate fair-housing enforcement is to reassign these obligations to a new agency devoted to this issue.[48] With HUD's wide array of issues—including regulating and working with the housing industry, addressing programmatic and political issues, and acquiring and allocating resources—it is difficult to get civil rights "to the top of the heap [at HUD] even with the most committed leadership," Pratt notes. The National Fair Housing Alliance echoes this suggestion, noting that FHEO "is fully intertwined in the HUD system. . . . This compromises what should be independent, objective investigations, putting them through the litmus test of public policy considerations and the very real issue of being ranked lower than other HUD priorities."[49] A separate agency, however, is not a magic wand to eliminate all of the problems and complexities of fair-housing enforcement. Nevertheless, such an administrative reshuffling would be likely to produce a reinvigorated and more effective fair housing effort.

INSTITUTIONAL ISSUES FOR CIVIL RIGHTS AGENCIES

The case studies in this book suggest that a policy's institutional home can shape agency initiatives in significant ways. The institutional homes approach directs attention to the structure and mission(s) of the government agency, agencies, or agency division(s) through which relevant policies are interpreted, articulated, and carried out. This approach hypothesizes that an advantaged institutional home will increase the odds of policy success—as measured by the degree to which agency goals as understood by employees are fulfilled—while a disadvantaged home will decrease these odds. To reiterate, an advantaged institutional home is one where agency employees consider the mission in question to be primary, other agency missions do not conflict with the mission in question, the agency's legitimacy will be judged by the achievement of that mission, and achievement of the agency's primary mission is relatively easy to convey to a broader audience. In a strong institutional home, the agency does not house numerous other programs, particularly ones with a tendency toward mismanagement or an unfavorable policy legacy. A disadvantaged home is one where the mission in question is secondary and may conflict with other missions, legitimacy may be gauged by the achievement of other agency goals, and fulfillment of the mission is difficult to communicate. A weak institutional home encompasses other programs with a tendency toward mismanagement or a policy legacy that contradicts the mission in question. I argue that the EEOC was able to develop into a comparatively strong institutional home (despite congressional intentions), while HUD's civil rights office was mired in a weak institutional home, thus providing key insights into the different trajectories of these agency policies. The EEOC's status as a stand-alone agency was an advantage in creating an organization with a singular sense of mission and a strong agency culture.

Advantaged institutional homes, however, do not exist only in stand-alone agencies. The Office of Federal Contract Compliance (in the Department of Labor) and the Office for Civil Rights (in HEW) had the support of their parent agencies in carrying out their missions of fighting discrimination. While HUD Secretary George Romney clearly backed the objective of desegregation, housing production staffers largely saw civil rights concerns as slowing their desperate drive to meet daunting production targets. Romney himself never solved the enigma of coordinating disparate efforts into a cohesive whole, and he left HUD feeling frustrated and defeated. Other civil rights agencies did not face such clashing missions. For instance, the civil rights bureaucracies in employment initially were not charged with creating jobs or reducing overall unemployment. Moreover, as argued in chapter 4, the ultimate goals of residential desegregation may take a longer time to realize, and short-term progress may seem less urgent and more difficult to convey to a larger audience than achievements in other areas of civil rights.

For better or for worse, EEOC staffers in the agency's early years stood firm in their conviction that racial discrimination was a more pressing issue than gender discrimination. The National Organization for Women asserted in 1971 that "the EEOC has compiled a record on combating sex discrimination so dismal that its negative effects far outweigh the one or two positive items on its record."[50] During the late 1960s and early 1970s, few HEW staffers disputed that school desegregation was the top civil rights priority, and health care discrimination (after 1966) an issue for the back burner.

Since that time, virtually all civil rights agencies have confronted additional legislative mandates in the face of constrained resources and, relatedly, lagging morale. Consider the case of OCR at HEW. Adding to OCR's continued enforcement obligations in health and education related to Title VI of the Civil Rights Act of 1964, Congress placed new obligations on the agency in prohibiting discrimination in federally assisted programs against the physically or mentally disabled (Section 504 of the Rehabilitation Act of 1973), women in federally assisted education programs (Title IX of the Education Amendments of 1973), and the aged (employment excepted).[51] The juggling act faced by HEW is captured by a memo, from the Ford Administration's outgoing head of

OCR to Jimmy Carter's presidential transition team, describing issues that would face the civil rights staff in coming months. The list of fifteen items includes (1) development and issuance of final regulations to implement Section 504 of the Rehabilitation Act of 1973; (2) development and issuance of Title VI standards on higher education admissions policies; (3) adherence to workload and timeframes specified in the *Adams* orders; (4) creation of strategies for complaint handling and conflict resolution; (5) promulgation of standards for equal educational opportunity in state higher education systems; (6) elimination of language barriers in public schools; and (7) development of policy positions for Title IX issues.[52] When increasing responsibilities collide with decreasing resources, only the highest-priority missions stand a real chance of effective execution.

THEORETICAL CONTRIBUTIONS AND LIMITATIONS

The institutional homes approach helps to refine scholarly thinking about concepts such as policy feedback, state capacity, and legitimation. While scholars have correctly pointed to the influence of policy histories on the creation of new policies, they often fail to explain which policy legacies are accessed and how these prior policies affect new policies. The institutional homes approach helps to clarify why some policy legacies (for instance, those tolerating or promoting segregation in housing) prove more influential than others (aggressive civil rights policies) in specific cases. The case studies of antidiscrimination policies also illustrate that the legacy of prior policies may be less constraining than the diffusion of delegitimation, in which scandals or mismanagement in one sector of an agency taint other agency activities. The relative strength of an institutional home is not solely determinative of policy outcomes. Surely, political will, the development of expertise, alliances with other governmental and private actors, and adept strategizing affect outcomes, as do the independent objectives of other branches of government.

Like other middle-range theories of social policy, the institutional homes approach does not purport to explain all aspects of the policy process. In comparing some policies, one may have to look no further than the provisions of the legislation to understand why one policy has been carried out more aggressively or more effectively than a comparable one. Nevertheless, government agencies, particularly regulatory ones, may have considerable autonomy in fulfilling their missions, and they may carry out the laws on the books in many different ways. Thus, the institutional homes approach may be applicable to a substantial number of cases.

The relative strength or weakness of a policy's institutional home is not, of course, a randomly occurring event. Congress may intentionally give a policy a weak institutional home because it does not want a law enforced aggressively. Congress, however, is not always successful in achieving its goals, as in the case of the EEOC, which by all indications was designed to be a weak agency with few strong-arm tactics at its disposal. Thus, while it is important to discern congressional intent in assigning a particular institutional home for a policy, this intent is not always clear and may be subverted, as in the case of the EEOC.

Like Lieberman's work on programs passed under the Social Security Act of 1935, I find that institutional arrangements—whatever their original intention—can have profound consequences on the effectiveness of policies addressing racial disadvantage.[53] Civil rights policies, particularly ones seeking to achieve desegregation, may have less-defined paths to effective administration than do the spending policies that Lieberman studies. Certainly, strong national leadership is essential, as Lieberman finds. Some of these policies, however, such as those in housing and education, unavoidably involve close federal interaction (whether in cooperation or conflict) with local institutions (school districts or the localities themselves). To be sure, leaving desegregation responsibilities to local bodies would have meant the withering of this goal; but a strong, national structure for enforcement is not enough for regulatory policies, where the path to effective administration is more complex. How the civil rights missions fit with other agency missions, and how agency staffers choose to fulfill the ambiguous mandates of civil rights laws, also loom as important factors in effective administration.

Recent scholarly work on the emergence of affirmative action in employment has resulted in important historical and theoretical contributions with regard to policy development. Because affirmative action in employment confounds many of our traditional understandings of policy evolution, it has proven valuable in spurring fresh theoretical thinking about why—despite no direct policy legacy, weak enforcement powers, and a lack of interest group pressure, among other factors—the employment bureaucracies were able to develop aggressive, race-conscious approaches to fighting discrimination. A single case study, however, takes scholarly thinking only so far.

While I have gained some theoretical leverage by utilizing a comparative approach, even the use of three cases falls short of the evidence necessary to prove the wide applicability of the institutional homes approach. For example, the institutional homes of civil rights and other regulatory policies may have different effects than the homes of spending policies. Nevertheless, this approach helps us to understand the ways in which the missions and structure of an agency can impede or enhance the fulfillment of bureaucratic objectives, and the ways in which different influences (other branches, pressure groups, the media, and so on) may affect agencies in contextually specific ways. In particular, this perspective offers a useful lens through which to consider agency attempts to establish legitimacy. Examining the institutional home for a certain policy possibility will not provide a foolproof prediction about whether the policy will be implemented successfully. This approach does give us a clearer, more refined understanding of the strategic context that political actors face, the choices they make within this context, and why certain actors are able to achieve the goals they set, while others fail.

CAN THIS BATTLE BE WON?

The policy lessons of these case studies are not confined to the odd contours of Nixon's civil rights activities. First, this study suggests that scholarly inattention to failed or less prominent policies may not only be a missed opportunity to mine fresh and interesting data sources.[54] This bias toward successful cases may also distort our historical understandings of policy development. Second, this study forges some new ground in understandings of blame avoidance strategies. In formulating a strategy to avoid blame, political actors must consider how the objects of their blame-shifting are likely to respond. Some targets are likely to fight back, resulting in a prolonged, ugly battle that renders involved parties susceptible to real political damage. Politicians may love a good fight, but if at all possible, they will choose ones they can win quickly and decisively.

In the cases studied here, Nixon acted most forcefully toward HUD's civil rights bureaucracy because it was the weakest of the three, and he could scale back civil rights activities indirectly. This indirect attack exemplified Nixon's blame avoidance approach to civil rights. It is not as if Nixon simply preferred to forgo credit that he could have claimed in the area of civil rights. Unable to effect significant reductions in school busing, Nixon attempted to ensure that the American public believed that he was not at fault. After playing a central role in establishing affirmative action policies in employment, his public stance on this issue became more tepid and ambivalent as the 1972 election drew near. Nixon probably would have been unable to win quickly and decisively against a stand-alone civil rights agency in housing. Such an agency, fighting for its life, would not have succumbed quietly. In addition, a stand-alone civil rights agency may have been better able to convey the importance of reducing residential segregation and to report progress. Moreover, it would have been particularly advantageous for the fair housing function to be situated in a stand-alone agency because of the potential (which was realized) for scandal and corruption within other HUD programs. Ironically, the scandals had nothing to do with suburban desegregation initiatives, as the inner-city programs were supposed to help rebuild largely segregated ghetto areas. HUD nevertheless became known as an agency that could do little right. Few noticed the effects of the moratorium on the residential desegregation drive amidst the din of housing industry interests expressing outrage at the spigot of federal subsidies being shut.

An affirmative action approach in housing would have to take a different form than the strategies used in education or employment. The evidence in this book suggests that the most effective means of monitoring discrimination (in intent or effect) is by locality. Metropolitan-level solutions, in which towns act to encourage economic and racial integration (where it does not exist already), seem to be the most promising avenue. Indeed, as explored in chapter 5, housing desegregation policies seemed to be heading in this direction before Nixon pulled the plug on all housing funding in early 1973, essentially ending HUD's attempts to foster "open communities." Given the marked tendency of federal courts at that time to back aggressive civil rights measures, there is reason to believe that efforts in this vein would have survived judicial scrutiny. Moreover, the federal government *has* compelled localities (such as Parma, Ohio) to encourage racial integration, though only in cases of blatant discrimination.

There is also the question of whether these aggressive efforts would have proven effective, fostering substantial reductions in segregation. Does the importance of institutional weakness in explaining the politics of housing desegregation mean that a more effective enforcement structure would have resulted in the rapid integration of neighborhoods? No. The halting desegregation that has occurred in other policy areas has been characterized by struggle, resistance, and administrative difficulties. The impact of these divergent policy outcomes, however, is not trivial. That desegregation efforts in employment and education led to measurable change is significant. So, too, is the fact that the federal government largely abandoned desegregation initiatives in primary and secondary education. The racial situation in America would look different now if housing had been (and still was) a higher priority in civil rights enforcement, and carried out with some success. The political and cultural chasms that exist among racial and ethnic groups in the United States would be smaller than they are today: still present, but smaller.

Of all policy areas of civil rights, residential integration has the greatest potential to alter the racial landscape. Stably integrated neighborhoods mean shared interests in quality schools, political representation, neighborhood services, quality of life, and so on. Backers of these neighborhoods need to develop more effective strategies for conveying the benefits of integration. To make a compelling case for residential desegregation, supporters of this objective must also address the counterexamples often used to argue that desegregation is not an important public policy goal. We need to know, with much greater precision, the dynamics of voluntary racial separation by affluent African Americans. Do families in Prince George's County (Maryland) and the Atlanta suburbs, living in rich, black communities, pay a price? If so, in what currency is this cost exacted: school quality, educational outcomes, neighborhood services, or job networks? Do the benefits of numerous role models for children, and a comfort level that does not exist in overwhelmingly white communities, outweigh these possible costs?

While residential integration has proven most difficult to achieve, integrated neighborhoods would make the realization of truly integrated educational institutions and workplaces substantially less painstaking. The responsibility for desegregation does not fall solely on administrative agencies, which do not have unlimited power to impose their policy solutions on other political actors and the public as a whole. Prior to passage of civil rights legislation, these agencies could do very little to encourage desegregation. Congress can also attempt to curtail agency activities, though this has proven remarkably difficult. The judiciary has been highly influential in setting the parameters of what agencies can and cannot do. Indeed, court appointments are one of the most significant, if least visible, means by which presidents can affect rights policies. Nevertheless, administrative agencies are crucial to explaining political outcomes because courts typically react to agency attempts to bring life to legislative mandates, and agencies have a big hand in shaping how laws affect actual lives. When agencies act passively, the chances for significant change are low. As we see in the more far-reaching results of civil rights efforts in employment and education, and the more truncated efforts in housing and health, institutional homes are a part of this story that should not be ignored.

Currently, there appears to be little reason for optimism that the federal government will revisit the issue of racial and economic segregation in any meaningful way. One might justify this neglect by pointing to the low and decreasing levels of segregation in America's fastest-growing metropolitan areas, arguing that the problem of residential segregation will *eventually* take care of itself. Perhaps so. But any serious discussion of policy options must acknowledge that doing nothing has costs as well. Father Theodore Hesburgh, a member of the USCCR from 1958 to 1973, and its chair from 1969 to 1972, observed in the early 1970s that "the price of solving our domestic problems, especially the problem of color inherent in most of them, is very high. The price of delay is even larger problems and ultimately a larger human cost."[55] Given its involvement in the creation of the problem, the federal government has a particularly sharp responsibility to address residential segregation. Despite this legacy, the government does very little as these human costs continue to accrue. These costs are paid mostly by African Americans, and also by Latinos, in the form of continued educational inequalities, truncated job opportunities, less advantageous neighborhood environments, the exacerbation of wealth disparities, and the naturalization of racial differences.

ABBREVIATIONS FOR NOTES

	College Park, Md. All HUD documents are located in Record Group 207.
LC	Library of Congress (Manuscript Division), Washington, D.C. The papers of the Leadership Conference on Civil Rights (LCCR), NAACP, the Urban League, Roy Wilkins, and Sen. Edward W. Brooke (R-MA) are housed here.
NAACP 1982	*National Association for the Advancement of Colored People Papers* (microfilm), Part 5: Campaign Against Racial Segregation, 1914–1955, Frederick, Md.: University Publications of America, 1982.
NARA	National Archives and Records Administration, College Park, Md.
NPM	Nixon Presidential Materials, National Archives and Records Administration, College Park, Md.
	WHSF White House Special Files
	WHCF White House Central Files
	SMOF Staff Member and Office Files
SCBC	Schomburg Center for Research in Black Culture, New York, N.Y. The papers of Robert C. Weaver are housed here.
SSC 1970	Senate Select Committee on Equal Educational Opportunity, "Part 5—De Facto Segregation and Housing Discrimination," August 25, 26, 27 and September 1, 1970.

ABBREVIATIONS FOR PERIODICALS

CQ	*Congressional Quarterly*
NJ	*National Journal*
NYT	*New York Times*
WP	*Washington Post*

NOTES

CHAPTER ONE

1. Gary Orfield and Chungmei Lee, "*Brown* at 50: King's Dream or *Plessy*'s Nightmare?" (Cambridge: The Civil Rights Project, Harvard University 2004). This report is available at http://www.civilrightsproject.harvard.edu/research/reseg04/brown50.pdf.

2. As quoted in Letter, Richard Van Dusen to National Council of Churches, United States Department of Housing and Urban Development (hereafter HUD), RG 207, Box 100, Reel 6-2, March 16, 1970.

3. Romney speech to National Association of Home Builders, Library of Congress, Manuscript Division (hereafter LC), Leadership Conference on Civil Rights Papers (hereafter LCCR), Part I, Box 105, Folder: HUD 1970, January 19, 1970.

4. Hugh Davis Graham, *The Civil Rights Era: Origins and Development of National Policy, 1960–1972* (New York: Oxford University Press, 1990); John David Skrentny, *The Ironies of Affirmative Action* (Chicago: University of Chicago Press, 1996); Nicholas Pedriana and Robin Stryker, "Political Culture Wars 1960s Style: Equal Employment Opportunity—Affirmative Action Law and the Philadelphia Plan," *American Journal of Sociology* 103 (3): 633–91; Dean J. Kotlowski, *Nixon's Civil Rights* (Cambridge: Harvard University Press, 2001).

5. I use the terms "desegregation" and "integration" interchangeably when referring to policy initiatives. The terms are used by some individuals to convey somewhat different realities. When the two are distinguished, "desegregation" may refer to a specific period of time, for instance, when the first black family moves into a previously all-white neighborhood. "Integration" is more likely to convey an ongoing process, where different racial or economic groups, in nontrivial numbers, share a neighborhood over a period of time. To those concerned with eliminating residential segregation, the goal is clearly an ongoing state of integration, rather than temporary desegregation followed by a return to segregation (in which the newly segregated group is likely to be a different racial group than the old one). In this work, when I discuss policy goals of desegregation or integration, I am referring to the same objective: a sustained change of living patterns that reflects reduced racial and economic concentrations.

6. Among presidents, Richard Nixon's legacy is particularly complex and multifaceted. On the domestic policy front, scholars continue to tussle over whether Nixon was a conservative, a liberal, or a pragmatist with no ties to political ideology. For an excellent examination of Nixon's many sides, see David Greenberg, *Nixon's Shadow: The History of an Image* (New York: Norton, 2003).

7. On the expansion of antidiscrimination policies to other groups, see John D. Skrentny, *The Minority Rights Revolution* (Cambridge: Harvard University Press, 2002).

8. Scholars tend to study other branches more frequently, in part because it is easier to access court decisions, congressional debates, and so on than it is to scrutinize administrative records. See Daniel P. Carpenter, *The Forging of Bureaucratic Autonomy* (Princeton: Princeton University Press, 2001). See also James Q. Wilson, "The Politics of Regulation," pp. 357–94 in *The Politics of Regulation*, ed. James Q. Wilson (New York: Basic, 1980); Wilson, *Bureaucracy: What Government Agencies Do and Why They Do It* (New York: Basic, 1989).

9. Carpenter, *Forging of Bureaucratic Autonomy*, 11.

10. Theda Skocpol, "Bringing the State Back In: Strategies of Analysis in Current Research," pp. 3–37 in *Bringing the State Back In*, ed. Peter B. Evans, Dietrich Rueschemeyer, and Theda Skocpol (New York: Cambridge University Press, 1985); Skocpol, *Protecting Soldiers and Mothers* (Cambridge, Mass.: Belknap, 1992); Hugh Heclo, *Modern Social Politics in Britain and Sweden: From Relief to Income Maintenance* (New Haven: Yale University Press, 1974); Dietrich Rueschemeyer and Theda Skocpol, *States, Social Knowledge and the Origins of Modern Social Policies* (Princeton: Princeton University Press, 1996).

11. Carpenter, *Forging of Bureaucratic Autonomy*, 4.

12. See, for example, Edwin Amenta, *Bold Relief: Institutional Politics and the Origins of American Social Policy* (Princeton: Princeton University Press, 1998); Theda Skocpol, "Political Response to Capitalist Crisis: Neo-Marxist Theories of the State and the Case of the New Deal," *Political Sociology* 10: 155–201.

13. R. Shep Melnick, *Between the Lines: Interpreting Welfare Rights* (Washington, D.C.: Brookings Institution, 1994).

14. Wilson, *Bureaucracy*, 250.

15. Wilson, "Politics of Regulation," 391.

16. On presidential lack of awareness, see Martha Derthick, *Policymaking for Social Security* (Washington, D.C.: Brookings Institution, 1979). On other factors contributing to lack of presidential control, see, for example, Max Weber, "Bureaucracy," in *From Max Weber: Essays in Sociology*, ed. by H. H. Gerth and C. Wright Mills (New York: Oxford University Press, 1946); Kenneth J. Meier, "Measuring Organizational Power: Resources and Autonomy of Government Agencies," *Administration and Society* 12 (3): 357–75; Meier, *Politics and the Bureaucracy: Policymaking in the Fourth Branch of Government*, 3rd ed., (Pacific Grove, Calif.: Brooks/Cole, 1993); Richard P. Nathan, *The Administrative Presidency* (New York: Wiley, 1983); Dennis Riley, *Controlling the Federal Bureaucracy* (Philadelphia: Temple University Press, 1987).

17. Robert Durant, *The Administrative Presidency Revisited: Public Lands, the BLM, and the Reagan Revolution* (Albany: State University of New York Press, 1992); Dan B. Wood and Richard W. Waterman, "The Dynamics of Political Control of the Bureaucracy," *American Political Science Review* 85, no. 3 (1991): 801–28. Other tools of the administrative presidency include the vesting of final decision-making in budgets to the Office of Management and Budget, and granting regulatory clearance and review powers to the Office of Information and Regulatory Affairs (within OMB). See William West, *Controlling the Bureaucracy: Institutional Constraints in Theory and Practice* (Armonk, N.Y.:

Sharpe, 1995); Marissa Martino Golden, *What Motivates Bureaucrats? Politics and Administration During the Reagan Years* (New York: Columbia University Press, 2000).

18. Gerald N. Rosenberg, *The Hollow Hope: Can Courts Bring about Social Change?* (Chicago: University of Chicago Press, 1991); Melnick, *Between the Lines.*

19. Randall L. Calvert, Matthew D. McCubbins, and Barry R. Weingast, "A Theory of Political Control and Agency Discretion," *American Journal of Political Science* 33 (3): 588–611. In their view, the appointment stage includes not only selection of personnel but also structuring of the agency and the delineation of agency powers, jurisdiction, and administrative procedures.

20. On agency capture, see Marver Bernstein, *Regulating by Independent Commission* (Princeton: Princeton University Press, 1955); Theodore J. Lowi, *The End of Liberalism: The Second Republic of the United States* (New York: Norton, 1979). On victories of the liberal sector over the business class, see, for instance, William G. Domhoff, *The Power Elite and the State: How Policy Is Made in America* (New York: de Gruyter, 1990); Craig J. Jenkins and Barbara G. Brents, "Social Protest, Hegemonic Competition, and Social Reform: A Political Struggle Interpretation of the Origins of the American Welfare State," *American Sociological Review* 54 (1989): 891–909. For an opposing viewpoint, see Edwin Amenta and Sunita Parikh, "Capitalists Did Not Want the Social Security Act: A Critique of the 'Capitalist Dominance' Thesis," *American Sociological Review* 56 (1991): 124–29.

21. See, for example, Philip Selznick, *TVA and the Grass Roots* (Berkeley: University of California Press, 1949).

22. Robert R. Detlefsen, *Civil Rights under Reagan* (San Francisco: Institute for Contemporary Studies Press, 1991); Herman Belz, *Equality Transformed* (New Brunswick, NJ: Transaction, 1991); Skrentny, *Ironies of Affirmative Action*; Skrentny, "State Capacity, Policy Feedbacks and Affirmative Action for Blacks, Women and Latinos," *Research in Political Sociology* 8 (1998): 279–310; Graham, *Civil Rights Era.*

23. Wayne A. Santoro and Gail M. McGuire, "Social Movement Insiders: The Impact of Institutional Activists on Affirmative Action and Comparable Worth Policies," *Social Problems* 44, no. 4 (1997): 503–19. I argue that social movement sympathizers may have the same effects on agency aggressiveness as actual movement participants.

24. For trends in public opinion over time, see Howard Schuman, Charlotte Steeh, Lawrence Bobo, and Maria Krysan, *Racial Attitudes in America: Trends and Interpretations* (Cambridge: Harvard University Press, 1997). On the importance of public opinion, see Paul Burstein, *Discrimination, Jobs and Politics: The Struggle for Equal Employment Opportunity in the United States since the New Deal* (Chicago: University of Chicago Press, 1985); Burstein, "Bringing the Public Back In: Should Sociologists Consider the Impact of Public Opinion on Public Policy?" *Social Forces* 77 (1): 27–62. Burstein (1985) links the passage of civil rights laws to public support, arguing that the Civil Rights Act of 1964 was enacted when the proportion of Americans believing the government was

moving too quickly on integration was at a historic low point of less than 30 percent, and the 1968 open housing bill passed just after resistance had fallen substantially.

25. Margaret Weir, *Politics and Jobs* (Princeton: Princeton University Press, 1992).

26. Schuman et al., *Racial Attitudes in America*.

27. Nathan Glazer, *Affirmative Discrimination* (New York: Basic, 1987), 214. This may not be the case when agency chiefs are appointed specifically to oversee retrenchment efforts; these appointees tend to be lifelong party loyalists rather than public figures with electoral ambitions of their own. The appointment of former Commerce Undersecretary James Lynn to replace George Romney is a prominent example. See Nathan, *Administrative Presidency*.

28. For an overview of historical institutionalism, see Kathleen Thelen and Sven Steinmo, "Historical Institutionalism in Comparative Politics," pp. 1–32 in *Structuring Politics: Historical Institutionalism in Comparative Analysis*, ed. Sven Steinmo, Kathleen Thelen, and Frank Longstreth (New York: Cambridge University Press, 1992). On variations in state autonomy, see Jill Quadagno, "Social Movements and State Transformation: Labor Unions and Racial Conflict in the War on Poverty," *American Sociological Review* 57 (1992): 616–34; Gregory Hooks, "From an Autonomous to a Captured State Agency: The Decline of the New Deal in Agriculture," *American Sociological Review* 55 (1990) 29–43; Bruce G. Carruthers, "When Is the State Autonomous? Culture, Organization Theory, and the Political Sociology of the State," *Sociological Theory* 12, no. 1 (1994): 19–44.

29. Nancy K. Cauthen and Edwin Amenta, "Not for Widows Only: Institutional Politics and the Formative Years of Aid to Dependent Children," *American Sociological Review* 61 (1996): 427–48. See also Skocpol, "Bringing the State Back In"; Skocpol, *Protecting Soldiers and Mothers*; Skrentny, *Ironies of Affirmative Action*; Robin H. Rogers-Dillon and John David Skrentny, "Administering Success: The Legitimacy Imperative and the Implementation of Welfare Reform," *Social Problems* 46, no. 1 (1999): 13–29. On operationalizing state capacity, see Skrentny, "State Capacity."

30. Skrentny, *Ironies of Affirmative Action*; Skrentny, "State Capacity"; Graham, *Civil Rights Era*.

31. Skocpol, *Protecting Soldiers and Mothers*; Weir, *Politics and Jobs*; Pedriana and Stryker, "Political Culture Wars"; Paul Pierson, *Dismantling the Welfare State?* (New York: Cambridge University Press, 1994).

32. Ann Shola Orloff, *The Politics of Pensions: A Comparative Analysis of Britain, Canada, and the United States, 1880–1940* (Madison: University of Wisconsin Press, 1993); Heclo, *Modern Social Politics*; John W. Kingdon, *Agendas, Alternatives and Public Policies* (Boston: Little, Brown, 1984); Deborah Stone, "Causal Stories and the Formation of Policy Agendas," *Political Science Quarterly* 104, no. 1 (1989): 281–300.

33. On various types of policy feedbacks, see Pierson, *Dismantling the Welfare State?* On various interpretations of policy legacies, see Skocpol, *Protecting Soldiers and Mothers*.

34. Weir, *Politics and Jobs*; Skocpol, *Protecting Soldiers and Mothers*; Theda

Skocpol and Edwin Amenta, "States and Social Policies," *Annual Review of Sociology* 12 (1986): 131–57.

35. Walter Powell and Paul DiMaggio, *The New Institutionalism in Organizational Analysis* (Chicago: University of Chicago Press, 1991); Rogers-Dillon and Skrentny, "Administering Success."

36. Robert Wuthnow, J. D. Hunter, A. Bergesen, and E. Kurzweil, *Cultural Analysis* (Boston: Routledge and Kegan Paul, 1984), 50.

37. Richard W. Scott, "Unpacking Institutional Arguments," pp. 164–82 in *The New Institutionalism in Organizational Analysis*, ed. Walter Powell and Paul DiMaggio (Chicago: University of Chicago Press, 1991). See also Carpenter, *Forging Bureaucratic Autonomy.*

38. John W. Meyer and W. Richard Scott, "Centralization and the Legitimacy Problem of Local Government," pp. 199–215 in *Organizational Environments: Ritual and Rationality*, ed. J. W. Meyer and W. R. Scott (Beverly Hills, Calif.: Sage, 1983), 202.

39. Wilson, *Bureaucracy.* A sense of mission is achieved "when an organization has a culture that is widely shared and warmly endorsed by operators and managers alike" (95).

40. Ibid., 101. On the relationship between bureaucratic responsiveness and organizational characteristics, see Dan B. Wood, "Does Politics Make a Difference at the EEOC?" *American Journal of Political Science* 34, no. 2 (1990): 503–30.

41. Glazer, *Affirmative Discrimination.*

42. Chris Bonastia, "Why Did Affirmative Action in Housing Fail During the Nixon Era? Exploring the 'Institutional Homes' of Social Policies," *Social Problems* 47, no. 4 (2000): 523–42. On the effects of media coverage on policy outcomes, see Peter A. Hall, "The Movement from Keynesianism to Monetarism: Institutional Analysis and British Economic Policy in the 1970s," pp. 90–114 in *Structuring Politics*; Wilson, *Bureaucracy*; Rogers-Dillon and Skrentny, "Administering Success."

43. Morris P. Fiorina, *Congress: Keystone of the Washington Establishment* (New Haven: Yale University Press, 1977); David Mayhew, *Congress: The Electoral Connection* (New Haven: Yale University Press, 1974).

44. R. Kent Weaver, "The Politics of Blame Avoidance," *Journal of Public Policy* 6, no. 4 (1986): 372.

45. Howard S. Bloom and H. Douglas Price, "Voter Response to Short-run Economic Conditions: The Asymmetric Effect of Prosperity and Recession," *American Political Science Review* 69 (1975): 1240–54; Samuel Kernell, "Presidential Popularity and Negative Voting: An Alternative Explanation of the Midterm Congressional Decline of the President's Party," *American Political Science Review* 72 (1977): 44–66; Gerald C. Wright, Jr., "Constituency Responses to Congressional Behavior: The Impact of the House Judiciary Committee Impeachment Votes," *Western Political Quarterly* 30, no. 3 (1977): 401–10.

46. Weaver, "Politics of Blame Avoidance," 376.

47. Richard J. Ellis, *Presidential Lightning Rods: The Politics of Blame Avoidance* (Lawrence: University Press of Kansas, 1994).

48. See, for example, Leon E. Panetta and Peter Gall, *Bring Us Together: The Nixon Team and the Civil Rights Retreat* (New York: Lipincott, 1971). On choos-

ing winnable battles, see Chris Bonastia, "Hedging His Bets: Why Nixon Killed HUD's Desegregation Efforts," *Social Science History* 28, no. 1 (2004): 19–52.

49. Richard Briffault, "Our Localism: Part I–The Structure of Local Government Law," *Columbia Law Review* 90, no. 1 (1990): 1–76.

50. Peter E. Mahoney, "The End(s) of Disparate Impact: Doctrinal Reconstruction, Fair Housing and Lending Law, and the Antidiscrimination Principle," *Emory Law Journal* 47, no. 409 (1998): 1–78.

51. U.S. Code, 1935, Vol. 29, secs. 160b, 160c, excerpted in Jo Ann Ooiman Robinson, ed., *Affirmative Action: A Documentary History* (Westport, Conn.: Greenwood, 2001).

52. Skrentny, *Ironies of Affirmative Action*.

53. Ibid; Graham, *Civil Rights Era*; Dean J. Kotlowski, "Richard Nixon and the Origins of Affirmative Action," *The Historian* 60, no. 3 (1998): 523–41; Pedriana and Stryker, "Political Culture Wars"; Thomas J. Sugrue, "Breaking Through: The Troubled Origins of Affirmative Action in the Workplace," pp. 31–52 in *Color Lines: Affirmative Action, Immigration, and Civil Rights Options for America*, ed. John David Skrentny (Chicago: University of Chicago Press, 2001). For previous work on civil rights enforcement in housing, see Michael N. Danielson, *The Politics of Exclusion* (New York: Columbia University Press, 1976); David H. McKay, *Housing and Race in Industrial Society* (Totowa, N.J.: Rowman and Littlefield, 1977); United States Commission on Civil Rights (hereafter USCCR), "The Federal Civil Rights Enforcement Effort—A Reassessment" (Washington, D.C.: U.S. Government Printing Office, 1973).

54. David Falk and Herbert M. Franklin, *Equal Housing Opportunity: The Unfinished Federal Agenda* (Washington, D.C.: Potomac Institute, 1976); USCCR, "Housing" (Washington, D.C.: U.S. Government Printing Office, 1961).

55. Douglas S. Massey and Nancy A. Denton, *American Apartheid* (Cambridge: Harvard University Press, 1993); McKay, *Housing and Race*.

56. Kenneth O'Reilly, *Nixon's Piano: Presidents and Racial Politics from Washington to Clinton* (New York: Free Press, 1995); Graham, *Civil Rights Era*.

57. Edward G. Carmines and James A. Stimson, *Issue Evolution: Race and the Transformation of American Politics* (Princeton: Princeton University Press, 1989).

58. O'Reilly, *Nixon's Piano*, 297.

59. Early in Nixon's first term, the White House attempted to craft a policy agenda that "might appeal to both black and white progressives on the one hand, and Southern whites and traditional fiscal conservatives on the other." After deciding that courting black votes was fruitless, the administration made some efforts to court Latino voters. See Paul Frymer and John David Skrentny, "Coalition-Building and the Politics of Electoral Capture during the Nixon Administration: African Americans, Labor, Latinos," *Studies in American Political Development* 12, no. 1 (1998): 131–61.

60. A. James Reichley, *Conservatives in an Age of Change: The Nixon and Ford Administrations* (Washington, D.C.: Brookings Institution, 1981).

61. Top Nixon domestic policy aide John Ehrlichman, among others, makes this assertion. John Ehrlichman, *Witness to Power: The Nixon Years*, pb. ed. (New York: Pocket Books, 1982).

CHAPTER TWO

1. John G. Stewart, "The Civil Rights Act of 1964: Tactics II," pp. 275–320 in *The Civil Rights Act of 1964: The Passage of the Law That Ended Racial Segregation*, ed. Robert D. Loevy (Albany: State University of New York Press, 1997).

2. *Congressional Quarterly* (hereafter CQ), "Civil Rights Act of 1964 Is Signed into Law," July 3, 1964, p. 1331.

3. CQ, "Strong Rights Bill Due to Leaders' Tactics, Southern Errors," June 19, 1964, pp. 1205–6.

4. Ibid., 1205.

5. For exhaustive accounts of the passage of the 1964 act, see Bureau of National Affairs, *The Civil Rights Act of 1964: Text, Analysis, Legislative History* (Washington, D.C.: BNA, 1964); Robert D. Loevy, *To End All Segregation: The Politics and the Passage of the Civil Rights Act of 1964* (New York: University Press of America, 1990); Charles Whalen and Barbara Whalen, *The Longest Debate: A Legislative History of the 1964 Civil Rights Act* (Cabin John, Md.: Seven Locks, 1985).

6. Genna Rae McNeil, *Groundwork: Charles Hamilton Houston and the Struggle for Civil Rights* (Philadelphia: University of Pennsylvania Press, 1983).

7. EO 8802.

8. Belz, *Equality Transformed.*

9. Sugrue, "Breaking Through."

10. Belz, *Equality Transformed*, 15.

11. Paul D. Moreno, *From Direct Action to Affirmative Action: Fair Employment Law and Policy in America, 1933–1972* (Baton Rouge: Louisiana State University Press, 1997), 185–86.

12. O'Reilly, *Nixon's Piano.*

13. Graham, *Civil Rights Era*; Belz, *Equality Transformed*; President's Committee on Equal Employment Opportunity, "President Announces 192 American Corporations Have Joined Plans for Progress," *The Committee Reporter* 2 (May 1964).

14. "A 'Plans for Progress'–Type Program in Housing," NPM, SMOF: Garment, Box 94. Members of the Nixon White House considered trying a similar effort that would encourage corporate leaders to back open housing efforts in their own communities.

15. Plans for Progress, "A Report: January 1966–August 1967" (Washington, D.C.: Plans for Progress, 1967).

16. Alfred W. Blumrosen, *Modern Law: The Law Transmission System and Equal Employment Opportunity* (Madison: University of Wisconsin Press, 1993).

17. Skrentny, *Ironies of Affirmative Action.*

18. "Clark-Case Memorandum," Appendix E-3 in Bureau of National Affairs, *Civil Rights Act of 1964.*

19. Bureau of National Affairs, *Civil Rights Act of 1964.*

20. AFL-CIO News Release, LC, LCCR, Part II, Box 35, Folder: EEOC—Miscellaneous Materials 1964–68, November 1, 1965.

21. Eleanor Holmes Norton, speech to Washington Press Club, LC, LCCR, Part 1, Box 100, Folder: EEOC News Releases and Publications, December 1, 1977.

22. Graham, *Civil Rights Era*; Skrentny, *Ironies of Affirmative Action*; Skrentny, "State Capacity"; Pedriana and Stryker, "Political Culture Wars."

23. Alfred W. Blumrosen, *Black Employment and the Law* (New Brunswick, N.J.: Rutgers University Press, 1971), 52.

24. Elliott Abrams, "The Quota Commission," *Commentary* 54, no. 4 (1972): 54–57.

25. See the recollections of former EEOC employees in the Southwest Texas State University Oral History Project, which can be accessed at www.eeoc.gov/35th/voices/swt.html.

26. CQ, "Nixon Administration Slows Civil Rights Movement," January 23, 1970, pp. 235–38.

27. Skrentny, *Ironies of Affirmative Action*. Of the 6,133 charges filed in the first year of the commission's existence, a little over half (53.1 percent) contained claims of racial discrimination. Over one-third of the complaints alleged discrimination on the basis of sex. The remaining complaints were made on the basis of religion or national origin, or were not specified. See Equal Employment Opportunity Commission, "35 Years of Ensuring the Promise of Opportunity: History," available at www.eeoc.gov/35th/history.

28. Blumrosen, *Black Employment*, 71.

29. Graham, *Civil Rights Era*, 199.

30. Testimony of William R. Morris, House Judiciary Committee/Civil Rights Oversight Committee (hereafter HJC) December 2, 1971.

31. EEOC, "Report of the White House Conference on Equal Employment Opportunity," August 19–20, 1965, Washington, D.C.

32. EEOC, "35 Years."

33. Ibid.

34. Blumrosen, *Modern Law*.

35. Skrentny, *Ironies of Affirmative Action*, 135.

36. CQ, "Nixon Administration Slows Civil Rights Movement."

37. EEOC, "Milestones in the History of the U.S. Equal Employment Opportunity Commission," available at www.eeoc.gov/35th/milestones.

38. The OFCC's legislative mandate did not extend to unions, as the EEOC's did.

39. Graham, *Civil Rights Era*.

40. Blumrosen, *Modern Law*.

41. Belz, *Equality Transformed*; Skrentny, *Ironies of Affirmative Action*; Graham, *Civil Rights Era*.

42. Hoff observes that the revised Philadelphia Plan focused on the racism of the construction industry in the North, rather than the equally discriminatory textile industry in the South. Nixon often expressed his concern that the South not be singled out in civil rights matters. See Joan Hoff, *Nixon Reconsidered* (New York: Basic, 1994). The GOP attack on discriminatory trade unions was prefigured in the 1960 Republican platform, which, unlike its Democratic counterpart, promised legislation "to end the discriminatory membership practices" in labor unions. See James L. Sundquist, *Politics and Policy: The Eisenhower, Kennedy and Johnson Years* (Washington, D.C.: Brookings Institution, 1968), 253.

43. National Public Radio, "Great Divide: History of Affirmative Action" (transcript), *All Things Considered*, September 16, 1991, 1–6.

44. Letter, Attorney General Mitchell to Secretary of Labor, September 22, 1969. LC, Papers of Edward W. Brooke, Box 422, Folder: Civil Rights, Nixon Administration, 1969–72.

45. Ehrlichman, *Witness to Power.*

46. Skrentny, *Ironies of Affirmative Action*; Stephen Skowronek, "Notes on the Presidency in the Political Order," *Studies in American Political Development* 1: 286–302; Kotlowski, *Nixon's Civil Rights*; Judith Stein, *Running Steel, Running America: Race, Economic Policy and the Decline of Liberalism* (Chapel Hill: University of North Carolina Press, 1998).

47. Belz, *Equality Transformed.*

48. Revised Order No. 4, issued in December 1971 to little notice, expanded affirmative action to include women as an affected class. See Graham*, Civil Rights Era.*

49. Gary Bryner, "Congress, Courts, and Agencies: Equal Employment Opportunity and the Limits of Policy Implementation," *Political Science Quarterly* 96, no. 3 (1981): 411–30.

50. *Federal Register* 35, no. 5 (February 5, 1970): 2587.

51. Hugh Davis Graham, "The Politics of Clientele Capture: Civil Rights Policy and the Reagan Administration," pp. 103–19 in *Redefining Equality*, ed. Neal Devins and Davison M. Douglas (New York: Oxford University Press, 1998).

52. Kotlowski, "Richard Nixon and the Origins of Affirmative Action," 538.

53. Stephen E. Ambrose, *Nixon: The Triumph of a Politician 1962–1972*, Vol. 2 (New York: Simon and Schuster, 1989).

54. On the weakening of the Philadelphia Plan, see Jon Katz, "Labor Dept. Mulls Plan to Cut Construction Minority Quota," *Washington Post* (hereafter WP), September 7, 1972, p. A1; Peter Milius, "Memo Said to Nullify Hiring Plan," WP, September 26, 1972, p. A7. On opposition to quotas, see Grayson Mitchell, "Quota Issue Seen Hurting McGovern," WP, October 20, 1972, p. A6.

55. Stein, *Running Steel, Running America.*

56. *National Journal* (hereafter NJ), "Equal Employment Opportunity Commission: Notes," February 13, 1971, p. 361. In the early 1970s, the OFCC instituted a requirement that federal agencies engaged in contracting undertake compliance reviews for at least half of their contractors; prior to that, compliance reviews typically had been carried out for 10 percent of contractors. At least one researcher, however, found that contractors often only pretended to adhere to fair employment standards, confident that the OFCC would not monitor them closely. See Harrell R. Rodgers, Jr., "Fair Employment Law for Minorities: An Evaluation of Federal Implementation," pp. 93–177 in *Implementation of Civil Rights Policy*, ed. Charles S. Bullock III and Charles M. Lamb (Monterey, Calif.: Brooks/Cole, 1984).

57. Jack Greenberg, *Crusaders in the Courts* (New York: Basic, 1994).

58. USCCR, "The Federal Civil Rights Enforcement Effort—A Reassessment."

59. Karen E. DeWitt, "Labor Report/Strengthened EEOC Accelerates Action Against Business, Labor Employee Discrimination," NJ, June 23, 1973, pp.

913–21; EEOC, "Milestones in the History of the U.S. Equal Employment Opportunity Commission."

60. DeWitt, "Labor Report/Strengthened EEOC Accelerates Action," 913. Many firms were particularly concerned about findings of sex discrimination, which was a relatively new area of scrutiny.

61. Ibid., 920.

62. Gerald R. Rosen, "Industry's New Watchdog in Washington," *Dun's*, June 1974, pp. 83–85.

63. EEOC, "35 Years"; Erin Kelly and Frank Dobbin, "How Affirmative Action Became Diversity Management: Employer Response to Anti-Discrimination Law, 1961–1996," pp. 87–117 in Skrentny, ed., *Color Lines*.

64. Eleanor Holmes Norton speech to Washington Press Club, LC, LCCR, Part 1, Box 100, Folder: EEOC News Releases and Publication, December 1, 1977.

65. CQ, "School Desegregation: How Far Will the Country Go?" December 11, 1970, pp. 2953–57.

66. Judith F. Buncher, ed., *The School Busing Controversy: 1970–75* (New York: Facts on File, 1975).

67. Doug McAdam, *Political Process and the Development of Black Insurgency, 1930–1970* (Chicago: University of Chicago Press, 1982), 174.

68. Tom W. Smith, "America's Most Important Problem—A Trend Analysis, 1946–1976," *Public Opinion Quarterly* 44, no. 2 (1980): 164–80; Schuman et al., *Racial Attitudes in America*.

69. HEW 1983, "OCR Historical Records, Title VI Implementation," reel 1, part 1, ch. 3, pp. 14–5.

70. Ibid., "OCR Historical Records, Title VI Implementation," reel 1, part 2, ch. 3, p. 47.

71. Memorandum, James M. Quigley to staff of the office of the Secretary and agencies, Feb. 8, 1965, in ibid., reel 2, part 1, ch. 3, p. 51.

72. Ibid., reel 2, part 1, ch. 3, pp. 67–8.

73. For an extended analysis of the Chicago situation, see Gary Orfield, *The Reconstruction of Southern Education: The Schools and the 1964 Civil Rights Act* (New York: Wiley-Interscience, 1969).

74. Under this new arrangement, direct Title VI appropriations were made by Congress. Under the prior approach, no separate Title VI funds were allocated to the various agencies within HEW. See HEW 1983, "OCR Title VI Report," reel 2, part 1, ch. 5, p. 2.

75. Ibid., reel 2, part 1, ch. 5, pp. 3–4.

76. Ibid., 18.

77. CQ, "Nixon's School Desegregation Policies Remain Unclear," February 14, 1969, p. 260.

78. Panetta and Gall, *Bring Us Together*.

79. See chapter 4 for a more detailed discussion of the 1968 Republican convention.

80. Rufus E. Miles, *The Department of Health, Education, and Welfare* (New York: Praeger, 1974).

81. Whites saying that the government should "see to it" went up to 47 percent

in 1970, then back down to 35 percent in 1972. The percentage of blacks saying that the government should do so declined to 86 in 1970 and 82 in 1972. See Schuman et al., *Racial Attitudes in America*.

82. Miles, *The Department of Health, Education, and Welfare*; CQ, February 14, 1969, pp. 255–61.

83. CQ, February 14, 1969.

84. "School Desegregation Statement by the Department of Justice and the Department of Health, Education, and Welfare," NPM, WHSF/SMOF: Harry Dent, Box 7, July 5, 1969.

85. Memo, Harry Dent to President Nixon, NPM, WHSF/SMOF: Harry Dent, Box 7, July 8, 1969.

86. Ibid., July 14, 1969.

87. Kotlowski, *Nixon's Civil Rights*.

88. Stephen C. Halpern, *On the Limits of the Law: The Ironic Legacy of Title VI of the 1964 Civil Rights Act* (Baltimore: Johns Hopkins University Press, 1995).

89. CQ, December 11, 1970, pp. 2953–57.

90. Panetta and Gall, *Bring Us Together*, 180.

91. Letter, HEW employees to President Nixon, March 3, 1970, NPM, WHCF/Subject Files, FG 23, box 2.

92. Buncher, *School Busing Controversy*, 101.

93. CQ, "The Nixon Administration and Civil Rights: 1969–1970," November 27, 1970, pp. 2853–58; *Time*, "Finch: First Casualty of the Nixon Cabinet," June 15, 1970, p. 12.

94. Ehrlichman, *Witness to Power*, 227, 232.

95. Robert B. Semple, "Busing and the President: The Evolution of a Policy," *New York Times* (hereafter NYT), March 19, 1972, p. 1.

96. CQ, "Nixon School Busing Policy: 'Fork in Tongue'?" August 28, 1971, p. 1829.

97. McAdam, *Political Process*.

98. Nixon's advisor on Southern politics, Harry Dent, had suggested immediately after the president took office that he should "freeze the [school desegregation] program until a study can be made" (NPM, WHSF/SMOF: Harry Dent, Box 7, January 23, 1969).

99. President's Message to the Congress on Busing, March 17, 1972. National Archives and Records Administration (hereafter NARA), RG 12, Office File of Commissioner of Education, Box 639, Folder: Busing.

100. Ibid.

101. NYT, "Roadblocks for the Nixon Proposals," April 23, 1972, Sec. IV, p. 2; John Herbers, "95 U.S. Rights Lawyers Score Nixon Busing View," NYT, April 26, 1972.

102. Ambrose, *Nixon*, 553; Ehrlichman, *Witness to Power*.

103. Miles, *The Department of Health, Education, and Welfare*; David Barton Smith, *Health Care Divided: Race and Healing a Nation* (Ann Arbor: University of Michigan Press, 1999); Jill Quadagno, "Promoting Civil Rights Through the Welfare State: How Medicare Integrated Southern Hospitals," *Social Problems* 47 (2000): 68–89; USCCR, "Federal Title VI Enforcement to

Ensure Nondiscrimination in Federally Assisted Programs" (Washington, D.C.: U.S. Government Printing Office, 1966). Southern hospital desegregation was coordinated by the Office of Equal Health Opportunity, formed within the Public Health Service in January 1966. As noted earlier, in summer 1967, Congress directed HEW to move Title VI responsibilities from its constituent programs to a new Office for Civil Rights that was accountable directly to the HEW secretary.

104. USCCR, "HEW and Title VI" (Washington, D.C.: Government Printing Office, 1970), vi.

105. Miles, *The Department of Health, Education, and Welfare*, 247.

106. United States General Accounting Office, "Compliance with Antidiscrimination Provision of Civil Rights Act by Hospitals and Other Facilities under Medicare and Medicaid," 14; reprinted in HJC 1973.

107. HJC 1973, p. 166, 174.

108. LCCR, "The Civil Rights Enforcement Program in the Health and Social Services Programs of the U.S. Dept. of Health, Education, and Welfare: Policy Paper for a New Direction and Approach," circa 1977. LC, LCCR, I:143, Folder: Health Task Force.

109. USCCR, "HEW and Title VI," 30.

110. People believing that they have received inadequate health care might be more likely to file a malpractice suit than a racial discrimination complaint.

111. Gregory D. Squires, Samantha Friedman, and Catherine E. Saidat, "Experiencing Residential Segregation: A Contemporary Study of Washington, D.C." *Urban Affairs Review* 38, no. 2 (2002): 155–83.

112. Letter, Law Offices of Rauh, Silard, and Lichtman to Patricia Roberts Harris, LC, Patricia Roberts Harris Papers, Box 53, Folder: OCR 1979, August 10, 1979.

113. "OCR Review," LC, Harris Papers, Box 298, Folder: OCR Review 5/16/80.

114. Halpern, *On the Limits of the Law*.

115. The Supreme Court's 1977 *Milliken II* decision (433 U.S. 267) allowed for special compensatory funds to be created to aid disadvantaged students in racially isolated schools. See Susan E. Eaton, Joseph Feldman, and Edward Kirby, "Still Separate, Still Unequal: The Limits of *Milliken II*'s Monetary Compensation to Segregated Schools," pp. 143–78 in *Dismantling Desegregation: The Quiet Reversal of "Brown v. Board of Education,"* ed. Gary Orfield, Susan E. Eaton, and the Harvard Project on School Desegregation (New York: New Press, 1996).

116. Lawrence J. McAndrews, "The Politics of Principle: Richard Nixon and School Desegregation," *Journal of Negro History* 83, no. 3 (1998): 187–200.

117. Leonard Garment, *Crazy Rhythm* (New York: Times Books, 1997), 217.

118. Massey and Denton, *American Apartheid*.

119. Reynolds Farley and William H. Frey, "Changes in the Segregation of Whites from Blacks during the 1980s: Small Steps toward a More Integrated Society," *American Sociological Review* 59 (1994): 23–45.

120. Massey and Denton, *American Apartheid*. There is some variation in researchers' calculations of segregation levels, due to such factors as researcher

methodology, the measure of segregation used, and the units that are being compared (e.g., census tracts, blocks, and so on).

121. Mark I. Gelfand, *A Nation of Cities: The Federal Government and Urban America, 1933–1965* (New York: Oxford University Press, 1975); Kenneth T. Jackson, *Crabgrass Frontier: The Suburbanization of the United States* (New York: Oxford University Press, 1985); Thomas J. Sugrue, *The Origins of the Urban Crisis: Race and Inequality in Postwar Detroit* (Princeton: Princeton University Press, 1996).

122. Joe T. Darden, "Black Residential Segregation since the 1948 *Shelley v. Kraemer* Decision," *Journal of Black Studies* 25, no. 6 (1995): 680–91; Karl E. Taeuber and Alma F. Taeuber, *Negroes in Cities: Residential Segregation and Neighborhood Change* (Chicago: Aldine, 1965); Thomas L. Van Valey, Wade Clark Roof, and Jerome E. Wilcox, "Trends in Residential Segregation: 1960–1970," *American Journal of Sociology* 82, no. 4 (1977): 826–44.

123. Darden, "Black Residential Segregation"; John R. Logan and Mark Schneider, "Racial Segregation and Racial Change in American Suburbs, 1970–1980," *American Journal of Sociology* 89, no. 4 (1984): 874–88; Douglas S. Massey and Nancy A. Denton, "Trends in the Residential Segregation of Blacks, Hispanics, and Asians: 1970–1980," *American Sociological Review* 52 (1987): 802–25; Stanley Lieberson and Donna K. Carter, "Temporal Changes and Urban Differences in Residential Segregation: A Reconsideration," *American Journal of Sociology* 88, no. 2 (1982): 296–310; Farley and Frey, "Changes in the Segregation of Whites from Blacks"; Reynolds Farley, "Black-White Residential Segregation: The Views of Myrdal in the 1940s and Trends of the 1980s," pp. 45–75 in *An American Dilemma Revisited: Race Relations in a Changing World*, ed. Obie Clayton, Jr. (New York: Russell Sage Foundation, 1996). Massey and Denton's (1993) analysis of the thirty metropolitan areas with the largest black populations found comparable, if slightly smaller, decreases.

124. Edward L. Glaeser and Jacob L. Vigdor, "Racial Segregation in the 2000 Census: Promising News" (Washington, D.C.: Brookings Institution, 2001). The difference between comparing black/white segregation and black/nonblack segregation essentially resides in the treatment of Latinos, since "Asian, Native American and Pacific Islander populations are generally too small to influence segregation (and their residential patterns generally resemble those of nonhispanic whites)."

125. Norman Fainstein, "Black Ghettoization and Social Mobility," pp. 123–41 in *The Bubbling Cauldron*, ed. Michael Peter Smith and Joe R. Feagin (Minneapolis: University of Minnesota Press, 1995), 135, 136. On African American isolation, see William Julius Wilson, *When Work Disappears: The World of the New Urban Poor* (New York: Knopf, 1996).

126. Massey and Denton, *American Apartheid*, 9.

127. Camille Zubrinsky Charles, "The Dynamics of Racial Residential Segregation," *Annual Review of Sociology* 29 (2003): 167–207.

128. Melvin L. Oliver and Thomas M. Shapiro, *Black Wealth/White Wealth* (New York: Routledge, 1995); John Yinger, *Closed Doors, Opportunity Lost: The Continuing Costs of Housing Discrimination* (New York: Russell Sage Foundation, 1995). For another excellent treatment of race and wealth disparities, see

Dalton Conley, *Being Black, Living in the Red* (Berkeley: University of California Press, 1999).

129. One reason for this differential is that more blacks find themselves having to obtain loans through financing companies rather than banks. Other factors may include the existence of tiered interests rates for mortgages below a certain amount (a policy having a disparate impact on minority and integrated neighborhoods) and the greater likelihood of white home-buyers receiving financial assistance from their parents.

130. Yinger, *Closed Doors, Opportunity Lost.*

131. David Rusk, "The 'Segregation' Tax: The Cost of Residential Segregation to Black Homeowners" (Washington, D.C.: Brookings Institution, 2001), 1.

132. Sugrue, *Origins of the Urban Crisis*, 9.

133. Jackson, *Crabgrass Frontier*, 217.

134. Pierson, *Dismantling the Welfare State?*

CHAPTER THREE

1. NAACP 1982, Remarks by Robert B. Pitts, Racial Relations Officer, FHA, before Conference on Housing for Minority Families, Seattle, Washington, part 5, reel 8.

2. Michael L. Lanza, *Agrarianism and Reconstruction Politics: The Southern Homestead Act* (Baton Rouge: Louisiana State University Press, 1990).

3. These laws were actually preceded by a local California law requiring all Chinese residents to relocate from their current area of residence to another one designated by the city. A federal court struck down the law in 1890. Chinese residents in the United States were also apparently the first victims of restrictive covenants barring their residence in areas of West Coast cities. A federal court ruled against these covenants in 1892. See Charles Abrams, *Forbidden Neighbors: A Study of Prejudice in Housing* (New York: Harper, 1955).

4. C. Vann Woodward, *The Strange Career of Jim Crow*, 3rd rev. ed. (New York: Oxford University Press, 1974), 100–101; Michael Jones-Correa, "The Origins and Diffusion of Racial Restrictive Covenants," *Political Science Quarterly* 115 (4): 541–67.

5. Loren Miller, "Louisville's Housing Anniversary," *The Crisis* June 1967, p. 255; Massey and Denton, *American Apartheid.*

6. Robert C. Weaver, *The Negro Ghetto* (New York: Harcourt, Brace, 1948).

7. USCCR, "Housing."

8. St. Clair Drake and Horace R. Cayton, *Black Metropolis: A Study of Negro Life in a Northern City* (Chicago: University of Chicago Press, [1945] 1993); Weaver, *Negro Ghetto.*

9. Drake and Cayton, *Black Metropolis.*

10. Ibid.; Stephen Grant Meyer, *As Long As They Don't Move Next Door: Segregation and Racial Conflict in American Neighborhoods* (Lanham, Md.: Rowman and Littlefield, 2000); Abrams, *Forbidden Neighbors.*

11. Abrams, *Forbidden Neighbors.*

12. Charles T. Male, *Real Estate Fundamentals* (New York: D. Van Nostrand, 1932).

13. In 1956, fifty such private developments were located, mostly in the industrial centers of the North and West. See George Grier and Eunice Grier, *Equality and Beyond: Housing Segregation and the Goals of the Great Society* (Chicago: Quadrangle, 1966).

14. USCCR, "Housing."

15. Ibid.; HUD, "Housing in the Seventies" (Washington, D.C.: U.S. Government Printing Office, 1973).

16. Jackson, *Crabgrass Frontier*, 203; Weaver, *Negro Ghetto*.

17. Jackson, *Crabgrass Frontier*; FHA, "Seventh Annual Report of the Federal Housing Administration" (Washington, D.C.: U.S. Government Printing Office, 1941).

18. Gelfand, *Nation of Cities*, 219–220.

19. Alan Wolfe, *America's Impasse: The Rise and Fall of the Politics of Growth* (New York: Pantheon, 1981), 82.

20. Abrams, *Forbidden Neighbors*, 156; Rose Helper, *Racial Policies and Practices of Real Estate Brokers* (Minneapolis: University of Minnesota Press, 1969.)

21. Quoted in "Government Relationship to Housing Supply," LC, Papers of the Urban League, Part III, Box 76, Folder 3. The main private-sector interests who relied extensively on covenants were property owners' and neighborhood improvement associations, and developers of subdivisions (Weaver, *Negro Ghetto*).

22. USCCR, "Housing."

23. Jackson, *Crabgrass Frontier*, 213; Weaver, *Negro Ghetto*.

24. Jackson, *Crabgrass Frontier*.

25. Paul F. Wendt, *The Role of the Federal Government in Housing* (Washington, D.C.: American Enterprise Association, 1956); USCCR, "Housing."

26. Robert C. Lieberman, *Shifting the Color Line: Race and the American Welfare State* (Cambridge: Harvard University Press, 1998).

27. The Public Works Administration required contractors to employ at least the same percentage of black workers as were recorded in the 1930 census for the city in question. See Moreno, *from Direct Action to Affirmative Action*.

28. Weaver, *Negro Ghetto*; USCCR, "Housing"; Gunnar Myrdal, *An American Dilemma: The Negro Problem and Modern Democracy* (New York: Harper, 1944), 350. In 1940, the Supreme Court revisited the issue of restrictive covenants in *Hansberry v. Lee* (311 U.S. 32), reversing an Illinois Supreme Court decision that upheld the validity of a racially restrictive covenant. Because the High Court decided the case on a technicality, however, *Hansberry* did not eliminate covenants or challenge the *Corrigan* precedent.

29. Wolfe, *America's Impasse*.

30. Note that during the Second Great Migration, significant numbers of blacks stayed in the South, moving from rural to urban areas. See Meyer, *As Long as They Don't Move Next Door*.

31. With respect to public war housing, practices varied widely. In San Diego, for instance, the manager of public war housing—an employee of the Federal

Public Housing Authority—instituted a policy of segregation, even though most of the housing was to be developed on vacant land in new communities and the city itself was not segregated. A small number of local authorities on the West Coast followed nonsegregation policies. See Weaver, *Negro Ghetto*.

32. Davis McEntire, *Residence and Race* (Berkeley and Los Angeles: University of California Press, 1960).

33. The Racial Relations Service claimed in 1952 that "Negro building trades workers have been paid over $78,000,000" in the construction of public housing projects, "largely due to the implementation by the racial relations personnel of specific non-discrimination policies adopted by the [RRS] many years prior to the rise of the FEPC approach" (NAACP 1982, "The Role of the Racial Relations Service in the Administration of Housing Programs of the Federal Government," part 5, reel 8).

34. USCCR, "Housing," 24.

35. Grier and Grier, *Equality and Beyond*.

36. Reginald A. Johnson, "Future Housing without the Legal Racial Restrictive Covenants," LC, National Urban League, Part III, Box 76, Folder 2, November 16, 1948.

37. Arnold R. Hirsch, " 'Containment' on the Home Front: Race and Federal Housing Policy from the New Deal to the Cold War," *Journal of Urban History* 26, no. 2 (2000): 158–89.

38. "HHFA Report on Civil Rights," NARA, General Records of the Department of Health, Education, and Welfare, RG 235, Box 133, Folder: Civil Rights, January 1961.

39. Letter, Robert Weaver to Albert M. Cole, Schomburg Center for Research in Black Culture (hereafter SCBC), Robert C. Weaver Papers, Reel 1, Correspondence, April 5, 1954.

40. Later, FHA refused to insure loans for discriminatory builders in states that had housing antidiscrimination laws. However, the agency would only step in if the state had found a violation, at which point the builder would have probably sold all homes on a discriminatory basis. As of 1961, FHA had never suspended a builder or developer for discrimination (see USCCR "Housing").

41. Robert Fredrick Burk, *The Eisenhower Administration and Black Civil Rights* (Knoxville: University of Tennessee Press, 1984), 117.

42. James Q. Wilson, *Negro Politics: The Search for Leadership* (Glencoe, Ill.: Free Press, 1960), 188.

43. Meyer, *As Long as They Don't Move Next Door*.

44. Congressional Quarterly Service, *Housing a Nation* (Washington, D.C.: Congressional Quarterly Service, 1966), 25.

45. This happened again in 1956, when prominent Democrats opposed the Powell Amendment to abolish school segregation, claiming it would endanger federal aid to education, and in 1966, when Sen. Muskie (D-ME) eliminated an antisegregation clause from Model Cities legislation in attempt to gain support for the bill. See Wolfe, *America's Impasse*, 87.

46. USCCR, "Housing," 19–20; Wendt, *The Role of the Federal Government in Housing*.

47. Gelfand, *Nation of Cities*, 212.

48. For a particularly egregious example of the indifference that public officials often displayed to families forced to relocate, see Robert A. Caro's *The Power Broker: Robert Moses and the Fall of New York* (New York: Vintage, 1974), which documents New York City's urban renewal activities under Robert Moses.

49. "Statement of Robert C. Weaver," LC, Papers of the National Urban League, Part III, Box 76, Folder 3, circa 1949.

50. "HHFA Report on Civil Rights," NARA, General Records of the Department of Health, Education, and Welfare, RG 235, Box 133, Folder: Civil Rights, January 1961.

51. Gelfand, *Nation of Cities*.

52. Burk, *Eisenhower Administration and Black Civil Rights*.

53. Gelfand, *Nation of Cities*, 236.

54. M. Carter McFarland, *Federal Government and Urban Problems: HUD: Successes, Failures, and the Fate of Our Cities* (Boulder, Colo.: Westview, 1978).

55. Quoted in NAACP 1982, "The Need for a White House Conference," Part 5, Reel 8, n.d.

56. Burk, *Eisenhower Administration and Black Civil Rights*, 113; Hirsch, " 'Containment' on the Home Front."

57. This was the case for many years at HEW, until a separate Office for Civil Rights was created with the authority to cut off funds. See HEW 1983, "OCR Historical Records, Title VI Implementation," Reel 1, Part 2, ch. 3, p. 47.

58. NAACP 1982, Address by Frank S. Horne to the Urban League of Buffalo, Part 5, Reel 8, April 28, 1954; see also Abrams, *Forbidden Neighbors*.

59. Nicholas Lemann, *The Promised Land: The Great Black Migration and How It Changed America* (New York: Vintage, 1991).

60. Quoted in NAACP 1982, Letter, George R. Metcalf to Walter White, Part 5, Reel 8, June 17, 1954.

61. *Congressional Quarterly Almanac*, "Housing Probe," (Washington, D.C.: Congressional Quarterly Service, 1954); Warren Unna, "Senators Pin FHA Scandal on 'Greedy,' " *Washington Post and Times Herald*, December 20, 1954, p. 1; *Wall Street Journal*, "Senate Group, in Scathing Report, Assails Both Builders, U.S. Officials for Greed, Dishonesty in F.H.A. Scandals," December 20, 1954, p. 2.

62. Gelfand, *Nation of Cities*; McFarland, *Federal Government and Urban Problems*.

63. LCCR, "Proposals for Executive Action to End Federally Supported Segregation and Other Forms of Racial Discrimination," NARA, General Records of the Department of Health, Education, and Welfare, RG 235, Box 133, Folder: Civil Rights, August 29, 1961, p. 45; Gelfand, *Nation of Cities*.

64. Sundquist, *Politics and Policy*; Grier and Grier, *Equality and Beyond*, 60.

65. Gelfand, *Nation of Cities*.

66. LCCR, "Proposals for Executive Action to End Federally Supported Segregation and Other Forms of Racial Discrimination," NARA, General Records of the Department of Health, Education, and Welfare, RG 235, Box 133, Folder: Civil Rights. August 29, 1961, p. 43.

67. Taylor Branch, *Parting the Waters: America in the King Years, 1954–63* (New York: Simon and Schuster, 1988).

68. Figures from HHFA-PHA Program Planning Division, Statistics Branch, filed in LC, Urban League, Part III, Box 73, Folder 8.

69. Massey and Denton, *American Apartheid.*

70. Sundquist, *Politics and Policy.*

71. Gelfand, *Nation of Cities.*

72. Graham, *Civil Rights Era.*

73. "Kentucky FH Law is First in South," *NCDH Trends in Housing*, April 1968. Some issues of this helpful newsletter are filed in LC, LCCR, Part I, Box 76, Folder: NCDH.

74. Gelfand, *Nation of Cities*; John B. Willmann, *The Department of Housing and Urban Development* (New York: Praeger, 1967).

75. Congressional Quarterly Service, *Revolution in Civil Rights*, 4th ed. (Washington, D.C.: Congressional Quarterly Service, 1968); Jill Quadagno, *The Color of Welfare: How Racism Undermined the War on Poverty* (New York: Oxford University Press, 1994).

76. HUD, "Housing in the Seventies."

77. Jackson, *Crabgrass Frontier*, 366, n. 66; Willmann, *The Department of Housing and Urban Development.*

78. Memo, HUD, "Equal Opportunity in HUD Operations and Programs," LC, NAACP, Part IV, Box A31, Folder: Government-National-HUD-Housing, January 9, 1967.

79. "Remarks of P. N. Brownstein, Assistant Secretary-Commissioner at Directors Conference," SCBC, Robert C. Weaver Papers (additions), Box 3, Folder 12, October 23, 1967.

80. Robert Weisbrot, *Freedom Bound: A History of America's Civil Rights Movement* (New York: Norton, 1990); National Advisory Commission on Civil Disorders, "Report of the National Advisory Commission on Civil Disorders" (Kerner Commission Report), *New York Times* ed. (New York: Dutton, 1968); McAdam, *Political Process.*

81. Graham, *Civil Rights Era*, 258.

82. National Committee Against Discrimination in Housing, "How the Federal Government Builds Ghettos" (New York: NCDH, 1968).

83. Memo, Joseph Califano to Lyndon Johnson, *Civil Rights During the Johnson Administration* (hereafter CRJA), Part 1, Reel 8, Box 47, October 28, 1965.

84. Memo, Hubert Humphrey to Lyndon Johnson, CRJA, Part 1, Reel 8, Box 47, September 13, 1966.

85. Oral history interview with Clarence Mitchell (Director, NAACP Washington Bureau), CRJA, Part 3, Reel 3.

86. On housing integration as a civil rights priority, see Quadagno, *The Color of Welfare.* For protest events, see McAdam, *Political Process.*

87. Mary Lou Finley, "The Open Housing Marches: Chicago, Summer '66." pp. 7–8 in *Chicago 1966: Open Housing Marches, Summit Negotiations, and Operation Bread basket*, ed. David J. Garrow (Brooklyn, N.Y.: Carlson, 1989), 7–8.

88. James R. Ralph, Jr., *Northern Protest: Martin Luther King, Jr., Chicago and the Civil Rights Movement* (Cambridge: Harvard University Press, 1993).

89. Ibid., 123.

90. *Chicago Tribune*, "King Asked to Stop March," August 23, 1966, p. 1;

Kathleen Connolly, "The Chicago Open Housing Conference," pp. 49–95 in Garrow, ed., *Chicago 1966*.

91. On September 4, 1966, a group of 200 individuals organized by the Congress of Racial Equality marched into Cicero, scuffling briefly with hecklers before the Chicago police and National Guard separated the two sides. See Ralph, *Northern Protest*; David Halvorsen, "Cancel Rights Marches," *Chicago Tribune*, August 27, 1966, p. 1.

92. Ralph, *Northern Protest*; CQ, "Civil Rights Housing Section at Center of Dispute," July 15, 1966, pp. 1465–66.

93. "NAACP Steps Up Campaign for Fair Housing Program" (press release), LC, NAACP, Part IV, Box A35, Folder: Housing General 1966–67, July 22, 1966.

94. Letter, National Association of Real Estate Boards to Board Presidents and Secretaries, LC, LCCR, Part I, Box 104, Folder: HUD 1966–69, June 8, 1966. In 1966, local real-estate boards with black members remained rare. See Barbara Bradshaw and Edward L. Holmgren, "Open Occupancy and Open Minds: A Study of Realtors," *Interracial Review* 39 (4).

95. *Congressional Record*, Aug. 5, 1966, p. 18396. Subsequent quotes from the floor debate are identified parenthetically in the main text. They are all from the *Congressional Record*.

96. CQ, July 15, 1966, p. 1465.

97. Fifty-four of the ninety-six senators present at the time voted to invoke cloture on the bill, ten votes short of the necessary two-thirds required to end debate. See Sundquist, *Politics and Policy*.

98. "Summary of a Statement by Stokeley Carmichael on the Civil Rights Bill of 1966," LC, NAACP, Part IV, Box A20, Folder: Civil Rights Bills, July 1, 1966.

99. Ralph, *Northern Protest*, 179.

100. CQ, "House Passes Civil Rights Bill, Retains Housing Section," August 12, 1966, pp. 1719–23.

101. Ibid.

102. Graham, *Civil Rights Era*, 274; *Wall Street Journal*, "House Approves Administration's Civil-Rights Bill," August 10, 1966.

103. With regard to the first point, note that congressional opponents objected to the proposed enforcement powers of the fair housing board on the basis of HEW's school desegregation guidelines and subsequent actions, rather than that of the EEOC, which was not terribly visible or powerful at the time.

104. These numbers come from the author's own tally of voting records provided in *Congressional Quarterly*. Note that it was the eighty-eighth Congress that voted on the 1964 Civil Rights Act, the eighty-ninth Congress that voted on 1966 fair housing legislation, and the ninetieth Congress that voted on the 1968 fair housing legislation. According to *CQ*'s own tally, twenty-six members opposed fair housing during the key vote in 1966 (the vote to recommit the bill) but favored it in 1968 (the previous question vote). Eight members supported it in 1966 but opposed it two years later.

105. Mara S. Sidney, "Images of Race, Class, and Markets: Rethinking the Origin of U.S. Fair Housing Policy," *Journal of Policy History* 13, no. 2 (2001): 181–214.

106. "NCDH says its work in 41 cities in 25 states finds tensions rising in

nation's racial ghettos because Negroes are locked in and want out," NCDH Press Release, LC, NAACP Papers, Part IV, Box A50, File: NCDH 1966–68, March 2, 1967.

107. Sidney, "Images of Race, Class, and Markets."

108. Oral history interview with Harold "Barefoot" Sanders, CRJA, Part 3, Reel 3.

109. The previous fall, Senate Judiciary Committee Chairman James O. Eastland (D-MS) had considered amending HR 2516 by adding the administration's open-housing provision, a move he described as "a dose of medicine which will be fatal" to the bill. See CQ, "Committee Roundup: Open Housing," September 1, 1967, pp. 1692–93.

110. George R. Metcalf, *Fair Housing Comes of Age* (New York: Greenwood, 1988).

111. Charles McL. Matthias, Jr., and Marion Morris, "Fair Housing Legislation: Not an Easy Row to Hoe," *Cityscape* 4, no. 3 (1999): 21–33. As noted earlier, twenty-three states had fair-housing laws at this time.

112. Massey and Denton, *American Apartheid*.

113. Rockford, Ill., the major city in Anderson's district, passed a strong open-housing law the night before the Rules Committee vote. Media outlets had reported prior to King's assassination that Anderson might switch his vote in the committee. On passage of the bill, see CQ, "Open-Housing Law Credited to Mitchell's Lobbying," April 24, 1968, pp. 1–4.

114. The law defines a riot as a public disturbance involving at least three people that endangers people or property.

115. Robert Weaver interview with James Mosby, SCBC, Robert C. Weaver Papers (Additions), Box 8, Folder 14, 1969. This interview provides an insider's discussion of the circumstances surrounding passage.

116. CQ, April 24, 1968, pp. 1–4.

117. Memo, Fred Panzer to Lyndon Johnson, CRJA, Part 1, Reel 8, Box 48, August 15, 1967.

118. Mara S. Sidney, *Unfair Housing: How National Policy Shapes Community Action* (Lawrence: University Press of Kansas, 2003).

119. "Understanding and Using the Supreme Court Decision Banning Racial Discrimination in Housing," NAACP Guidelines for Branches, LC, Roy Wilkins Papers, Box 25, Folder: Housing Discrimination, August 1968.

120. Charles J. Orlebeke, "The Evolution of Low-Income Housing Policy, 1949 to 1999," *Housing Policy Debate* 11, no. 2 (2000): 489–520.

121. Metcalf, *Fair Housing Comes of Age*; Danielson, *The Politics of Exclusion*; Falk and Franklin, *Equal Housing Opportunity*; William R. Morris, "The 1968 Housing Act: New Hope for Negroes," *The Crisis*, November 1968, pp. 313–17.

Chapter Four

1. Peter N. Carroll, *It Seemed Like Nothing Happened: The Tragedy and Promise of America in the 1970s* (New York: Holt, Rinehart, and Winston, 1982), 56.

2. *Newsweek*, "The Troubled American: A Special Report on the White Majority," October 6, 1969, p. 29.

3. *Newsweek*, "How It Feels to Be Caught in the Middle," October 6, 1969, p. 36; Karl Fleming, "The Square American Speaks Out," *Newsweek*, October 6, 1969, p. 57.

4. Dan T. Carter, *The Politics of Rage: George Wallace, the Origins of the New Conservatism, and the Transformation of American Politics* (New York: Simon and Schuster, 1995), 368; Ambrose, *Nixon*.

5. Samuel Lubell, *The Hidden Crisis in American Politics* (New York: Norton, 1970), pp. 70–71.

6. Daniel Yergin and Joseph Stanislaw, *The Commanding Heights: The Battle Between Government and the Marketplace That Is Remaking the Modern World* (New York: Simon and Schuster, 1998); James T. Patterson, *Grand Expectations: The United States, 1945–1974* (New York: Oxford University Press, 1996).

7. Terry H. Anderson, *The Movement and the Sixties: Protest in America from Greensboro to Wounded Knee* (New York: Oxford University Press, 1995); Thomas Byrne Edsall and Mary D. Edsall, *Chain Reaction: The Impact of Race, Rights, and Taxes on American Politics* (New York: Norton, 1991); O'Reilly, *Nixon's Piano*. Nixon's statements at the private meeting with Southern delegates are quoted in Jules Witcover, *The Resurrection of Richard Nixon* (New York: Putnam, 1970), 343–34.

8. Statement by Governor George Romney, LC, Papers of Edward W. Brooke, Box 189, Folder: George Romney, August 9, 1968. On the "mini-revolt," see also Witcover, *Resurrection of Richard Nixon*; Richard Milhous Nixon, *RN: The Memoirs of Richard Nixon* (New York: Touchstone, [1978] 1990).

9. Reichley, *Conservatives in an Age of Change*.

10. Theodore H. White, *The Making of the President–1968* (New York: Atheneum, 1969), 147.

11. There is an odd side-note to the connection between Romney and Nixon: in 1964, a mentally ill man barged into Governor Romney's office with a gun and knife, claiming that Nixon had sent him. On a more conventional note, Nixon deemed Romney as the individual having the best chance to defeat right-wing candidate Barry Goldwater during the 1964 Republican primaries. See "Romney-Personal" in LC, Brooke Papers, Box 164, Folder: George Romney.

12. Taking a shot at Romney's intellect after his comments about being brainwashed, Democratic Senator and presidential candidate Eugene McCarthy joked that, "in his case, a little light rinse would have been more than enough." See *Daily Telegraph*, "Obituary of George Romney," July 31, 1995.

13. On Romney's first campaign, see "Romney: 1962 Campaign," LC, Papers of Edward W. Brooke, Box 644, Folder: George Romney. On Detroit riots, see Weisbrot, *Freedom Bound*. On Romney's early career, see Garry Wills, *Nixon Agonistes: The Crisis of the Self-Made Man* (New York: Mentor, 1979).

14. HJC 1971/2; LC, Brooke Papers, Box 189, Folder: George Romney.

15. Nathan, *Administrative Presidency*, 28.

16. On funding, see A. James Reichley, "George Romney Is Running Hard at HUD," *Fortune*, December 1970, pp. 100–103, 134–35; HJC 1971/2. On

Romney as salesman, see William Lilley III, "Housing Report/Romney Faces Political Perils with Plan to Integrate Suburbs," NJ, October 17, 1970, pp. 2251–63.

17. NYT, "Transcript of Nixon's Program on Television Introducing His Cabinet Members," December 12, 1968, p. 37.

18. Lilley, "Housing Report/Romney Faces Political Perils," 2263.

19. William Lilley III, "CPR Report/Romney Lines Up HUD Money Programs to Back Operation Breakthrough Housing Push," NJ, January 31, 1970, p. 232–41.

20. HUD, "Housing in the Seventies"; Metcalf, *Fair Housing Comes of Age*; Danielson, *Politics of Exclusion*; Falk and Franklin, *Equal Housing Opportunity*; William R. Morris, "The 1968 Housing Act: New Hope for Negroes," *The Crisis*, November 1968, pp. 313–17.

21. Memo, George Romney to President Nixon, "The HUD Inheritance," HUD, Box 74, February 14, 1969.

22. "HUD Decentralized to 23 Area Cities" (HUD Press Release), October 28, 1970, in LC, LCCR, Box 1, Part 105, Folder: HUD. In the same location, see also HUD press releases of November 7, 1969 ("Organizational Overhaul Announced by Romney"), November 30, 1969 ("HUD-FHA Field Offices Get Key Role in Processing Housing Projects"), and August 18, 1970 ("HUD Set to Decentralize Its Program Operations").

23. The Equal Opportunity Office was reshuffled in April 1972. Prior to this reorganization, HUD's internal organization did not allow for coordination between the antidiscrimination protections in Title VIII of the Fair Housing Act and the funding cut-off authority granted under Title VI of the 1964 Civil Rights Act. See USCCR, "The Federal Civil Rights Enforcement Effort—A Reassessment."

24. Civil rights groups such as the NAACP later expressed concern to Romney that local officials were failing at times to carry out the policies of HUD's Washington office. See Letter, William R. Morris to George Romney, LC, NAACP, Part VI, Box F11, Folder: HUD 1971, March 2, 1971.

25. Quoted in unsigned memo, "Draft for a HUD Policy on Open Communities," HUD, Papers of Richard C. Van Dusen, Box 10, circa 1969–70.

26. National Advisory Commission on Civil Disorders, "Report," pp. 474–75. During his 1968 presidential campaign, Nixon criticized the Kerner Commission report because it "blamed everybody for the riots except the perpetrators of the riots," and because its recommendations relied too heavily on federal programs. See CQ, November 27, 1970.

27. SSC 1970.

28. Lilley, "Housing Report/Romney Faces Political Perils," 2253.

29. Kevin P. Phillips, "Squeezing the Suburbs," WP, June 22, 1971.

30. See Memo, Tom Stoel to Leonard Garment, CRNA, Reel 20, Box 19, 870-6, March 11, 1971.

31. Memo, David L. Norman to Ray Price, BHL, George W. Romney Papers, Box 13, Folder: The President—Ehrlichman—1971, June 3, 1971.

32. Mahoney, "The End(s) of Disparate Impact."

33. "Fair Housing Program Issues," BHL, Romney Papers, Box 4, Folder: HUD Civil Rights Policy, n.d.; William Lilley III, "Housing Report/Administration

and Congress Follow Courts in Promoting Residential Integration," NJ, November 12, 1971, pp. 2431–39.

34. Memo, Alexander C. Ross to Jerris Leonard, "The Provision of Low-Income Housing by Recipients of Federal Funds," BHL, Romney Papers, Box 14, Folder: President, November 20, 1970.

35. "HUD: Civil Rights Policy Choices," BHL, Romney Papers, Box 4, Folder: HUD's Civil Rights Policy, n.d.

36. Danielson, *Politics of Exclusion.*

37. Ibid.; Lilley, "CPR Report."

38. Quoted in Letter, Richard C. Van Dusen to Rev. James A. Hamilton, HUD, Box 100, Rel. 6-2, March 6, 1970.

39. USCCR, "Federal Civil Rights Enforcement: One Year Later" (Washington, D.C.: U.S. Government Printing Office, 1971).

40. Reichley, "George Romney Is Running Hard," 134.

41. Skrentny, *Ironies of Affirmative Action.*

42. The issue of open housing may call for different collective mobilization strategies than issues such as employment discrimination. Open housing protest marches—like those led by Martin Luther King, Jr., in Chicago—may be counterproductive means of drawing support for ending discrimination in housing. White fears of residential desegregation are typically not based on the movement of small numbers of African Americans moving to their neighborhoods *as such*, but on widespread racial transition (often a self-fulfilling prophecy). Consequently, large marches may reinforce white fears that they will be overwhelmed by African American families in a short period of time.

43. Wilson, *Negro Politics.*

44. *Newsweek*, October 6, 1969, p. 45.

45. Proposed Departmental Circular from George Romney, BHL, Papers of Albert Applegate, Box 3, Folder: Fair Housing 1969–70, n.d..

46. See, for instance, Memo, Lawrence M. Cox to George Romney, HUD, Van Dusen Papers, Box 10, Open Communities File, July 20, 1970. This file contains extensive material on internal deliberations within the agency. The Open Communities Task Force included Assistant Secretary for Metropolitan Planning and Management Samuel Jackson, Assistant Secretary for Equal Opportunity Samuel Simmons, General Counsel Sherman Unger, and Under Secretary Richard Van Dusen.

47. Memo, Henry B. Schechter to John C. Chapin, "Selection of Localities for Open Communities Demonstrations," HUD, Van Dusen Papers, Box 10, Open Communities File, August 15, 1969.

48. Danielson, *Politics of Exclusion*; Lilley, "Housing Report/Romney Faces Political Perils."

49. Hugh McDonald, "How Warren Became Integration Test City," *Detroit News*, July 22, 1970, p. 6A.

50. Transcript of Warren, Michigan, Meeting, BHL, Applegate Papers, Box 9, Folder: Romney Interviews, July 27, 1970, pp. 28–29; Hugh McDonald, "U.S. Picks Warren as Prime Target in Move to Integrate All Suburbs," *Detroit News*, July 21, 1970, p. 1A.

51. Reichley, "George Romney Is Running Hard," 135.

52. Transcript of Warren meeting, 29; Hugh McDonald and Gary Schuster, "No Forced Integration, But Open Housing Is Essential, Romney Says," *Detroit News*, July 28, 1970, p. 1A.

53. Transcript of Warren meeting, 32.

54. Don Lenhausen and Howard Kohn, "Romney Tells the Suburbs He Won't Force Integration," *Detroit Free Press*, July 28, 1970, p. 1A; Walter S. Mossberg, "A Blue-Collar Town Fears Urban Renewal Perils Its Way of Life," *Wall Street Journal*, November 2, 1970, p. 1; Michael Wowk, "Romney Is Hissed by Warren Crowd; He Keeps a Smile," *Detroit News*, July 28, 1970, p. 1A. At the time, Romney's wife Lenore was running for a U.S. Senate seat. She won the Republican primary against an opponent who tried to use the Warren issue against her, but lost in the general election to Philip A. Hart. On Lenore Romney and the Warren issue, see Clark Hoyt, "Romney Trip Hit as Election Ploy," *Detroit Free Press*, July 31, 1970, p. 2A.

55. Jerry M. Flint, "Michiganites Jeer Romney over Suburbs' Integration," NYT, July 29, 1970, p. 27; NYT, "Suburbs Reject Housing Program," November 8, 1970, p. 55. According to the U.S. Census Bureau, Warren's 2000 population of 138,247 was 91.3 percent non-Hispanic white, 2.7 percent African American, 3.1 percent Asian/Pacific Islander, and 1.4 percent Hispanic.

56. See the exchange of memos between Romney and Ehrlichman in BHL, Romney Papers, Box 13, Folder: The President-Ehrlichman 1970.

57. H. R. Haldeman, *The Haldeman Diaries: Inside the Nixon White House* (New York: Putnam, 1994), 210–11; Ehrlichman, *Witness to Power*, 192, 194; *Detroit Free Press*, "Nixon Calls Talks as GOP Slams His Election Tactics," November 8, 1970, p. 1A.

58. Memo, Eugene Gulledge to George Romney, HUD, Box 100, October 16, 1970.

59. Monroe W. Karmin, "Romney's Departure Grows More Likely," *Wall Street Journal*, December 16, 1970.

60. Letter, Romney to Nixon, BHL, Romney Papers, Box 4, Folder: HUD's Civil Rights Policy, November 16, 1970.

61. John Herbers, "Mitchell Is Said to Advise Romney to Take New Post," NYT, November 22, 1970, p. 1.

62. Danielson, *Politics of Exclusion*, 227–28. Despite his objections to the phrase, Romney said at the Warren meeting that he opposed "forced integration." He also used the phrase earlier in his career. In a 1964 speech before the Wolverine State Missionary Baptist Convention in Detroit, then-Governor Romney promised to enforce civil rights laws, but he warned that such efforts "must not be accomplished abnormally, or the abnormality will lead to weakness of the total effort and the sore of abnormal, forced integration will fester and become inflamed" (Address to Wolverine State Missionary Baptist Convention, LC, Brooke Papers, Box 644, Folder George Romney, July 31, 1964).

63. Nixon's statement shared media attention with the wedding of his daughter Tricia, who was married on the day after the statement was released.

64. Romney and Under Secretary Richard Van Dusen had tried to convince top White House and Justice Department officials that federal authority was justified and necessary to forge demonstrable progress in the area of suburban

integration. Reportedly, Romney and Van Dusen were unable to convince Attorney General John N. Mitchell and presidential assistant John Ehrlichman. Ehrlichman and Mitchell were both knowledgeable about laws concerning land use, as the former was a zoning lawyer in Seattle for eighteen years and the latter developed expertise on zoning as a municipal bond attorney. See Ken W. Clawson, "Top Nixon Aides Urged Housing Shift," WP, June 12, 1971, p. A6.

65. For example, Evans and Novak characterized Nixon's school desegregation statement as "a masterpiece of equivocation, a hollow egg laid after a long and noisy incubation period." See Rowland Evans, Jr., and Robert D. Novak, *Nixon in the White House: The Frustration of Power* (New York: Random House, 1971), p. 149.

66. "Statement by the President on Federal Policies Relative to Equal Housing Opportunity," NPM, White House Central Files: Staff Member and Office Files, Leonard Garment, Box 94, Alpha-Subject Files, June 11, 1971.

67. *Los Angeles Times*, "Nixon's Actions Cheer Fair Housing Backers," June 16, 1971; *Milwaukee Journal*, "No Leadership on Housing," June 14, 1971; Saul Friedman, "Housing Policy Battle Lines Drawn," *Detroit Free Press*, June 17, 1971.

68. Lilley, "Housing Report/Romney Faces Political Perils," 2259.

69. Glazer, *Affirmative Discrimination*, 212.

70. *Newsweek*, "Trouble in Pontiac," September 20, 1971, p. 33; Eric Wentworth, "Schools: To Bus or Not to Bus," WP, February 21, 1972, p. A1; *U.S. News & World Report*, "Chaos over School Busing: Tale of Two Cities," March 16, 1970, pp. 29–33.

71. Christine H. Rossell, "The Convergence of Black and White Attitudes on School Desegregation Issues," pp. 120–38 in *Redefining Equality*, ed. Neal Devins and Davison M. Douglas (New York: Oxford University Press, 1998). Tellingly, black Americans were not polled about their views on the principle of school desegregation or desegregation techniques until 1972.

72. "Strategy Paper: The Anti-Busing Crisis," LC, National Urban League, Part 3, Box 17, Folder 7, n.d.

73. "Dear Editor" letter, LC, National Urban League, Part 3, Box 17, Folder 7, August 29, 1972.

74. Jonathan Kelley, "The Politics of School Busing," *Public Opinion Quarterly* 38, no. 1 (1974): 23–39.

75. Ehrlichman, *Witness to Power*, 200; Memo, Harry Dent to Bryce Harlow, NPM, WHCF/SF, FG 23, Box 2, April 28, 1970.

76. The only busing-related legislation to pass during the first Nixon Administration, a 1971 higher education bill that tried to stop the implementation of busing orders requiring "racial balance" until all appeals had been exhausted, had minimal effect. See David E. Rosenbaum, "Bill to Bar Busing Killed in Senate as Closure Fails," NYT, October 13, 1972, p. 1.

77. The employment question asked, "Should the government in Washington see to it that black people get fair treatment in jobs or should the government in Washington leave these matters to the states and local communities?" Forty percent of whites chose "see to it," 42 percent chose "stay out," and 18 percent expressed "no interest" in the issue. See Schuman et al., *Racial Attitudes in America*.

78. CQ, "Growing Issue: Communities vs. Low-Income Housing," January 8, 1972, p. 51.

79. On limits of opinion surveys, see Gary Orfield, "Segregated Housing and School Resegregation," pp. 291–330 in *Dismantling Desegregation: The Quiet Reversal of "Brown v. Board of Education,"* ed. Gary Orfield, Susan E. Eaton, and the Harvard Project on School Desegregation (New York: New Press, 1996), 299. For public opinion on school desegregation, see Steven A. Shull, *The President and Civil Rights Policy: Leadership and Change* (New York: Greenwood, 1989). The percentage of Americans identifying civil rights as "the most important problem facing this country today" peaked from fall of 1963 (following King's "I Have a Dream" speech) through early 1965, at levels above 40 percent. Except for a brief spike in 1968 (presumably after King's death), the percentage of respondents answering "civil rights" declined steadily, to the low single-digits by the mid-1970s. See Smith, "America's Most Important Problem."

80. Phyllis Helper, "Housing and Urban Development: Biggest Open Housing Section Takes Effect; U.S. Plans Enforcement," NJ, January 10, 1970, pp. 76–78; CQ, July 15, 1966; CQ, August 12, 1966.

81. Letter, Richard B. Morris (NAREB Chairman) to Maurice G. Reed (NAREB president), LC, NAACP, Part IV, Box A50, Folder: NCDH 1966–68, January 24, 1966.

82. Helper, "Housing and Urban Development"; Lilley, "Housing Report/Romney Faces Political Perils."

83. Memo, Charles Colson to Hugh Sloan, NPM, SMOF: Charles Colson, Box 56, NAREB file, March 13, 1970.

84. Quadagno, *Color of Welfare*; Jeanne R. Lowe, "Race, Jobs, and Cities: What Business Can Do," *Saturday Review*, February 22, 1969, pp. 32–33. One proposal floated in the White House suggested that the "Plans for Progress" program that encouraged large corporations to increase minority recruitment voluntarily might be adapted to the area of housing. Discussing members of the "Business Establishment" who could be expected to support efforts to expand equal opportunity in housing, the memo identifies potential allies as the housing industry, including materials suppliers and home furnishing producers as well as home builders; manufacturers in other industries that are relocating to the suburbs and facing shortages of semi-skilled and unskilled labor; and "a core of sophisticated businessmen (limited in number perhaps) who understand fully the urban problem and the complex interrelationships within it" (Memo from Charles B. Markham, NPM, Papers of Leonard Garment, Box 94, November 1970).

85. USCCR, "Equal Opportunity in Suburbia" (Washington, D.C.: U.S. Government Printing Office, 1974).

86. On NAHB motivation, see Lilley, "Housing Report/Romney Faces Political Perils," 2252. On NAHB's support for HUD proposal, see National Association of Home Builders, "Barba Urges Retention of Tested FHA Housing Programs in HUD's Proposed Revision of Nation's Housing Laws," *NAHB Washington Scope* 8, no. 24 (June 12, 1970): 1–2.

87. William Lilley III, "Housing Report/Courts Lead Revolutionary Trend toward Desegregation of Residential Areas," NJ, November 27, 1971, p. 2342.

88. "Statement of Mayor Richard J. Daley," CRNA, Reel 20, Box 19, 935-8, March 8, 1971.

89. Republican city mayors were not always the Nixon Administration's biggest fans either. For example, they were the most vocal critics of the administration when it announced it would divert Model Cities funds to aid school desegregation. See Letter, Floyd Hyde to John Ehrlichman, BHL, Romney Papers, Box 13, Folder: The President—Ehrlichman—1970, May 12, 1970.

90. Christopher Wallace, "Mayors Rip U.S. Policy on Suburban Housing," *Boston Globe*, June 13, 1971, p. 1; Peter Braestrup, "Romney Calls for Warning to the Suburbs by Mayors," WP, June 15, 1971, p. A2; James B. Steele, "Mayors Soften Blow at Nixon Housing Policy, Ask Fund Cutoff over Bias," *Philadelphia Inquirer*, June 17, 1971.

91. Danielson, *Politics of Exclusion*, 231; *Los Angeles Times*, June 16, 1971.

92. The NAACP insisted that in virtually all cases where local governments attempt to bar low-income housing, "the reason is racial, not economic" (see Gloster B. Current, "All Together Now!" The 62nd Annual Convention: A Symphony of Understanding, *The Crisis*, August–September, pp. 205–61).

93. *Houston Chronicle*, "Minority Leaders Assail Nixon on Housing Stance," June 12, 1971. From an opposing political perspective, conservative columnist Kevin Phillips likened the housing statement to the president's earlier document on school desegregation, predicting "a heavy opening barrage of conservative rhetoric followed by subsequent activity in the other direction" (Phillips, "Squeezing the Suburbs").

94. NAACP, "Housing Resolutions," HUD, Van Dusen Papers, Box 25, June 29–July 4, 1970.

95. Lilley, "Housing Report/Courts Lead Revolutionary Trend," 2346–47.

96. The 1966 open housing bill, which in most other respects was quite similar to the 1968 law, would have created such an agency based on the National Labor Relations Board. See chapter 3.

97. See SSC 1970.

98. National Committee Against Discrimination in Housing, "Response to Questions as to How the Federal Fair Housing Law Can Be Made More Effective," SSC, pp. 2916–19.

99. "HUD Fair Housing and Equal Opportunity Budget Justification" in testimony before the House Appropriations/HUD-Space-Science Veterans Subcommittee, April 18, 1972, p. 886.

100. USCCR, "Federal Civil Rights Enforcement: One Year Later." For legal arguments about the extent of HUD's power, see SSC 1970 and HJC 1971/2.

101. "Department of Housing and Urban Development Response to Questions of the U.S. Commission on Civil Rights," HUD, Box 132, Rel 6, August 18, 1972.

102. "Civil Rights Compliance and Enforcement," *Challenge* (HUD), filed in NPM, HU 2-3 Housing, 1974. In fiscal year 1972, HUD processed 2159 Title VIII complaints, 394 Title VI (Civil Rights Act of 1964) complaints, and eight complaints covered under Kennedy's Executive Order 11063. Of the 1500 complaints closed in FY 1972, 227 were successfully conciliated; 130 were unsuccessfully conciliated; fourteen were conciliated in a manner deemed partially

successful; 264 were closed by state or local agencies; 301 were withdrawn or closed because required information was not provided; and 564 ended in a determination not to resolve. HUD estimated the average processing time for Title VIII complaints (in FY 1971) to be five-and-a-half months ("Department of Housing and Urban Development Response to Questions of the United States Commission on Civil Rights," HUD, Box 132, Rel 6, August 18, 1972). On USCCR's complaints, see USCCR, "The Federal Civil Rights Enforcement Effort—1974 (vol. 2: To Provide . . . For Fair Housing)," (Washington, D.C.: U.S. Government Printing Office, 1974).

103. SSC 1970, 2919; "Questions on Department of Housing and Urban Development Fair Housing Policy" from Rep. Don Edwards, HUD, Box 121, Rel 6-2, 1971. This policy also caused delays in the processing of complaints, as a good portion of complaints sent to state and local agencies were returned to HUD because those agencies lacked sufficient resources to investigate.

104. Memo, Pat Buchanan to Ken Cole, NPM, FG 90 (USSCR), November 26, 1971; *Wall Street Journal*, "Civil Rights Commission Gives Administration Mixed Progress Rating," May 11, 1971.

105. George Romney, "Remarks for Annual Meeting of the Leadership Council for Metropolitan Open Communities," LC, LCCR, Part 1, Box 127, Folder: Fair Housing, June 1, 1971.

106. The Department of Justice filed 135 Title VIII suits between January 1969 and June 1973; at least twenty originated in individual complaints forwarded from HUD to Justice. HUD conciliated 1,218 complaints during this same period (HUD, "Housing in the Seventies").

107. Information sheet, Black Jack Improvement Association, HUD, Van Dusen Papers, Box 31 (Folder: Black Jack, Missouri Project St. Louis), circa 1969–70.

108. Danielson, *Politics of Exclusion*, 233.

109. Ibid.; USCCR, "The Federal Civil Rights Enforcement Effort—A Reassessment."

110. John Herbers, "U.S. Acts to Spread Subsidized Housing," NYT, September 30, 1971, p. 1.

111. HJC 1971/2.

112. Ibid., 380.

CHAPTER FIVE

1. Carter, *Politics of Rage*, 425.

2. On the contents of bureaucrats' briefcases, see NJ, "Critics of Bureaucrats: Nixon and Wallace," December 16, 1972, p. 1935. Attacks on bureaucrats came from the left as well. For example, Mario Savio, a leader of the Berkeley free speech movement, maintained, "In our free-speech fight, we have come up against what may emerge as the greatest problem of our nation—depersonalized, unresponsive bureaucracy." See Allen J. Matusow, *The Unraveling of America: A History of Liberalism in the 1960s* (New York: Harper Torchbooks, 1984), 317.

3. HGOC 1971, 18.

4. Matusow, *Unraveling of America*.

5. Memo, Floyd H. Hyde to George Romney, BHL, Romney Papers, Box 41, Folder: Future of HUD, November 21, 1972.

6. Santoro and McGuire, "Social Movement Insiders."

7. Memo, Richard C. Van Dusen to John Ehrlichman, BHL, Romney Papers, Box 7, Folder: Housing Programs, March 18, 1969.

8. Memo, Samuel J. Simmons to George Romney, HUD, Van Dusen Papers, Box 24, November 21, 1969; Memo, Samuel J. Simmons to George Romney, HUD, Van Dusen Papers, Box 25, June 7, 1971.

9. *Clarion-Ledger* (Jackson, Miss.), "Feds Eye Quotas for Housing Mix," September 15, 1970.

10. Memo, Samuel J. Simmons to Richard C. Van Dusen, HUD, Van Dusen Papers, Box 25, April 7, 1970. A 1985 *Dallas Morning News* series on subsidized housing found that the agency still did not have racial occupancy data for these programs. See George Rodrigue, "Racial Data on Subsidized Housing Not Compiled," *Dallas Morning News*, February 13, 1985, p. 15A.

11. HUD press release, LC, LCCR, Part I, Box 106, Folder: 1971–72, February 22, 1972; Romney speech to National Association of Home Builders, LC, LCCR, Part I, Box 105, Folder: HUD 1970, January 19, 1970.

12. Lilley, "Housing Report/Romney Faces Political Perils" and "Housing Report/Administration and Congress Follow Courts."

13. "Affeldt's Statement," HUD, Van Dusen Papers, Box 25, July 18, 1970.

14. NJ, October 17, 1970; Memo, Eugene A. Gulledge to George Romney, BHL, Romney Papers, Box 7, Folder: Gulledge, June 19, 1972.

15. Craig Flournoy and George Rodrigue, "Fair-Housing Failure: 5 Administrations Have Refused to Enforce Anti-Discrimination Laws," *Dallas Morning News*, February 15, 1985.

16. Lilley, "Housing Report/Romney Faces Political Perils," 2255.

17. Letter, George Romney to Richard Nixon, HUD, Van Dusen Papers, Box 74, undated response to February 18, 1969 memorandum.

18. Memo, Samuel J. Simmons to George Romney, HUD, Van Dusen Papers, Box 26, Equal Opportunity 71-2 folder, February 18, 1972. Under Romney, HUD's emphasis on reducing processing time for grant applications also made addressing civil rights concerns difficult.

19. Testimony of Aileen C. Hernandez, HJC, November 3, 1971, p. 113.

20. HUD, "Answers to Questions of Hon. John S. Monagan, Chairman, Legal and Monetary Affairs Subcommittee, for Inclusion in the Record of the Hearing Held May 24, 1971," Appendix A of Testimony before HGOC 1971.

21. SSC 1970, 2775. On lack of equal opportunity staff, see USCCR, "The Federal Civil Rights Enforcement Effort—1974 (vol. 2: To Provide . . . For Fair Housing)."

22. Milton P. Semer and Julian H. Zimmerman, "Impact of Judicial and Administrative Decisions on Legislative Policy Development and Implementation of Housing Programs," *Housing in the Seventies Working Papers 1* (Washington, D.C.: U.S. Government Printing Office, 1976).

23. Memo, Leonard Garment to John Ehrlichman, CRNA, Reel 20, Box 19, February 26, 1971, pp. 836–45.

24. Lilley, "Housing Report/Courts Lead Revolutionary Trend." CQ, January 8, 1972, pp. 51–55.

25. In response to the ruling, the county commissioners formed their own housing authority to rescind the Atlanta Housing Authority's right to build in unincorporated parts of the county. The county did not build housing until the mid-1980s, and those units were allotted for elderly individuals only. See George Rodrigue, "14 Years After Ruling, Atlanta's White Suburbs Resist Low-Rent Housing," *Dallas Morning News*, February 13, 1985, p. 15A.

26. This desegregation plan is discussed more extensively in chapter 6. On outcomes for movers, see, for example, Julie E. Kaufman and James E. Rosenbaum, "The Education and Employment of Low-Income Black Youth in White Suburbs," *Educational Evaluation and Policy Analysis* 14, no. 3 (1992): 229–40; James E. Rosenbaum and Susan Popkin, "Employment and Earnings of Low-Income Blacks Who Move to Middle-Class Suburbs," pp. 342–56 in *The Urban Underclass*, ed. Christopher Jencks and Paul E. Peterson (Washington, D.C.: Brookings Institution, 1991); James E. Rosenbaum, "Changing the Geography of Opportunity by Expanding Residential Choice: Lessons from the Gautreaux Program," *Housing Policy Debate* 6, no. 1 (1995): 231–69. On the program as a whole, see Alexander Polikoff, "Sustainable Integration or Inevitable Resegregation: The Troubling Questions," pp. 43–71 in *Housing Desegregation and Federal Policy*, ed. John M. Goering (Chapel Hill: University of North Carolina Press, 1986); Laura Janota, "Door Closes on Historic Housing-Assistance Program," *Chicago Daily Herald*, October 1, 1998, p. 11.

27. Lilley, "Housing Report/Courts Lead Revolutionary Trend," 2348.

28. Fair-share plans allocating specific numbers of units to communities made those localities responsible for constructing the housing itself or arranging for private-sector sponsors to do so. See George Sternlieb and David Listokin, "Exclusionary Zoning: State of the Art, Strategies for the Future," *Housing in the Seventies Working Papers 1* (Washington, D.C.: U.S. Government Printing Office).

29. Memo, Dana Meade to Ken Cole, CRNA, Reel 20, Box 19, 983, December 16, 1971; Memo, Pat Buchanan to Dana Meade, CRNA, Reel 20, Box 19, 1048, December 27, 1971.

30. John Herbers, "Proposal to Disperse Housing Snagged," NYT, April 24, 1972, p. 14.

31. See, for example, Romney speeches to National Housing Conference (March 6, 1972) and Community Development Seminar (March 30, 1972), LC, LCCR, Part I, Box 105, Folder: HUD. HUD provided technical assistance to metropolitan areas voluntarily adopting "fair share" plans, including Dayton, Washington, D.C., San Bernadino County (Calif.), and Minneapolis-St. Paul. See "Department of Housing and Urban Development Response to Questions of the U.S. Commission on Civil Rights," HUD, Subj-Corr Files, Box 132, Rel 6, Aug. 18, 1972.

32. NJ, November 12, 1971; NJ, November 27, 1971. One radical approach would be to cut off mortgage assistance to homes in segregated communities, thus giving these towns strong incentives to take serious pro-integrative actions (HUD, Van Dusen Papers, Box 77, Nixon Statement Folder).

33. In 1972, two-thirds of Section 235 buyers were categorized as non-minority white, 22 percent as black, 11 percent as Spanish American and 2 percent as "other." See HUD, "Housing in the Seventies."

34. USCCR, "Federal Civil Rights Enforcement: One Year Later." Segregation in traditional public housing was, if anything, an even bigger problem. Most buildings were highly segregated internally, and site selection decisions often intensified, rather than alleviated, neighborhood racial segregation. This problem was exacerbated by the lack of coordination among agencies involved in public housing (Memo, Samuel Simmons to George Romney and Richard Van Dusen, HUD, Van Dusen Papers, Box 25, Equal Opportunity folder, July 21, 1970).

35. HJC 1971/2.

36. William Lilley III and Timothy B. Clark, "Urban Report/Federal Programs Spur Abandonment of Housing in Major Cities," NJ, January 1, 1972, pp. 26–33; Brian D. Boyer, "HUD Scandal Profited All But Taxpayer," *Detroit Free Press*, March 19, 1972, p. 3; Boyer, *Cities Destroyed for Cash: The FHA Scandal at HUD* (Chicago: Follett, 1973); Metcalf, *Fair Housing Comes of Age*; *St. Louis Globe-Democrat*, "St. Louis' Housing Debacle" (editorial), March 11–12, 1972, p. 2F.

37. WP, "Romney Finds FHA Unprepared to Handle 'Fast-Buck Artists,'" May 6, 1972, p. E36. On Romney's earlier dismissals of the problem, see HBCC 1970.

38. Jack Rosenthal, "Romney, in Shift, Freezes Disputed Home Aid to Poor," NYT, January 15, 1971; NYT, "White House Said to Plan Freeze on Public Housing," December 23, 1972, p. 1; CQ, "Housing Bill: Congressional Delay Foreseen," December 16, 1972, pp. 3150–53.

39. Romney speech to National Housing Conference, LC, LCCR, Part I, Box 105, Folder: HUD 1970, March 6, 1972; WP, ". . . And Secretary Romney Steps Out" (editorial), November 28, 1972, p. A14.

40. Some have argued that Romney simply was not very smart. Robert Mc-Namara, who encouraged Romney to enter politics when they both worked in the Detroit auto industry, later concluded that Romney "has no brains" (Wills, *Nixon Agonistes*, 194). Historian Allen Matusow shares this view: "Square-jawed and compassionate, a capitalist with a heart, Romney had everything except brains" (Matusow, *Unraveling of America*, 399).

41. HGOC 1972. Romney noted in congressional testimony that the federal government's housing inventory was greater in 1964 than in 1972.

42. HGOC 1972, p. 314.

43. R. Allen Hays, *The Federal Government and Urban Housing*, 2nd ed. (Albany: State University of New York Press, 1995); Don Ball, "How Milwaukee Does It," *Detroit News*, December 22, p. 1971; Ball, "Profit Lid Placed on FHA Sales," *Detroit News*, March 16, 1972. Romney hired Katz in March 1972 as a HUD consultant on FHA big-city housing programs.

44. On the concerns of advocacy groups, see, for instance, Testimony of Edward Rutledge, Executive Director, National Committee Against Discrimination in Housing, SSC, 2678. On long-time FHA employees, see Gelfand, *A Nation of Cities*; Massey and Denton, *American Apartheid*; Jackson, *Crabgrass Frontier*; USCCR, "Housing."

45. Most observers agree that serious fair housing efforts should attempt to increase economic and racial integration throughout metropolitan areas and to revitalize ghettos. See, for example, George C. Galster, "The Evolving Challenges of Fair Housing Since 1968: Open Housing, Integration, and the Reduction of Ghettoization," *Cityscape* 4, no. 3 (1999) 123–38.

46. Memo, Ken Cole to Dana Mead, NPM, HS (Housing), Box 2, April 28, 1972; Memo, Ken Cole to Dana Mead, NPM, HS, Box 2, May 22, 1972.

47. The incident prompted the secretary's wife, Lenore Romney, to write a personal letter to John Ehrlichman expressing grave disappointment in the president. "Loyalty works both ways," she reminded the White House. See Letter, Lenore Romney to John Ehrlichman, NPM, WHSF/SMOF, John D. Ehrlichman, Alpha-Subject File: George Romney, August 8, 1972.

48. Letter, George Romney to Richard Nixon, NPM, WHSF/SMOF, John D. Ehrlichman, Alpha-Subject File: George Romney, August 10, 1972.

49. Romney Press Conference, BHL, Romney Papers, Box 41, Folder: Resignation Press Conference, November 27, 1972.

50. WP, ". . . And Secretary Romney Steps Out" (editorial).

51. Remarks by Romney to National Association of Home Builders, BHL, Romney Papers, Box 41, Folder: NAHB Houston, January 8, 1973; Hays, *Federal Government and Urban Housing*.

52. Letter, George Romney to Richard Nixon, BHL, Romney Papers, Box 14, Folder: The President-Ehlrichman-1972, December 28, 1972; Susanna McBee, "U.S. Housing Program Hit by President," WP, January 18, 1972, p. A2.

53. Richard Nixon, "Radio Address about the State of the Union Message on Community Development," March 4, 1973, available at www.nixonfoundation.org/Research_Center/PublicPapers.cfm.

54. Susanna McBee, "Subsidized Housing Frozen Before Justification by HUD," WP, December 3, 1973, p. A1.

55. Henry B. Schechter, "Critique of 'Housing in the Seventies'" (Congressional Research Service. Washington, D.C.: U.S. Government Printing Office, 1974), x; Anthony Downs, "Federal Housing Subsidies: Their Nature and Effectiveness and What We Should Do about Them" (Washington, D.C.: National Association of Home Builders, 1972).

56. CQ, "Housing: First Battle in War over Spending?" January 1, 1973, p. 40; CQ, "Housing Programs: Administration-Congress Clash," January 27, 1973, p. 139. Under special revenue–sharing, groups of related categorical programs would be replaced by block grants that gave states and localities freedom to spend as they saw fit within broad functional categories such as health, education, and community development. General revenue–sharing, enacted by Congress early in 1972, gave virtually unrestricted grants to states and localities (Hays, *Federal Government and Urban Housing*). When Nixon first proposed general revenue–sharing, Assistant Secretary Samuel Simmons worried that states and localities would not treat minorities fairly without federal oversight (Memo, Samuel Simmons to George Romney, HUD, Box 120, Rel 6, February 19, 1971).

57. Author telephone interview with Samuel Simmons, September 18, 2001.

58. On increase in subsidized housing, see HUD, "Housing in the Seventies." On the declining economy, see Ambrose, *Nixon*, 457.

59. McBee, "U.S. Housing Program Hit by President," p. A2.

60. USCCR, "The Federal Civil Rights Enforcement Effort—1974 (vol. 7: To Preserve, Protect, and Defend the Constitution)," (Washington, D.C.: U.S. Government Printing Office, 1974).

61. Hays, *Federal Government and Urban Housing*. Section 8 vouchers can have a pro-integrative effect in cases where recipients receive quality counseling about their housing options.

62. Pat Buchanan quoted in William Safire, *Before the Fall: An Inside View of the Pre-Watergate White House* (New York: Da Capo Press. 1975), 544.

63. Belz, *Equality Transformed*; Skrentny, *Ironies of Affirmative Action*; Graham, *Civil Rights Era*.

64. Ehrlichman, *Witness to Power*.

65. On dividing core Democratic constituencies, see Ehrlichman, *Witness to Power*. On lowering construction costs, see Stein, *Running Steel, Running America*. On tagging Democrats with the "race and quota" label, see Skrentny, *Ironies of Affirmative Action*.

66. Richard Nixon, "Radio Address on the Philosophy of Government" (October 21, 1972, Item 356), available at www.nixonfoundation.org/Research_Center/PublicPapers.cfm.

67. Halpern, *On the Limits of the Law*. Nixon's March 1972 proposed busing moratorium—which ultimately went nowhere in Congress—was announced two days after George Wallace decisively won the Democratic presidential primary in Florida.

68. Safire, *Before the Fall*, 267.

69. Ambrose, *Nixon*; Weisbrot, *Freedom Bound*.

70. Memo, Len Garment to John Ehrlichman, CRNA, Reel 20, Box 19, 848, March 15, 1971.

71. Carter, *Politics of Rage*, 423.

72. Howell Raines, "George Wallace, Symbol of the Fight to Maintain Segregation, Dies at 79," NYT, September 15, 1998, p. B10.

73. HUD, "1973 Appeals: Note to the Secretary," BHL, Romney Papers, Box 2, Folder: Budget—December 1971.

74. Nixon framed both the proposed busing freeze and the actual housing freeze partially in terms of equity. In justifying the housing freeze, Nixon argued, "It is now clear that all too frequently the needy haven't been the primary beneficiaries of these programs . . . [and] that the programs have been riddled with inequities." See Monroe W. Karmin, "Nixon's Moratorium on Subsidized Housing Stirs Debate among Its Critics, Advocates," *Wall Street Journal*, March 16, 1973, p. 34.

75. Ehrlichman, *Witness to Power*, 194–95.

76. Kotlowski, *Nixon's Civil Rights*, 3.

77. Graham, *Civil Rights Era*, 302.

78. Hugh Davis Graham, "Richard Nixon and Civil Rights: Explaining an Enigma," *Presidential Studies Quarterly* 26: 93–106.

CHAPTER SIX

1. Byron York, "HUD Makes Last Try to Keep Itself Alive," *Baltimore Sun*, December 25, 1994, p. 1F.

2. Orlebeke, "The Evolution of Low-Income Housing Policy, 1949 to 1999," 489–520.

3. Rochelle L. Stanfield, "Fair Housing: Still Doors to Open After 11 Years," NJ, May 5, 1979, pp. 1–8.

4. Mathias and Morris, "Fair Housing Legislation," 21–33.

5. Either the aggrieved person or the subject of the complaint may elect to have the charges heard in federal court. See Bill Lan Lee, "An Issue of Public Importance: The Justice Department's Enforcement of the Fair Housing Act," *Cityscape* 4, no. 3 (1999): 35–56.

6. Michael H. Schill and Samantha Friedman, "The Fair Housing Amendments Act of 1988: The First Decade," *Cityscape* 4, no. 3 (1999): 57–78; Massey and Denton, *American Apartheid*; Lee, "An Issue of Public Importance."

7. John Yinger, "Sustaining the Fair Housing Act," *Cityscape* 4, no. 3 (1999): 93–106.

8. Leonard S. Rubinowitz and James E. Rosenbaum, *Crossing the Class and Color Lines: From Public Housing to White Suburbia* (Chicago: University of Chicago Press, 2000).

9. Gary Orfield, "Segregated Housing and School Resegregation," in *Dismantling Desegregation: The Quiet Reversal of "Brown v. Board of Education."*

10. Rabinowitz and Rosenbaum, *Crossing the Class and Color Lines*; Rosenbaum, "Changing the Geography of Opportunity"; Janota, "Door Closes on Historic Housing-Assistance Program."

11. Clients were offered apartments as they became available, regardless of their locational preference. Few refused the offer, since they were unlikely to receive another offer. See Rosenbaum, "Changing the Geography of Opportunity."

12. Ibid.; Rosenbaum and Popkin, "Employment and Earnings of Low-Income Blacks."

13. Suburban movers received significantly more verbal harassment than city movers, though the groups reported very similar rates of being threatened or victimized by violence at the hands of peers. Ibid.; Kaufman and Rosenbaum, "The Education and Employment of Low-Income Black Youth in White Suburbs."

14. HUD, "Moving to Opportunity for Fair Housing Demonstration Program: Current Status and Initial Findings," September 1999, available at http://www.hud.gov, 6. The Moving to Opportunity program aimed to address economic rather than racial integration, though the former can help to bring about the latter. The Section 8 program, administered by state and local housing agencies contracting with the federal government, offers tenant-based assistance to very low-income households. Recipients typically contribute 30 percent of their income to rent, with the program paying the remainder, up to a locally defined maximum. See Margery Austin Turner, Susan Popkin, and Mary Cunningham, "Section 8 Mobility and Neighborhood Health: Emerging Issues and Policy Challenges" (Washington, D.C.: Urban Institute, 2000).

15. Margery Austin Turner, Remarks at Integration Works Conference, Philadelphia, December 1 and 2, 2000.

16. HUD, "Moving to Opportunity for Fair Housing Demonstration Program"; John Goering, "Comments on Future Research and Housing Policy," pp. 383–498 in *Choosing a Better Life? Evaluating the Moving to Opportunity Social Experiment*, ed. John Goering and Judith D. Feins (Washington, D.C.: Urban Institute Press, 2003).

17. John Goering, Judith D. Feins and Todd M. Richardson, "What Have We Learned about Housing Mobility and Poverty Deconcentration?" pp. 3–36 in *Choosing a Better Life?* ed. Goering and Feins; Susan J. Popkin, Laura E. Harris, and Mary K. Cunningham, "Families in Transition: A Qualitative Analysis of the MTO Experience" (Washington, D.C.: Urban Institute, 2002). For more data on the benefits on relocation, see Mary K. Cunningham and Noah Sawyer, "Moving to Better Neighborhoods with Mobility Counseling" (Washington, D.C.: Urban Institute, 2005).

18. Goering, Feins, and Richardson, "What Have We Learned about Housing Mobility and Poverty Deconcentration?"

19. W. Dennis Keating, *The Suburban Racial Dilemma: Housing and Neighborhoods* (Philadelphia: Temple University Press, 1994).

20. Ibid.; Council on Affordable Housing, "About COAH," available at http://www.state.nj.us/dca/coah/about.shtml (2005); David L. Kirp, John P. Dwyer, and Larry A. Rosenthal, *Our Town: Race, Housing and the Soul of Suburbia* (New Brunswick, N.J.: Rutgers University Press, 1995).

21. Kirp, Dwyer, and Rosenthal, *Our Town*, 70.

22. The use of explicit racial quotas to maintain a racially diverse tenant population was struck down in 1988 when the Supreme Court refused to review an Appeals Court ruling, which required the Starrett City (Brooklyn, N.Y.) apartment complex to discontinue its policy of limiting the number of apartments rented to black and Latino applicants to prevent the departure of white tenants. Starrett City management was sued by the Reagan Administration in 1984. See *U.S. v. Starrett City Associates* (1988) (840 F.2d 1096); Linda Greenhouse, "High Court Voids Quotas on Races in Housing Units," NYT, November 8, 1988, p. A1; Yinger, *Closed Doors, Opportunity Lost*.

23. Polikoff, "Sustainable Integration or Inevitable Resegregation"; Rose Helper, "Introduction to American Policies and Programs," in *Urban Housing Segregation of Minorities in Western Europe and the United States*, ed. Elizabeth D. Huttman (Durham, N.C.: Duke University Press, 1991); Juliette Saltman, *A Fragile Movement: The Struggle for Neighborhood Stabilization* (New York: Greenwood, 1990); Keating, *Suburban Racial Dilemma*. Several planned communities have sought racial and economic integration from their inception and have had some success in achieving this goal. Examples include Columbia, Md.; Reston, Va.; and Roosevelt Island in New York City.

24. Keating, *Suburban Racial Dilemma*, 29, 34.

25. Lee, "An Issue of Public Importance." Since 1981, the Department of Justice has had oversight and coordination responsibility for Title VI of the 1964 Civil Rights Act. See USCCR, "Federal Title VI Enforcement to Ensure Nondiscrimination in Federally Assisted Programs" (Washington, D.C.: U.S. Government Printing Office, 1996).

26. Joseph L. Wagner, "Desegregation an Uphill Battle for Parma Still," *Cleveland Plain Dealer*, November 26, 2000, p. 1A.

27. Nancy A. Denton and Richard D. Alba, "Suburban Racial and Ethnic Change at the Neighborhood Level: The Declining Number of All-White Neighborhoods," paper presented at conference on Suburban Racial Change, Harvard University, March 26, 1998. On the neighborhood racial composition preferences of individuals from various racial and ethnic groups, see, for example, Reynolds Farley, Charlotte Steeh, Tara Jackson, Maria Krysan, and Keith Reeves, "Continued Racial Residential Segregation in Detroit: 'Chocolate City, Vanilla Suburbs' Revisited," *Journal of Housing Research* 4 (1993): 1–38; Reynolds Farley, Elaine L. Fielding, and Maria Krysan, "The Residential Preferences of Blacks and Whites: A Four-Metropolis Analysis," *Housing Policy Debate* 8, no. 4 (1997): 763–800; Lawrence Bobo and Camille L. Zubrinsky, "Attitudes Toward Integration: Perceived Status Differences, Mere In-Group Preference, or Racial Prejudice?" *Social Forces* 74, no. 3 (1996): 883–909; Camille Zubrinsky Charles, "Neighborhood Racial-Composition Preferences: Evidence from a Multi-Ethnic Metropolis," *Social Problems* 47, no. 3 (2000): 379–407; Charles, "The Dynamics of Racial Residential Segregation,": 167–207. In the latter articles, Charles finds that African Americans, Latinos, Asians and whites all "exhibit preferences for both meaningful integration and a substantial presence of same-race neighbors," but "whites exhibit the strongest preference for same-race neighbors and blacks the weakest" (179).

28. Ingrid Gould Ellen, *Sharing America's Neighborhoods: The Prospects for Stable Racial Integration* (Cambridge: Harvard University Press, 2000). Ellen argues that large stabilizing institutions such as universities and military bases reassure current and prospective residents about the stability of the neighborhood. As a result, these neighborhoods are more likely to be stably integrated. Note also that Ellen's finding that substantial proportions of rental housing increase the chances for stable integration runs counter to Keating's contention that mostly owner-occupied housing is advantageous.

29. Orfield, "Segregated Housing and School Resegregation."

30. Steven G. Rivkin, "Residential Segregation and School Integration," *Sociology of Education* 67 (1994): 285, 291. Judicial decisions, including a number by the Supreme Court, have described "housing segregation as something separate and mysterious—something that simply happened—and that local officials could do little about." In *Milliken*, for instance, Justice Potter Stewart, the decisive fifth vote in the case, opined in a footnote to the decision that housing segregation was the result of "unknown or unknowable causes" (See Orfield, "Segregated Housing and School Resegregation," 292, 296).

31. Neil M. Gold, "The Mismatch of Jobs and Low-Income People in Metropolitan Areas and Its Implications for the Central City Poor," pp. 443–86 in *Report of the Commission on Population Growth and the American Future* (Washington, D.C.: U.S. Government Printing Office, 1972); Darden, "Black Residential Segregation."

32. See, for example, Wilson, *When Work Disappears*; Philip Kasinitz and Jan Rosenberg, "Missing the Connection: Social Isolation and Employment on the Brooklyn Waterfront," *Social Problems* 43, no. 2 (1996): 180–96; Katherine S. Newman, *No Shame in My Game: The Working Poor in the Inner City* (New York: Vintage Books and Russell Sage Foundation, 1999). These studies also

suggest that some employers engage in "place discrimination," refusing to hire individuals who live in poor inner-city neighborhoods. For a more skeptical view about the importance of spatial mismatch, see Christopher Jencks and Susan Mayer, "Residential Segregation, Job Proximity, and Black Job Opportunities," pp. 187–222 in *Inner-City Poverty in the United States*, ed. Laurence Lynn and Michael McGeary (Washington, D.C.: National Academy Press, 1990).

33. Wells argues convincingly that too much of the public and academic debate about the consequences of school desegregation has concentrated on short-term gains in standardized test scores. As she observes, in *Brown v. Board of Education* (1954) and several earlier cases, the Supreme Court stressed the importance of desegregation in offering minority students access to institutions with greater resources, higher status, and valuable social networks of faculty and students. See Amy Stuart Wells, "The 'Consequences' of School Desegregation: The Mismatch Between the Research and the Rationale," *Hastings Constitutional Law Quarterly* 28, no. 771 (2001).

34. Carol Ascher, "The Changing Face of Racial Isolation and Desegregation in Urban Schools," *ERIC/CUE Digest*, 91 (1993); Kenneth Jost, "Rethinking School Integration," *CQ Researcher* 6, no. 39 (1996) 913–936.

35. Megan Twohey, "Desegregation is Dead," NJ, September 18, 1999, pp. 2614–20.

36. Gary Orfield and Chungmei Lee, "*Brown* at 50: King's Dream or *Plessy's* Nightmare?"

37. Mark Walsh, "High Court Closes Historic Desegregation Case," *Education Week*, April 24, 2002.

38. Rochelle L. Stanfield, "Reagan Courting Women, Minorities, But It May Be Too Late to Win Them," NJ, May 28, 1983, p. 1119; Blumrosen, *Modern Law*.

39. Michael Wines, "Administration Says It Merely Seeks a 'Better Way' to Enforce Civil Rights," NJ, January 27, 1982, pp. 536–41; Nadine Cohodas, "Affirmative Action Assailed in Congress, Administration," CQ, September 12, 1981, p. 1749.

40. EEOC, "Enforcement Efforts in the 1980s," available at www.eeoc.gov /35th/1980s/enforcement.

41. Felicity Barringer, "EEOC's Two-Part Mission Pulling Its Employees in Opposing Directions," WP, March 12, 1984, p. A17.

42. Anne B. Fisher, "Businessmen Like to Hire by the Numbers," *Fortune*, September 16, 1985, p. 26.

43. Ibid., 28; *Harvard Law Review*, "Rethinking *Weber*: The Business Response to Affirmative Action," 102, no. 3 (1989): 658–71; Kelly and Dobbin, "How Affirmative Action Became Diversity Management."

44. In the 1990s, Supreme Court decisions involving employment discrimination law related primarily to cases involving women, older workers, and the disabled.

45. Hugh Davis Graham, "The Politics of Clientele Capture."

46. Durant, *The Administrative Presidency Revisited*; Wood and Waterman, "The Dynamics of Political Control of the Bureaucracy"; West, *Controlling the Bureaucracy*; Golden, *What Motivates Bureaucrats?*

47. Graham, "The Politics of Clientele Capture."

48. Remarks by Sara K. Pratt, National Fair Housing Research and Policy Forum, Washington, D.C., March 13, 2004.

49. Author telephone interview with Sara Pratt, March 31, 2004; National Fair Housing Alliance, *2004 Fair Housing Trends Report* (Washington, D.C.: National Fair Housing Alliance, 2004).

50. Anderson, *The Movement and the Sixties*, 338.

51. "OCR Review," LC, Harris Papers, Box 298, Folder: OCR Review 5/16/80, pp. I–1.

52. Letter, Martin H. Gerry to HEW Under Secretary, Domestic Policy Staff Files: Gutierrez, Box 29, OCR-HEW Legislative Proposals, November 19, 1976. Jimmy Carter Presidential Materials, Atlanta, Georgia.

53. Lieberman, *Shifting the Color Line*, 98.

54. Edwin Amenta, Chris Bonastia, and Neal Caren, "U.S. Social Policy in Comparative and Historical Perspective: Concepts, Images, Arguments, and Research Strategies," *Annual Review of Sociology* 27: 213–34.

55. Quoted by George Romney in Speech to National Association of Home Builders, Houston, BHL, Romney Papers, Box 41, Folder: NAHB Houston, January 8, 1973.

WORKS CITED

Abrams, Charles. 1955. *Forbidden Neighbors: A Study of Prejudice in Housing*. New York: Harper.

Abrams, Elliott. 1972. "The Quota Commission." *Commentary* 54 (4): 54–57.

Alba, Richard D., and John R. Logan. 1993. "Minority Proximity to Whites in Suburbs: An Individual-Level Analysis of Segregation." *American Journal of Sociology* 98 (6): 1388–427.

Ambrose, Stephen E. 1989. *Nixon: The Triumph of a Politician 1962–1972, vol. 2*. New York: Simon and Schuster.

Amenta, Edwin. 1998. *Bold Relief: Institutional Politics and the Origins of American Social Policy*. Princeton: Princeton University Press.

Amenta, Edwin, Chris Bonastia, and Neal Caren. 2001. "U.S. Social Policy in Comparative and Historical Perspective: Concepts, Images, Arguments, and Research Strategies." *Annual Review of Sociology* 27: 213–34.

Amenta, Edwin, and Sunita Parikh. 1991. "Capitalists Did Not Want the Social Security Act: A Critique of the 'Capitalist Dominance' Thesis." *American Sociological Review* 56: 124–29.

Anderson, Terry H. 1995. *The Movement and the Sixties: Protest in America from Greensboro to Wounded Knee*. New York: Oxford University Press.

Arnold, Mark R. 1969. "Courts May Rule on Challenge to Suburban Zoning." *National Observer*, October 20.

Ascher, Carol. 1993. "The Changing Face of Racial Isolation and Desegregation in Urban Schools." *ERIC/CUE Digest* 91.

Ball, Don. 1971. "How Milwaukee Does It." *Detroit News*, December 22.

———. 1972. "Profit Lid Placed on FHA Sales." *Detroit News*, March 16.

Barringer, Felicity. 1984. "EEOC's Two-Part Mission Pulling Its Employees in Opposing Directions." *Washington Post*, March 12, p. A17.

Baumgartner, Frank R., and Bryan D. Jones. 1993. *Agendas and Instability in American Politics*. Chicago: University of Chicago Press.

Belz, Herman. 1991. *Equality Transformed*. New Brunswick, N.J.: Transaction.

Bernstein, Marver. 1955. *Regulating by Independent Commission*. Princeton: Princeton University Press.

Bloom, Howard S., and H. Douglas Price. 1975. "Voter Response to Short-run Economic Conditions: The Asymmetric Effect of Prosperity and Recession." *American Political Science Review* 69: 1240–54.

Blumrosen, Alfred W. 1971. *Black Employment and the Law*. New Brunswick, N.J.: Rutgers University Press.

———. 1993. *Modern Law: The Law Transmission System and Equal Employment Opportunity*. Madison: University of Wisconsin Press.

Bobo, Lawrence, and Camille L. Zubrinsky. 1996. "Attitudes Toward Integration: Perceived Status Differences, Mere In-Group Preference, or Racial Prejudice?" *Social Forces* 74 (3): 883–909.

Bonastia, Chris. 2000. "Why Did Affirmative Action in Housing Fail During the Nixon Era? Exploring the 'Institutional Homes' of Social Policies." *Social Problems* 47 (4): 523–42.

———. 2004. "Hedging His Bets: Why Nixon Killed HUD's Desegregation Efforts." *Social Science History* 28 (1): 19–52.

Boyer, Brian D. 1972. "HUD Scandal Profited All But Taxpayer." *Detroit Free Press*, March 19, p. 3.

———. 1973. *Cities Destroyed for Cash: The FHA Scandal at HUD*. Chicago: Follett.

Bradshaw, Barbara Robinson, and Edward L. Holmgren. 1966. "Open Occupancy and Open Minds: A Study of Realtors." *Interracial Review* 39 (4).

Braestrup, Peter. 1971. "Romney Calls for Warning to the Suburbs by Mayors." *Washington Post*, June 15, p. A2.

Branch, Taylor. 1988. *Parting the Waters: America in the King Years, 1954–63*. New York: Simon and Schuster.

Briffault, Richard. 1990. "Our Localism: Part I—The Structure of Local Government Law." *Columbia Law Review* 90 (1): 1–76.

Bryner, Gary. 1981. "Congress, Courts, and Agencies: Equal Employment Opportunity and the Limits of Policy Implementation." *Political Science Quarterly* 96 (3): 411–30.

Buncher, Judith F., ed. 1975. *The School Busing Controversy: 1970–75*. New York: Facts on File.

Bureau of National Affairs. 1964. *The Civil Rights Act of 1964: Text, Analysis, Legislative History*. Washington, D.C.: BNA.

Burk, Robert Fredrick. 1984. *The Eisenhower Administration and Black Civil Rights*. Knoxville: University of Tennessee Press.

Burstein, Paul. 1985. *Discrimination, Jobs and Politics: The Struggle for Equal Employment Opportunity in the United States since the New Deal*. Chicago: University of Chicago Press.

———. 1998. "Bringing the Public Back In: Should Sociologists Consider the Impact of Public Opinion on Public Policy?" *Social Forces* 77 (1): 27–62.

Calvert, Randall L., Matthew D. McCubbins, and Barry R. Weingast. 1989. "A Theory of Political Control and Agency Discretion." *American Journal of Political Science* 33 (3): 588–611.

Canter, Donald. 1971. "HUD Aide Talks Revenue Sharing." *San Francisco Examiner*, March 3.

Carmines, Edward G., and James A. Stimson. 1989. *Issue Evolution: Race and the Transformation of American Politics*. Princeton: Princeton University Press.

Caro, Robert A. 1974. *The Power Broker: Robert Moses and the Fall of New York*. New York: Vintage.

Carpenter, Daniel P. 2001. *The Forging of Bureaucratic Autonomy*. Princeton: Princeton University Press.

Carroll, Peter N. 1982. *It Seemed Like Nothing Happened: The Tragedy and Promise of America in the 1970s*. New York: Holt, Rinehart, and Winston.

Carruthers, Bruce G. 1994. "When Is the State Autonomous? Culture, Organization Theory, and the Political Sociology of the State." *Sociological Theory* 12 (1): 19–44.

Carter, Dan T. 1995. *The Politics of Rage: George Wallace, the Origins of the New Conservatism, and the Transformation of American Politics*. New York: Simon and Schuster.

Cauthen, Nancy K., and Edwin Amenta. 1996. "Not for Widows Only: Institutional Politics and the Formative Years of Aid to Dependent Children." *American Sociological Review* 61: 427–48.

Charles, Camille Zubrinsky. 2000. "Neighborhood Racial-Composition Preferences: Evidence from a Multi-Ethnic Metropolis." *Social Problems* 47 (3): 379–407.

———. 2003. "The Dynamics of Racial Residential Segregation." *Annual Review of Sociology* 29: 167–207.

Chicago Tribune. 1966. "King Asked to Stop March." August 23, p. 1.

Clarion-Ledger (Jackson, Miss.). 1970. "Feds Eye Quotas for Housing Mix." September 15.

Clawson, Ken W. 1971. "Top Nixon Aides Urged Housing Shift." *Washington Post*, June 12, p. A6.

Cohodas, Nadine. 1981. "Affirmative Action Assailed in Congress, Administration." *Congressional Quarterly*, September 12, p. 1749.

Congressional Quarterly. 1964a. "Strong Rights Bill Due to Leaders' Tactics, Southern Errors." June 19, 1205–6.

———. 1964b. "Civil Rights Act of 1964 Is Signed into Law." July 3, p. 1331.

———. 1966a. "Civil Rights Housing Section at Center of Dispute." July 15, pp. 1465–66.

———. 1966b. "House Passes Civil Rights Bill, Retains Housing Section." August 12, pp. 1719–23.

———. 1967. "Committee Roundup: Open Housing." September 1, pp. 1692–93.

———. 1968. "Open-Housing Law Credited to Mitchell's Lobbying." April 24, pp. 1–4.

———. 1969. "Nixon's School Desegregation Policies Remain Unclear." February 14, pp. 255–61.

———. 1970a. "Nixon Administration Slows Civil Rights Movement." January 23, pp. 235–38.

———. 1970b. "The Nixon Administration and Civil Rights: 1969–1970." November 27, pp. 2853–58.

———. 1970c. "School Desegregation: How Far Will the Country Go?" December 11, pp. 2953–57.

———. 1971. "Nixon School Busing Policy: 'Fork in Tongue'?" August 28, p. 1829.

———. 1972a. "Growing Issue: Communities vs. Low-Income Housing." January 8, pp. 51–55.

———. 1972b. "Housing Bill: Congressional Delay Foreseen." December 16, pp. 3150–53.

———. 1973a. "Housing: First Battle in War over Spending?" January 1, p. 40.

———. 1973b. "Housing Programs: Administration-Congress Clash." January 27, p. 139.

Congressional Quarterly Almanac. 1954. "Housing Probe." Washington, D.C.: Congressional Quarterly Service.

Congressional Quarterly Service. 1966. *Housing a Nation.* Washington, D.C.: Congressional Quarterly Service.

———. 1968. *Revolution in Civil Rights.* 4th ed. Washington, D.C.: Congressional Quarterly Service.

Conley, Dalton. 1999. *Being Black, Living in the Red.* Berkeley: University of California Press.

Connolly, Kathleen. 1989. "The Chicago Open-Housing Conference." Pp. 49–95 in *Chicago 1966: Open Housing Marches, Summit Negotiations, and Operation Breadbasket,* edited by David J. Garrow. Brooklyn, N.Y.: Carlson.

Council on Affordable Housing. "About COAH." Available at http://www.state .nj.us/dca/coah/about.shtml. Accessed 2001, 2005.

Cunningham, Mary K., and Noah Sawyer. 2005. "Moving to Better Neighborhoods with Mobility Counseling." Washington, D.C.: Urban Institute.

Current, Gloster B. 1971. "All Together—Now! The 62nd Annual Convention: A Symphony of Understanding." *The Crisis,* August–September, pp. 205–6.

Daily Telegraph. 1995. "Obituary of George Romney." July 31.

Danielson, Michael N. 1976. *The Politics of Exclusion.* New York: Columbia University Press.

Darden, Joe T. 1995. "Black Residential Segregation since the 1948 *Shelley v. Kraemer* Decision." *Journal of Black Studies* 25 (6): 680–91.

Denton, Nancy A. 1999. "Half Empty or Half Full: Segregation and Segregated Neighborhoods 30 Years After the Fair Housing Act." *Cityscape* 4 (3): 107–22.

Denton, Nancy A., and Richard D. Alba. 1998. "Suburban Racial and Ethnic Change at the Neighborhood Level: The Declining Number of All-White Neighborhoods." Paper presented at conference on Suburban Racial Change, Harvard University, March 26.

Denton, Nancy, and Douglas Massey. 1988. "Residential Segregation of Blacks, Hispanics, and Asians by Socioeconomic Status and Generation." *Social Science Quarterly* 69: 797–817.

Derthick, Martha. 1979. *Policymaking for Social Security.* Washington, D.C.: Brookings Institution.

Detlefsen, Robert R. 1991. *Civil Rights under Reagan.* San Francisco: Institute for Contemporary Studies Press.

Detroit Free Press. 1970. "Nixon Calls Talks as GOP Slams His Election Tactics." November 8, p. 1A.

DeWitt, Karen E. 1973. "Labor Report/Strengthened EEOC Accelerates Action Against Business, Labor Employee Discrimination." *National Journal,* June 23, pp. 913–21.

Domhoff, G. William. 1990. *The Power Elite and the State: How Policy Is Made in America.* New York: de Gruyter.

Downs, Anthony. 1972. "Federal Housing Subsidies: Their Nature and Effectiveness and What We Should Do about Them." Washington, D.C.: National Association of Home Builders.

Drake, St. Clair, and Horace R. Cayton. [1945] 1993. *Black Metropolis: A Study of Negro Life in a Northern City.* Chicago: University of Chicago Press.

Durant, Robert. 1992. *The Administrative Presidency Revisited: Public Lands, the BLM, and the Reagan Revolution.* Albany: State University of New York Press.

Eaton, Susan E., Joseph Feldman, and Edward Kirby. 1996. "Still Separate, Still Unequal: The Limits of *Milliken II*'s Monetary Compensation to Segregated Schools." Pp. 143–78 in *Dismantling Desegregation: The Quiet Reversal of "Brown v. Board of Education,"* edited by Gary Orfield, Susan E. Eaton and the Harvard Project on School Desegregation. New York: New Press.

Edsall, Thomas Byrne, and Mary D. Edsall. 1991. *Chain Reaction: The Impact of Race, Rights, and Taxes on American Politics.* New York: Norton.

Ehrlichman, John. 1982. *Witness to Power: The Nixon Years.* Paperback ed. New York: Pocket Books.

Ellen, Ingrid Gould. 2000. *Sharing America's Neighborhoods: The Prospects for Stable Racial Integration.* Cambridge: Harvard University Press.

Ellis, Richard J. 1994. *Presidential Lightning Rods: The Politics of Blame Avoidance.* Lawrence: University Press of Kansas.

Ellison, Christopher G., and W. Allen Martin, eds. 1999. "Sources and Consequences of Residential Segregation." *Racial and Ethnic Relations in the United States.* Los Angeles: Roxbury.

Equal Employment Opportunity Commission (EEOC). 1965. "Report of the White House Conference on Equal Employment Opportunity." August 19–20, Washington, D.C.

———. 2002a. "35 Years of Ensuring the Promise of Opportunity: History." Available at www.eeoc.gov/35th/history.

———. 2002b. "Milestones in the History of the U.S. Equal Employment Opportunity Commission." Available at www.eeoc.gov/35th/milestones.

———. 2002c. "Enforcement Efforts in the 1980s." Available at www.eeoc.gov/35th/1980s/enforcement.

Evans, Rowland, Jr., and Robert D. Novak. 1971. *Nixon in the White House: The Frustration of Power.* New York: Random House.

Fainstein, Norman. 1995. "Black Ghettoization and Social Mobility." Pp. 123–41 in *The Bubbling Cauldron*, edited by Michael Peter Smith and Joe R. Feagin. Minneapolis: University of Minnesota Press.

Falk, David, and Herbert M. Franklin. 1976. *Equal Housing Opportunity: The Unfinished Federal Agenda.* Washington, D.C.: Potomac Institute.

Farley, Reynolds. 1996. "Black-White Residential Segregation: The Views of Myrdal in the 1940s and Trends of the 1980s." Pp. 45–75 in *An American Dilemma Revisited: Race Relations in a Changing World*, edited by Obie Clayton, Jr. New York: Russell Sage Foundation.

Farley, Reynolds, Elaine L. Fielding, and Maria Krysan. 1997. "The Residential Preferences of Blacks and Whites: A Four-Metropolis Analysis." *Housing Policy Debate* 8 (4): 763–800.

Farley, Reynolds, and William H. Frey. 1994. "Changes in the Segregation of Whites from Blacks during the 1980s: Small Steps toward a More Integrated Society." *American Sociological Review* 59: 23–45.

Farley, Reynolds, Howard Schuman, Suzanne Bianchi, Diane Colasanto, and Shirley Hatchett. 1978. "Chocolate City, Vanilla Suburbs: Will the Trend toward Racially Separate Communities Continue?" *Social Science Research* 7: 319–44.

Farley, Reynolds, Charlotte Steeh, Tara Jackson, Maria Krysan, and Keith Reeves. 1993. "Continued Racial Residential Segregation in Detroit: 'Chocolate City, Vanilla Suburbs' Revisited." *Journal of Housing Research* 4: 1–38.

Farley, Reynolds, Charlotte Steeh, Maria Krysan, Tara Jackson, and Keith Reeves. 1994. "Stereotypes and Segregation: Neighborhoods in the Detroit Area." *American Journal of Sociology* 100 (3): 750–80.

Federal Housing Administration (FHA). 1941. "Seventh Annual Report of the Federal Housing Administration." Washington, D.C.: U.S. Government Printing Office.

Finley, Mary Lou. 1989. "The Open Housing Marches: Chicago, Summer '66." Pp. 1–47 in *Chicago 1966: Open Housing Marches, Summit Negotiations, and Operation Breadbasket*, edited by David J. Garrow. Brooklyn, N.Y.: Carlson.

Fiorina, Morris P. 1977. *Congress: Keystone of the Washington Establishment.* New Haven: Yale University Press.

Fisher, Anne B. 1985. "Businessmen Like to Hire by the Numbers." *Fortune*, September 16, pp. 26–31.

Fleming, Karl. 1969. "The Square American Speaks Out." *Newsweek*, October 6, pp. 48–59.

Flint, Jerry M. 1970. "Michiganites Jeer Romney over Suburbs' Integration." *New York Times*, July 29, p. 27.

Flournoy, Craig, and George Rodrigue. 1985a. "Separate and Unequal: Illegal Segregation Pervades Nation's Subsidized Housing." *Dallas Morning News*, February 10.

———. 1985b. "Houses Divided: Officially Sanctioned Segregation Is Rule, Not Exception, in East Texas." *Dallas Morning News*, February 12.

———. 1985c. "Fair-Housing Failure: 5 Administrations Have Refused to Enforce Anti-Discrimination Laws." *Dallas Morning News*, February 15.

Friedman, Saul. 1971. "Housing Policy Battle Lines Drawn." *Detroit Free Press*, June 17.

Frymer, Paul, and John David Skrentny. 1998. "Coalition-Building and the Politics of Electoral Capture during the Nixon Administration: African Americans, Labor, Latinos." *Studies in American Political Development* 12 (1): 131–61.

Galster, George C. 1999. "The Evolving Challenges of Fair Housing since 1968: Open Housing, Integration, and the Reduction of Ghettoization." *Cityscape* 4 (3): 123–38.

Garment, Leonard. 1997. *Crazy Rhythm*. New York: Times Books.

Gelfand, Mark I. 1975. *A Nation of Cities: The Federal Government and Urban America, 1933–1965*. New York: Oxford University Press.

Glaeser, Edward L., and Jacob L. Vigdor. 2001. "Racial Segregation in the 2000 Census: Promising News." Washington, D.C.: Brookings Institution.

Glazer, Nathan. 1987. *Affirmative Discrimination*. New York: Basic.

Goering, John. 2003. "Comments on Future Research and Housing Policy." Pp. 383–408 in *Choosing a Better Life? Evaluating the Moving to Opportunity*

Social Experiment, edited by John Goering and Judith D. Feins. Washington, D.C.: Urban Institute Press.

Goering, John, Judith D. Feins, and Todd M. Richardson. 2003. "What Have We Learned about Housing Mobility and Poverty Deconcentration?" Pp. 3–36 in *Choosing a Better Life? Evaluating the Moving to Opportunity Social Experiment*, edited by John Goering and Judith D. Feins. Washington, D.C.: Urban Institute Press.

Gold, Neil M. 1972. "The Mismatch of Jobs and Low-Income People in Metropolitan Areas and Its Implications for the Central City Poor." Pp. 443–86 in *Report of the Commission on Population Growth and the American Future*. Washington, D.C.: U.S. Government Printing Office.

Golden, Marissa Martino. 2000. *What Motivates Bureaucrats? Politics and Administration During the Reagan Years*. New York: Columbia University Press.

Graham, Hugh Davis. 1990. *The Civil Rights Era: Origins and Development of National Policy, 1960–1972*. New York: Oxford University Press.

———. 1996. "Richard Nixon and Civil Rights: Explaining an Enigma." *Presidential Studies Quarterly* 26: 93–106.

———. 1998. "The Politics of Clientele Capture: Civil Rights Policy and the Reagan Administration." Pp. 103–19 in *Redefining Equality*, edited by Neal Devins and Davison M. Douglas. New York: Oxford University Press.

Greenberg, David. 2003. *Nixon's Shadow: The History of an Image*. New York: Norton.

Greenberg, Jack. 1994. *Crusaders in the Courts*. New York: Basic.

Greenhouse, Linda. 1988. "High Court Voids Quotas on Races in Housing Units." *New York Times*, November 8, p. A1.

Grier, George, and Eunice Grier. 1966. *Equality and Beyond: Housing Segregation and the Goals of the Great Society*. Chicago: Quadrangle.

Haldeman, H. R. 1994. *The Haldeman Diaries: Inside the Nixon White House*. New York: Putnam.

Hall, Peter A. 1992. "The Movement from Keynesianism to Monetarism: Institutional Analysis and British Economic Policy in the 1970s." Pp. 90–114 in *Structuring Politics: Historical Institutionalism in Comparative Analysis*, edited by Sven Steinmo, Kathleen Thelen, and Frank Longstreth. New York: Cambridge University Press.

Halpern, Stephen C. 1995. *On the Limits of the Law: The Ironic Legacy of Title VI of the 1964 Civil Rights Act*. Baltimore: Johns Hopkins University Press.

Halvorsen, David. 1966. "Cancel Rights Marches." *Chicago Tribune*, August 27, p. 1.

Harvard Law Review. 1989. "Rethinking *Weber*: The Business Response to Affirmative Action." 102 (3): 658–71.

Hays, R. Allen. 1995. *The Federal Government and Urban Housing*. 2nd ed. Albany: State University of New York Press.

Heclo, Hugh. 1974. *Modern Social Politics in Britain and Sweden: From Relief to Income Maintenance*. New Haven: Yale University Press.

Helper, Phyllis. 1970. "Housing and Urban Development: Biggest Open Housing Section Takes Effect; U.S. Plans Enforcement." *National Journal*, January 10, pp. 76–78.

Helper, Rose. 1969. *Racial Policies and Practices of Real Estate Brokers*. Minneapolis: University of Minnesota Press.

———. 1991. "Introduction to American Policies and Programs." In *Urban Housing Segregation of Minorities in Western Europe and the United States*, edited by Elizabeth D. Huttman. Durham, N.C.: Duke University Press.

Herbers, John. 1970. "Mitchell Is Said to Advise Romney to Take New Post." *New York Times*, November 22, p. 1.

———. 1971. "U.S. Acts to Spread Subsidized Housing." *New York Times*, September 30, p. 1.

———. 1972a. "Proposal to Disperse Housing Snagged." *New York Times* April 24, p. 14.

———. 1972b. "95 U.S. Rights Lawyers Score Nixon Busing View." *New York Times*, April 26, p. 33.

Hirsch, Arnold R. 2000. " 'Containment' on the Home Front: Race and Federal Housing Policy from the New Deal to the Cold War." *Journal of Urban History* 26 (2): 158–89.

Hoff, Joan. 1994. *Nixon Reconsidered*. New York: Basic.

Hooks, Gregory. 1990. "From an Autonomous to a Captured State Agency: The Decline of the New Deal in Agriculture." *American Sociological Review* 55: 29–43.

Houston Chronicle. 1971. "Minority Leaders Assail Nixon on Housing Stance." June 12.

Hoyt, Clark. 1970. "Romney Trip Hit as Election Ploy." *Detroit Free Press*, July 31, p. 2A.

Hunter, Marjorie. 1968. "Civil Rights Bill Wins Final Vote." *New York Times*, April 11, p. 1.

Jackson, Kenneth T. 1985. *Crabgrass Frontier: The Suburbanization of the United States*. New York: Oxford University Press.

Janota, Laura. 1998. "Door Closes on Historic Housing-Assistance Program." *Chicago Daily Herald*. October 1, p. 11.

Jencks, Christopher, and Susan Mayer. 1990. "Residential Segregation, Job Proximity, and Black Job Opportunities." Pp. 187–222 in *Inner-City Poverty in the United States*, edited by Laurence Lynn and Michael McGeary. Washington, D.C.: National Academy Press.

Jenkins, J. Craig, and Barbara G. Brents. 1989. "Social Protest, Hegemonic Competition, and Social Reform: A Political Struggle Interpretation of the Origins of the American Welfare State." *American Sociological Review* 54: 891–909.

Jones-Correa, Michael. 2000–01. "The Origins and Diffusion of Racial Restrictive Covenants." *Political Science Quarterly* 115 (4): 541–67.

Jost, Kenneth. 1996. "Rethinking School Integration." *CQ Researcher* 6 (39): 913–36.

Karmin, Monroe W. 1970. "Romney's Departure Grows More Likely." *Wall Street Journal*, December 16.

———. 1973. "Nixon's Moratorium on Subsidized Housing Stirs Debate among Its Critics, Advocates." *Wall Street Journal*, March 16, p. 34.

Kasinitz, Philip, and Jan Rosenberg. 1996. "Missing the Connection: Social Isolation and Employment on the Brooklyn Waterfront." *Social Problems* 43 (2): 180–96.

Katz, Jon. 1972. "Labor Dept. Mulls Plan to Cut Construction Minority Quota." *Washington Post*, September 7, p. A1.

Kaufman, Julie E., and James E. Rosenbaum. 1992. "The Education and Employment of Low-Income Black Youth in White Suburbs." *Educational Evaluation and Policy Analysis* 14 (3): 229–40.

Keating, W. Dennis. 1994. *The Suburban Racial Dilemma: Housing and Neighborhoods*. Philadelphia: Temple University Press.

Kelley, Jonathan. 1974. "The Politics of School Busing." *Public Opinion Quarterly* 38 (1): 23–39.

Kelly, Erin, and Frank Dobbin. 2001. "How Affirmative Action Became Diversity Management: Employer Response to Anti-Discrimination Law, 1961–1996," Pp. 87–117 in *Color Lines: Affirmative Action, Immigration, and Civil Rights Options for America*, edited by John David Skrentny. Chicago: University of Chicago Press.

Kernell, Samuel. 1977. "Presidential Popularity and Negative Voting: An Alternative Explanation of the Midterm Congressional Decline of the President's Party." *American Political Science Review* 72: 44–66.

Kingdon, John W. 1984. *Agendas, Alternatives and Public Policies*. Boston: Little, Brown.

Kirp, David L., John P. Dwyer, and Larry A. Rosenthal. 1995. *Our Town: Race, Housing and the Soul of Suburbia*. New Brunswick, N.J.: Rutgers University Press.

Kotlowski, Dean J. 1998a. "Richard Nixon and the Origins of Affirmative Action." *The Historian* 60 (3): 523–41.

———. 1998b. "Nixon's Southern Strategy Revisited." *Journal of Policy History* 10 (2): 207–38.

———. 2001. *Nixon's Civil Rights*. Cambridge: Harvard University Press.

Lanza, Michael L. 1990. *Agrarianism and Reconstruction Politics: The Southern Homestead Act*. Baton Rouge: Louisiana State University Press.

Lee, Bill Lan. 1999. "An Issue of Public Importance: The Justice Department's Enforcement of the Fair Housing Act." *Cityscape* 4 (3): 35–56.

Lemann, Nicholas. 1991. *The Promised Land: The Great Black Migration and How It Changed America*. New York: Vintage.

Lenhausen, Don, and Howard Kohn. 1970. "Romney Tells the Suburbs He Won't Force Integration." *Detroit Free Press*, July 28, pp. 1A, 8A.

Lieberman, Robert C. 1998. *Shifting the Color Line: Race and the American Welfare State*. Cambridge: Harvard University Press.

Lieberson, Stanley, and Donna K. Carter. 1982. "Temporal Changes and Urban Differences in Residential Segregation: A Reconsideration." *American Journal of Sociology* 88 (2): 296–310.

Lilley, William III. 1970a. "CPR Report/Romney Lines Up HUD Money Programs to Back Operation Breakthrough Housing Push." *National Journal*, January 31, 232–41.

———. 1970b. "Housing Report/Romney Faces Political Perils with Plan to Integrate Suburbs." *National Journal*, October 17, pp. 2251–63.

———. 1971a. "Housing Report/Administration and Congress Follow Courts in Promoting Residential Integration." *National Journal*, November 12, pp. 2431–39.

———. 1971b. "Housing Report/Courts Lead Revolutionary Trend toward Desegregation of Residential Areas." *National Journal*, November 27, pp. 2346–47.

Lilley, William, III, and Timothy B. Clark. 1972. "Urban Report/Federal Programs Spur Abandonment of Housing in Major Cities." *National Journal*, January 1, pp. 26–33.

Loevy, Robert D. 1990. *To End All Segregation: The Politics and the Passage of the Civil Rights Act of 1964*. New York: University Press of America.

Los Angeles Times. 1971. "Nixon's Actions Cheer Fair Housing Backers." June 16.

Logan, John R., and Mark Schneider. 1984. "Racial Segregation and Racial Change in American Suburbs, 1970–1980." *American Journal of Sociology* 89 (4): 874–88.

Lowe, Jeanne R. 1969. "Race, Jobs, and Cities: What Business Can Do." *Saturday Review*. February 22, pp. 32–33.

Lowi, Theodore J. 1979. *The End of Liberalism: The Second Republic of the United States*. New York: Norton.

Lubell, Samuel. 1970. *The Hidden Crisis in American Politics*. New York: Norton.

Mahoney, Peter E. 1998. "The End(s) of Disparate Impact: Doctrinal Reconstruction, Fair Housing and Lending Law, and the Antidiscrimination Principle." *Emory Law Journal* 47 (409): 1–78.

Malbin, Michael J. 1973. "Employment Report/Agency Differences Persist over Goals and Timetables in Nondiscrimination Plans." *National Journal*, September 22, pp. 1400–11.

Male, Charles T. 1932. *Real Estate Fundamentals*. New York: Van Nostrand.

Massey, Douglas S., and Nancy A. Denton. 1987. "Trends in the Residential Segregation of Blacks, Hispanics, and Asians: 1970–1980." *American Sociological Review* 52: 802–25.

———. 1988. "Suburbanization and Segregation in U.S. Metropolitan Areas." *American Journal of Sociology* 94 (3): 592–626.

———. 1993. *American Apartheid*. Cambridge: Harvard University Press.

Mathias, Charles McC., Jr., and Marion Morris. 1999. "Fair Housing Legislation: Not an Easy Row to Hoe." *Cityscape* 4 (3): 21–33.

Matusow, Allen J. 1984. *The Unraveling of America: A History of Liberalism in the 1960s*. New York: Harper Torchbooks.

Mayhew, David. 1974. *Congress: The Electoral Connection*. New Haven: Yale University Press.

McAdam, Doug. 1982. *Political Process and the Development of Black Insurgency, 1930–1970*. Chicago: University of Chicago Press.

McAndrews, Lawrence J. 1998. "The Politics of Principle: Richard Nixon and School Desegregation." *Journal of Negro History* 83 (3): 187–200.

McBee, Susanna. 1973a. "U.S. Housing Program Hit by President." *Washington Post*, January 18, p. A2.

———. 1973b. "Subsidized Housing Frozen before Justification by HUD." *Washington Post*, December 3, p. A1.

McDonald, Hugh. 1970a. "U.S. Picks Warren as Prime Target in Move to Integrate All Suburbs." *Detroit News*, July 21, p. 1A.

———. 1970b. "How Warren Became Integration Test City." *Detroit News*, July 22, p. 1A.

———. 1970c. "Warren Was Given Romney Ultimatum." *Detroit News*, July 24, p. 1A.

McDonald, Hugh, and Gary Schuster. 1970. "No Forced Integration, But Open Housing Is Essential, Romney Says." *Detroit News*, July 28, p. 1A.

McEntire, Davis. 1960. *Residence and Race*. Berkeley and Los Angeles: University of California Press.

McFarland, M. Carter. 1978. *Federal Government and Urban Problems: HUD: Successes, Failures, and the Fate of Our Cities*. Boulder, Colo.: Westview.

McKay, David H. 1977. *Housing and Race in Industrial Society*. Totowa, N.J.: Rowman and Littlefield.

McNeil, Genna Rae. 1983. *Groundwork: Charles Hamilton Houston and the Struggle for Civil Rights*. Philadelphia: University of Pennsylvania Press.

Meier, Kenneth J. 1980. "Measuring Organizational Power: Resources and Autonomy of Government Agencies." *Administration and Society* 12 (3): 357–75.

———. 1993. *Politics and the Bureaucracy: Policymaking in the Fourth Branch of Government*. 3rd ed. Pacific Grove, Calif.: Brooks/Cole.

Melnick, R. Shep. 1994. *Between the Lines: Interpreting Welfare Rights*. Washington, D.C.: Brookings Institution.

Metcalf, George R. 1988. *Fair Housing Comes of Age*. New York: Greenwood.

Meyer, John W., and W. Richard Scott. 1983. "Centralization and the Legitimacy Problem of Local Government." Pp. 199–215 in *Organizational Environments: Ritual and Rationality*, edited by J. W. Meyer and W. R. Scott. Beverly Hills, Calif.: Sage.

Meyer, Stephen Grant. 2000. *As Long As They Don't Move Next Door: Segregation and Racial Conflict in American Neighborhoods*. Lanham, Md.: Rowman and Littlefield.

Miles, Rufus E., Jr. 1974. *The Department of Health, Education, and Welfare*. New York: Praeger.

Milius, Peter. 1972. "Memo Said to Nullify Hiring Plan." *Washington Post*, September 26, p. A7.

Miller, Loren. 1967. "Louisville's Housing Anniversary." *The Crisis*, June, p. 255.

Milwaukee Journal. 1971. "No Leadership on Housing." June 14.

Mitchell, Grayson. 1972. "Quota Issue Seen Hurting McGovern." *Washington Post*, October 20, p. A6.

Moreno, Paul D. 1997. *From Direct Action to Affirmative Action: Fair Employment Law and Policy in America, 1933–1972*. Baton Rouge: Louisiana State University Press.

Morris, William R. 1968. "The 1968 Housing Act: New Hope for Negroes." *The Crisis*, November, pp. 313–17.

Mossberg, Walter S. 1970. "A Blue-Collar Town Fears Urban Renewal Perils Its Way of Life." *Wall Street Journal*, November 2, p. 1.

Myrdal, Gunnar. 1944. *An American Dilemma: The Negro Problem and Modern Democracy*. New York: Harper.

Nathan, Richard P. 1983. *The Administrative Presidency*. New York: Wiley.

National Advisory Commission on Civil Disorders. 1968. "Report of the National Advisory Commission on Civil Disorders" (Kerner Commission Report). *New York Times* ed. New York: Dutton.

National Association of Home Builders. 1970. "Barba Urges Retention of Tested FHA Housing Programs in HUD's Proposed Revision of Nation's Housing Laws." *NAHB Washington Scope* 8, no. 24 (June 12): 1–2.

National Committee Against Discrimination in Housing. 1968. "How the Federal Government Builds Ghettos." New York: NCDH.

National Fair Housing Alliance. 2004. *2004 Fair Housing Trends Report*. Washington, D.C.: National Fair Housing Alliance. Available at www.nationalfairhousing.org, accessed June 2004.

National Journal. 1971. "Equal Employment Opportunity Commission: Notes." February 13, p. 361.

———. 1972. "Critics of Bureaucrats: Nixon and Wallace." December 16, p. 1935.

National Public Radio. 1991. "Great Divide: History of Affirmative Action." Transcript from *All Things Considered*, September 16, pp. 1–6.

Newman, Katherine S. 1999. *No Shame in My Game: The Working Poor in the Inner City*. New York: Vintage Books and Russell Sage Foundation.

Newsweek. 1969a. "The Troubled American: A Special Report on the White Majority." October 6, pp. 29–34.

———. 1969b. "How It Feels to Be Caught in the Middle." October 6, pp. 34–48.

———. 1971. "Trouble in Pontiac." September 20, p. 33.

New York Times. 1968. "Transcript of Nixon's Program on Television Introducing His Cabinet Members." December 12, p. 37.

———. 1970. "Suburbs Reject Housing Program." November 8, p. 55.

———. 1971. "How Do You Break the Ring Around the City?" January 10, sec. IV, p. 3.

———. 1972a. "Roadblocks for the Nixon Proposals." April 23, sec. IV, p. 2.

———. 1972b. "White House Said to Plan Freeze on Public Housing." December 23, p. 1.

Nixon, Richard. 1972. "Radio Address on the Philosophy of Government." October 21, Item 356. This and other public papers are available at www.nixonfoundation.org/Research_Center/PublicPapers.cfm.

———. 1973. "Radio Address about the State of the Union Message on Community Development." March 4, Item 68. Available at www.nixonfoundation.org/Research_Center/PublicPapers.cfm.

———. [1978] 1990. *RN: The Memoirs of Richard Nixon*. New York: Touchstone.

Oliver, Melvin L., and Thomas M. Shapiro. 1995. *Black Wealth/White Wealth*. New York: Routledge.

O'Reilly, Kenneth. 1995. *Nixon's Piano: Presidents and Racial Politics from Washington to Clinton*. New York: Free Press.

Orfield, Gary. 1969. *The Reconstruction of Southern Education: The Schools and the 1964 Civil Rights Act*. New York: Wiley-Interscience.

————. 1996a. "Turning Back to Segregation." Pp. 1–22 in *Dismantling Deseg-regation: The Quiet Reversal of* Brown v. Board of Education, edited by Gary Orfield, Susan E. Eaton, and the Harvard Project on School Desegregation. New York: New Press.

———— 1996b. "Segregated Housing and School Resegregation." Pp. 291–330 in *Dismantling Desegregation: The Quiet Reversal of* Brown v. Board of Education, edited by Gary Orfield, Susan E. Eaton, and the Harvard Project on School Desegregation. New York: New Press.

Orfield, Gary, and Chungmei Lee. 2004. "*Brown* at 50: King's Dream or *Plessy's* Nightmare?" The Civil Rights Project, Harvard University, Cambridge, Mass. Available at http://www.civilrightsproject.harvard.edu/research/reseq04/brown50.pdf.

Orlebeke, Charles J. 2000. "The Evolution of Low-Income Housing Policy, 1949 to 1999." *Housing Policy Debate* 11 (2): 489–520.

Orloff, Ann Shola. 1993. *The Politics of Pensions: A Comparative Analysis of Britain, Canada, and the United States, 1880–1940*. Madison: University of Wisconsin Press.

Orloff, Ann Shola, and Theda Skocpol. 1984. "Why Not Equal Protection? Explaining the Politics of Public Social Spending in Britain, 1900–1911, and the United States, 1880s–1920." *American Sociological Review* 49: 726–50.

Panetta, Leon E., and Peter Gall. 1971. *Bring Us Together: The Nixon Team and the Civil Rights Retreat*. New York: Lipincott.

Patterson, James T. 1996. *Grand Expectations: The United States, 1945–1974*. New York: Oxford University Press.

Pedriana, Nicholas, and Robin Stryker. 1997. "Political Culture Wars 1960s Style: Equal Employment Opportunity—Affirmative Action Law and the Philadelphia Plan." *American Journal of Sociology* 103 (3): 633–91.

Phillips, Kevin P. 1971. "Squeezing the Suburbs." *Washington Post*, June 22.

Pierson, Paul. 1994. *Dismantling the Welfare State?* New York: Cambridge University Press.

Plans for Progress. 1967. "A Report: January 1966–August 1967." Washington, D.C.: Plans for Progress.

Polikoff, Alexander. 1986. "Sustainable Integration or Inevitable Resegregation: The Troubling Questions." Pp. 43–71 in *Housing Desegregation and Federal Policy*, edited by John M. Goering. Chapel Hill: University of North Carolina Press.

Popkin, Susan J., Laura E. Harris, and Mary K. Cunningham. 2002. "Families in Transition: A Qualitative Analysis of the MTO Experience." Washington, D.C.: Urban Institute.

Powell, Walter, and Paul DiMaggio. 1991. *The New Institutionalism in Organizational Analysis*. Chicago: University of Chicago Press.

President's Committee on Equal Employment Opportunity. 1964. "President Announces 192 American Corporations Have Joined Plans for Progress." *The Committee Reporter* 2 (May).

Quadagno, Jill. 1994. *The Color of Welfare: How Racism Undermined the War on Poverty*. New York: Oxford University Press.

———. 1992. "Social Movements and State Transformation: Labor Unions and Racial Conflict in the War on Poverty." *American Sociological Review* 57: 616–34.

———. 2000. "Promoting Civil Rights Through the Welfare State: How Medicare Integrated Southern Hospitals." *Social Problems* 47: 68–89.

Rabkin, Jeremy. 1980. "Office for Civil Rights." Pp. 304–53 in *The Politics of Regulation*, edited by James Q. Wilson. New York: Basic Books.

Raines, Howell. 1998. "George Wallace, Symbol of the Fight to Maintain Segregation, Dies at 79." *New York Times*, September 15, p. B10.

Ralph, James R., Jr. 1993. *Northern Protest: Martin Luther King, Jr., Chicago and the Civil Rights Movement*. Cambridge: Harvard University Press.

Reichley, A. James. 1970. "George Romney Is Running Hard at HUD." *Fortune*, December, pp. 100–103, 134–35.

———. 1981. *Conservatives in an Age of Change: The Nixon and Ford Administrations*. Washington, D.C.: Brookings Institution.

Riley, Dennis. 1987. *Controlling the Federal Bureaucracy*. Philadelphia: Temple University Press.

Rivkin, Steven G. 1994. "Residential Segregation and School Integration." *Sociology of Education* 67: 279–92.

Robinson, Jo Ann Ooiman, ed. 2001. *Affirmative Action: A Documentary History*. Westport, Conn.: Greenwood.

Rodgers, Harrell R., Jr. 1984. "Fair Employment Law for Minorities: An Evaluation of Federal Implementation." Pp. 93–177 in *Implementation of Civil Rights Policy*, edited by Charles S. Bullock III and Charles M. Lamb. Monterey, Calif.: Brooks/Cole.

Rodrigue, George. 1985a. "Racial Data on Subsidized Housing Not Compiled." *Dallas Morning News*, February 13, p. 15A.

———. 1985b. "14 Years After Ruling, Atlanta's White Suburbs Resist Low-Rent Housing." *Dallas Morning News*, February 13, p. 15A

Rodrigue, George, Craig Flournoy, and David Tarrant. 1985. "Segregation in Dallas: How Integration in Housing Failed." *Dallas Morning News*, February 14, p. 1A.

Rogers-Dillon, Robin H., and John David Skrentny. 1999. "Administering Success: The Legitimacy Imperative and the Implementation of Welfare Reform." *Social Problems* 46 (1): 13–29.

Rosen, Gerald R. 1974. "Industry's New Watchdog in Washington." *Dun's*, June, pp. 83–85.

Rosenbaum, David E. 1972. "Bill to Bar Busing Killed in Senate as Closure Fails." *New York Times*, October 13, p. 1.

Rosenbaum, James E. 1995. "Changing the Geography of Opportunity by Expanding Residential Choice: Lessons from the Gautreaux Program." *Housing Policy Debate* 6 (1): 231–69.

Rosenbaum, James E., and Susan Popkin. 1991. "Employment and Earnings of Low-Income Blacks Who Move to Middle-Class Suburbs." Pp. 342–56 in *The Urban Underclass*, edited by Christopher Jencks and Paul E. Peterson. Washington, D.C.: Brookings Institution.

Rosenberg, Gerald N. 1991. *The Hollow Hope: Can Courts Bring about Social Change?* Chicago: University of Chicago Press.

Rosenthal, Jack. 1971. "Romney, in Shift, Freezes Disputed Home Aid to Poor." *New York Times*, January 15.

Rossell, Christine H. 1998. "The Convergence of Black and White Attitudes on School Desegregation Issues." Pp. 120–138 in *Redefining Equality*, edited by Neal Devins and Davison M. Douglas. New York: Oxford University Press.

Rubinowitz, Leonard S., and James E. Rosenbaum. 2000. *Crossing the Class and Color Lines: From Public Housing to White Suburbia*. Chicago: University of Chicago Press.

Rueschemeyer, Dietrich, and Theda Skocpol. 1996. *States, Social Knowledge and the Origins of Modern Social Policies*. Princeton: Princeton University Press.

Rusk, David. 2001. "The 'Segregation' Tax: The Cost of Residential Segregation to Black Homeowners." Washington, D.C.: Brookings Institution.

Safire, William. 1975. *Before the Fall: An Inside View of the Pre-Watergate White House*. New York: Da Capo.

Saltman, Juliet. 1990. *A Fragile Movement: The Struggle for Neighborhood Stabilization*. New York: Greenwood.

Santoro, Wayne A., and Gail M. McGuire. 1997. "Social Movement Insiders: The Impact of Institutional Activists on Affirmative Action and Comparable Worth Policies." *Social Problems* 44 (4): 503–19.

Schechter, Henry B. 1974. "Critique of 'Housing in the Seventies.'" Congressional Research Service. Washington, D.C.: U.S. Government Printing Office.

Schill, Michael H., and Samantha Friedman. 1999. "The Fair Housing Amendments Act of 1988: The First Decade." *Cityscape* 4 (3): 57–78.

Schuman, Howard, Charlotte Steeh, Lawrence Bobo, and Maria Krysan. 1997. *Racial Attitudes in America: Trends and Interpretations*. Cambridge: Harvard University Press.

Scott, W. Richard. 1991. "Unpacking Institutional Arguments." Pp. 164–82 in *The New Institutionalism in Organizational Analysis*, edited by Walter Powell and Paul DiMaggio. Chicago: University of Chicago Press.

Selznick, Philip. 1949. *TVA and the Grass Roots*. Berkeley: University of California Press.

Semer, Milton P., and Julian H. Zimmerman. 1976. "Impact of Judicial and Administrative Decisions on Legislative Policy Development and Implementation of Housing Programs." *Housing in the Seventies Working Papers 1*. Washington, D.C.: U.S. Government Printing Office.

Semple, Robert B., Jr. 1972. "Busing and the President: The Evolution of a Policy." *New York Times*, March 19, p. 1.

Shull, Steven A. 1989. *The President and Civil Rights Policy: Leadership and Change*. New York: Greenwood.

Sidney, Mara S. 2001. "Images of Race, Class, and Markets: Rethinking the Origin of U.S. Fair Housing Policy." *Journal of Policy History* 13 (2): 181–214.

———. 2003. *Unfair Housing: How National Policy Shapes Community Action*. Lawrence: University Press of Kansas.

Skocpol, Theda. 1980. "Political Response to Capitalist Crisis: Neo-Marxist Theories of the State and the Case of the New Deal." *Political Sociology* 10: 155–201.

———. 1985. "Bringing the State Back In: Strategies of Analysis in Current Research." Pp. 3–37 in *Bringing the State Back In*, edited by Peter B. Evans,

Dietrich Rueschemeyer, and Theda Skocpol. New York: Cambridge University Press.

———. 1992. *Protecting Soldiers and Mothers*. Cambridge, Mass.: Belknap.

———. 1995. "African Americans in U.S. Social Policy." Pp. 129–51 in *Classifying by Race*, edited by Paul E. Peterson. Princeton: Princeton University Press.

Skocpol, Theda, and Edwin Amenta. 1986. "States and Social Policies." *Annual Review of Sociology* 12: 131–57.

Skowronek, Stephen. 1986. "Notes on the Presidency in the Political Order." *Studies in American Political Development* 1: 286–302.

Skrentny, John David. 1996. *The Ironies of Affirmative Action*. Chicago: University of Chicago Press.

———. 1998. "State Capacity, Policy Feedbacks and Affirmative Action for Blacks, Women and Latinos." *Research in Political Sociology* 8: 279–310.

———. 2002. *The Minority Rights Revolution*. Cambridge: Harvard University Press.

Smith, David Barton. 1999. *Health Care Divided: Race and Healing a Nation*. Ann Arbor: University of Michigan Press.

Smith, Tom W. 1980. "America's Most Important Problem—A Trend Analysis, 1946–1976." *Public Opinion Quarterly* 44 (2): 164–80.

Squires, Gregory D., Samantha Friedman, and Catherine E. Saidat. 2002. "Experiencing Residential Segregation: A Contemporary Study of Washington, D.C." *Urban Affairs Review* 38 (2): 155–83.

Stanfield, Rochelle L. 1979. "Fair Housing: Still Doors to Open After 11 Years." *National Journal*, May 5, pp. 1–8.

———. 1983. "Reagan Courting Women, Minorities, But It May Be Too Late to Win Them." *National Journal*, May 28, pp. 1118–23.

Steele, James B. 1971. "Mayors Soften Blow at Nixon Housing Policy, Ask Fund Cutoff over Bias." *Philadelphia Inquirer*, June 17.

Stein, Judith. 1998. *Running Steel, Running America: Race, Economic Policy and the Decline of Liberalism*. Chapel Hill: University of North Carolina Press.

Sternlieb, George, and David Listokin. 1976. "Exclusionary Zoning: State of the Art, Strategies for the Future." *Housing in the Seventies Working Papers 1*. Washington, D.C.: U.S. Government Printing Office.

Stewart, John G. 1997. "The Civil Rights Act of 1964: Tactics II." Pp. 275–320 in *The Civil Rights Act of 1964: The Passage of the Law That Ended Racial Segregation*, edited by Robert D. Loevy. Albany: State University of New York Press.

St. Louis Globe-Democrat. 1972. "St. Louis' Housing Debacle" (editorial). March 11–12, p. 2F.

Stone, Deborah. 1989. "Causal Stories and the Formation of Policy Agendas." *Political Science Quarterly* 104 (2): 281–300.

Sugrue, Thomas J. 1996. *The Origins of the Urban Crisis: Race and Inequality in Postwar Detroit*. Princeton: Princeton University Press.

———. 2001. "Breaking Through: The Troubled Origins of Affirmative Action in the Workplace." Pp. 31–52 in *Color Lines: Affirmative Action, Immigration, and Civil Rights Options for America*, edited by John David Skrentny. Chicago: University of Chicago Press.

Sundquist, James L. 1968. *Politics and Policy: The Eisenhower, Kennedy and Johnson Years*. Washington, D.C.: Brookings Institution.

Taeuber, Karl E., and Alma F. Taeuber. 1965. *Negroes in Cities: Residential Segregation and Neighborhood Change*. Chicago: Aldine.

Thelen, Kathleen, and Sven Steinmo. 1992. "Historical Institutionalism in Comparative Politics." Pp. 1–32 in *Structuring Politics: Historical Institutionalism in Comparative Analysis*, edited by Sven Steinmo, Kathleen Thelen, and Frank Longstreth. New York: Cambridge University Press.

Time. 1970. "Finch: First Casualty of the Nixon Cabinet." June 15, p. 12.

———. 1972. "Retreat from Integration." March 27, p. 21.

Turner, Margery Austin. 2000. Remarks at Integration Works Conference, Philadelphia, December 1 and 2.

Turner, Margery Austin, Susan Popkin, and Mary Cunningham. 2000. "Section 8 Mobility and Neighborhood Health: Emerging Issues and Policy Challenges." Washington, D.C.: Urban Institute.

Twohey, Megan. 1999. "Desegregation is Dead." *National Journal*, September 18, pp. 2614–20.

United States Commission on Civil Rights (USCCR). 1961. "Housing." Washington, D.C.: U.S. Government Printing Office.

———. 1966. "Title VI . . . One Year After: A Survey of Desegregation of Health and Welfare Services in the South." Washington, D.C.: U.S. Government Printing Office.

———. 1970. "HEW and Title VI." Washington, D.C.: U.S. Government Printing Office.

———. 1971. "Federal Civil Rights Enforcement: One Year Later." Washington, D.C.: U.S. Government Printing Office.

———. 1973. "The Federal Civil Rights Enforcement Effort—A Reassessment." Washington, D.C.: U.S. Government Printing Office.

———. 1974a. "Equal Opportunity in Suburbia." Washington, D.C.: U.S. Government Printing Office.

———. 1974b. "The Federal Civil Rights Enforcement Effort—1974 (vol. 2: To Provide . . . For Fair Housing)." Washington, D.C.: U.S. Government Printing Office.

———. 1974c. "The Federal Civil Rights Enforcement Effort—1974 (vol. 7: To Preserve, Protect, and Defend the Constitution)." Washington, D.C.: U.S. Government Printing Office.

———. 1996. "Federal Title VI Enforcement to Ensure Nondiscrimination in Federally Assisted Programs." Washington, D.C.: U.S. Government Printing Office.

United States Department of Housing and Urban Development (HUD). 1973. "Housing in the Seventies." Washington, D.C.: U.S. Government Printing Office.

———. 1999. "Moving to Opportunity for Fair Housing Demonstration Program: Current Status and Initial Findings." September. Available at http://www.hud.gov.

United States General Accounting Office. 1973. "Compliance with Antidiscrimination Provision of Civil Rights Act by Hospitals and Other Facilities Under Medicare and Medicaid," p. 14; reprinted in HJC 1973.

Unna, Warren. 1954. "Senators Pin FHA Scandal on 'Greedy.'" *Washington Post and Times Herald,* December 20, p. 1.

U.S. News & World Report. 1970. "Chaos over School Busing: Tale of Two Cities." March 16, pp. 29–33.

Van Valey, Thomas L., Wade Clark Roof, and Jerome E. Wilcox. 1977. "Trends in Residential Segregation: 1960–1970." *American Journal of Sociology* 82 (4): 826–44.

Wagner, Joseph L. 2000. "Desegregation an Uphill Battle for Parma Still." *Cleveland Plain Dealer,* November 26, p. 1A.

Wall Street Journal. 1954. "Senate Group, in Scathing Report, Assails Both Builders, U.S. Officials for Greed, Dishonesty in F.H.A. Scandals." December 20, p. 2.

———. 1966. "House Approves Administration's Civil-Rights Bill." August 10.

———. 1971a. "Secretary of Housing Romney Indicates He Will Compromise Any Rifts with Nixon." January 7.

———. 1971b. "Civil Rights Commission Gives Administration Mixed Progress Rating." May 11.

Wallace, Christopher. 1971. "Mayors Rip U.S. Policy on Suburban Housing." *Boston Globe,* June 13, p. 1.

Walsh, Mark. 2002. "High Court Closes Historic Desegregation Case." *Education Week,* April 24.

Washington Post. 1972a. "Romney Finds FHA Unprepared to Handle 'Fast-Buck Artists.'" May 6, p. E36.

———. 1972b. ". . . And Secretary Romney Steps Out" (editorial). November 28, p. A14.

Watzman, Sanford. 1970. "HUD Dragging Feet on Fair Housing." *Cleveland Plain Dealer,* March 5, p. 1.

Weaver, R. Kent. 1986. "The Politics of Blame Avoidance." *Journal of Public Policy* 6 (4): 371–98.

Weaver, Robert C. 1948. *The Negro Ghetto.* New York: Harcourt, Brace.

Weber, Max. 1946. "Bureaucracy." In *From Max Weber: Essays in Sociology,* edited by H. H. Gerth and C. Wright Mills. New York: Oxford University Press.

Weir, Margaret. 1992. *Politics and Jobs.* Princeton: Princeton University Press.

———. 1995. "The Politics of Racial Isolation in Europe and America." In *Classifying by Race,* edited by Paul E. Peterson. Princeton: Princeton University Press.

Weir, Margaret, Ann Shola Orloff, and Theda Skocpol. 1988. "The Future of Social Policy in the United States: Political Constraints and Possibilities." Pp. 421–45 in *The Politics of Social Policy in the United States,* edited by Margaret Weir, Ann Shola Orloff, and Theda Skocpol. Princeton: Princeton University Press.

Weisbrot, Robert. 1990. *Freedom Bound: A History of America's Civil Rights Movement.* New York: Norton.

Wells, Amy Stuart. 2001. "The 'Consequences' of School Desegregation: The Mismatch Between the Research and the Rationale." *Hastings Constitutional Law Quarterly* 28 (771).

Wendt, Paul F. 1956. *The Role of the Federal Government in Housing.* Washington, D.C.: American Enterprise Association.

Wentworth, Eric. 1972. "Schools: To Bus or Not to Bus." *Washington Post*, February 21, p. A1.

West, William. 1995. *Controlling the Bureaucracy: Institutional Constraints in Theory and Practice*. Armonk, N.Y.: Sharpe.

Whalen, Charles, and Barbara Whalen. 1985. *The Longest Debate: A Legislative History of the 1964 Civil Rights Act*. Cabin John, Md.: Seven Locks.

White, Theodore H. 1969. *The Making of the President—1968*. New York: Atheneum.

Willmann, John B. 1967. *The Department of Housing and Urban Development*. New York: Praeger.

Wills, Garry. [1969] 1979. *Nixon Agonistes: The Crisis of the Self-Made Man*. New York: Mentor.

Wilson, James Q. 1960. *Negro Politics: The Search for Leadership*. Glencoe, Ill.: Free Press.

———. 1980. "The Politics of Regulation." Pp. 357–94 in *The Politics of Regulation*, edited by James Q. Wilson. New York: Basic.

———. 1989. *Bureaucracy: What Government Agencies Do and Why They Do It*. New York: Basic.

Wilson, William Julius. 1996. *When Work Disappears: The World of the New Urban Poor*. New York: Alfred A. Knopf.

Wines, Michael. 1982. "Administration Says It Merely Seeks a 'Better Way' to Enforce Civil Rights." *National Journal*, January 27, pp. 536–41.

Witcover, Jules. 1970. *The Resurrection of Richard Nixon*. New York: Putnam.

Wolfe, Alan. 1981. *America's Impasse: The Rise and Fall of the Politics of Growth*. New York: Pantheon.

Wood, B. Dan. 1990. "Does Politics Make a Difference at the EEOC?" *American Journal of Political Science* 34 (2): 503–30.

Wood, B. Dan, and Richard W. Waterman. 1991. "The Dynamics of Political Control of the Bureaucracy." *American Political Science Review* 85 (3): 801–28.

Woodward, C. Vann. 1974. *The Strange Career of Jim Crow*. 3rd rev. ed. New York: Oxford University Press.

Wowk, Michael. 1970. "Romney Is Hissed by Warren Crowd; He Keeps a Smile." *Detroit News*, July 28, p. 1A.

Wright, Gerald C., Jr. 1977. "Constituency Responses to Congressional Behavior: The Impact of the House Judiciary Committee Impeachment Votes." *Western Political Quarterly* 30 (3): 401–10.

Wuthnow, Robert, J. D. Hunter, A. Bergesen, and E. Kurzweil. 1984. *Cultural Analysis*. Boston: Routledge and Kegan Paul.

Yergin, Daniel, and Joseph Stanislaw. 1998. *The Commanding Heights: The Battle Between Government and the Marketplace That Is Remaking the Modern World*. New York: Simon and Schuster.

Yinger, John. 1995. *Closed Doors, Opportunity Lost: The Continuing Costs of Housing Discrimination*. New York: Russell Sage Foundation.

———. 1999. "Sustaining the Fair Housing Act." *Cityscape* 4 (3): 93–106.

York, Byron. 1994. "HUD Makes Last Try to Keep Itself Alive." *Baltimore Sun* December 25, p. 1F.

INDEX

Southern Christian Leadership Conference (SCLC), 78–79
Southern Homestead Act (1866), 58
Sparkman, John, 73
Standard Metropolitan Statistical Areas (SMSAs), 53, 54
state autonomy, and institutional capability, 10–12
Stennis, John, 46
Stewart, Potter, 204n30
Student Nonviolent Coordinating Committee, 80
subsidized housing, 20–21, 89–90, 100, 105, 129; and the controversy in Warren, Michigan, 105–8; role of business elites in, 113–15
suburbs, 100, 102, 129, 147; post-WWII employment in, 154; promotion of racial balance in, 150–51; and suburban integration, 18, 110–11, 192–93n64; success of fair housing policy in, 151. *See also* residential desegregation, in the suburbs
Sugrue, Thomas J., 56
Swann v. Charlotte-Mecklenburg Board of Education (1971), 47, 51, 155
Sylvester, Edward C., 33

Taylor, Robert, 71
Thomas, Clarence, 156
Thurmond, Strom, 46
Turner, Margery, 148

Underwriting Manual (FHA), 63, 66
unemployment rates, 104–8
Unger, Sherman, 101
United Airlines, 40
United Auto Workers (UAW), 71, 79
United States Conference of Mayors, 74
United Steelworkers, 79
Urban Development Corporation, 150
Urban League. *See* National Urban League
Urban Renewal Administration (URA), 70
U.S. Chamber of Commerce, 75
U.S. Commission on Civil Rights (USCCR), 39, 49, 69, 114, 117, 118, 124
U.S. Congress, 4, 7, 22, 57, 68, 75–76, 148, 158, 162, 165, 187n104; and anger at Nixon's housing freeze, 137–38; and general revenue-sharing, 200n56; urban renewal policies of, 69–70. *See also* fair housing legislation

U.S. Department of Agriculture, Farmers Home Administration program, 137
U.S. Department of Defense (DOD), 34
U.S. Department of Health, Education, and Welfare (HEW), 46–47, 49–51, 96; monitoring responsibilities of, 43; Office of Civil Rights (OCR), 22, 40–41, 44, 49, 81, 97, 122–23, 126, 139, 160–61, 185n57; Office of Education (OE), 42, 43; Public Health Service, 42; Surplus Property Division, 42; Vocational Rehabilitation Administration, 42; Welfare Administration, 42
U.S. Department of Housing and Urban Development (HUD), 2, 3, 5, 8, 14, 17, 22–24, 67, 74, 114, 115, 121–24, 134, 142–43, 144, 158; ability to issue civil fines, 145; and advocacy group pressure, 115–18; Affirmative Fair Housing Regulations of, 127; bureaucracy of, 95–96, 163–64, 196n2; civil rights office of, 11, 37; creation of, 74–77; and creation of Open Communities taskforce, 103–8; failure of, 4, 6–7, 12, 21, 110–13, 117, 195–96n102; five primary desegregation programs of, 102; and formation of fair housing policies, 91–96; the "goals and timetables" approach of, 116–17; and grants for comprehensive planning, 102–3; lethargy of, 100; Office of Equal Opportunity (later the Office of Fair Housing and Equal Opportunity [FHEO]), 102, 116, 117–18, 159, 190n23; and Operation Breakthrough, 103; payments to commercial lenders by, 89; progress of (1969–72), 96–103; prospects for change in, 90, 159; scandals at, 3, 131–35, 199n34; site selection guidelines of, 119–20; and time limits for complaint resolutions, 145–46; workable program requirement of, 102. *See also* Moving to Opportunity (MTO) program
U.S. Department of Justice (DOJ), 43, 145; Civil Rights Division, 48, 152, 154, 155
U.S. Department of Labor, 34, 158
U.S. Fair Employment Practices Committee (FEPC), 27
U.S. Housing Authority (USHA), 63–65